TASK FORCE HELMAND

A SOLDIER'S STORY OF LIFE, DEATH AND COMBAT ON THE AFGHAN FRONT LINE

DOUG BEATTIE MC

with Philip Gomm

POCKET
BOOKS

LONDON • SYDNEY • NEW YORK • TORONTO

First published in Great Britain by Simon & Schuster UK Ltd, 2009
This edition first published by Pocket Books, 2010
An imprint of Simon & Schuster UK Ltd
A CBS COMPANY

1 3 5 7 9 10 8 6 4 2

Simon & Schuster UK Ltd
1st Floor
222 Gray's Inn Road
London WC1X 8HB

www.simonandschuster.co.uk

Simon & Schuster Australia
Sydney

A CIP catalogue record for this book is available
from the British Library.

ISBN: 978-1-84739-790-4

Typeset in Bembo by M Rules
Printed by CPI Cox & Wyman, Reading, Berkshire RG1 8EX

The names of some serving soldiers and Afghans
have been changed to protect their identity.

Doug Beattie became a soldier at the age of 16. During a quarter of a century in the British Army he served in almost every major theatre of operation, including Iraq where he was regimental sergeant major to Colonel Tim Collins. He was first sent to Afghanistan in 2006. In early 2008 he returned for a second tour of the country before finally retiring. He first met co-writer Philip Gomm in Helmand Province.

Praise for Doug Beattie

An Ordinary Soldier

'Beattie's gripping account of the two-week battle is exhilarating, bloody, moving and terrifying. But that's only half of an action-packed career . . .'
News of the World

'Of the battalion of courageous tales to emerge from the Iraq and Afghanistan conflicts, this extraordinary account by an "ordinary soldier" is one of the finest'
Daily Mail

'A riveting read. Beattie vividly describes the horror of killing'
Sunday Times

'A profound and humbling account of a truly epic piece of soldiering'
Damien Lewis, author of *Apache Down*

'Because of the immediacy of the narrative, it gives a remarkably true idea of the confusion and horror of close-quarter fighting . . . What singles out the quality and courage of officers such as Beattie is his determination to face whatever risks are involved for himself, rather than let others make fatal mistakes . . . But *An Ordinary Soldier* will not only give an idea . . . of just what they have been through, but also an insight into the spirit which has made the British Army what it is'
Times Literary Supplement

'Doug Beattie has written a thrilling modern war story'
Yorkshire Post

I am no hero, but I served alongside heroes

CONTENTS

Acknowledgements   ix
Maps   xii
Preface   xix
Prologue – Shabia   xxi

Part One – The Beginning: Kajaki

1 Loyalties and Disloyalties   3
2 A Defeated Army   24
3 The Sopranos Without the Humour   37
4 Compound 808   61
5 Job Done   86

Part Two – The Middle: Marjah

6 A Disaster Waiting to Happen   103
7 Boulevards   128
8 The Glorious Twelfth   160
9 Bunch of Pikeys   181

Part Three – The End: Attal

10 Point of the Spear   201
11 Killed in Action   231

12   Fuckin' Afghans   237
13   Smelling of Lavender   254
14   Task Force Beattie   274
15   Nine Lives Gone   292

     Epilogue   315
     Glossary   323
     Picture Credits   327
     Index   329

ACKNOWLEDGEMENTS

Over so many years, there are three people who have supported me through thick and thin above all others. My wife Margaret, and my children, Leigh and Luke. They have always been there for me; at my side when I have not been away with the army – on tour and on exercise – and in my heart when I have.

Their love has kept me going through the worst of times. Now I hope the best of times is yet to come so I can share it with them and my grandson Tristan.

As with *An Ordinary Soldier* I am pleased to acknowledge the advice and co-operation of those at the Ministry of Defence who smoothed the passage towards publication of *Task Force Helmand*. Thank you to the staff at the Directorate of Defence Public Relations (Army). Sincerest thanks also to my one-time commanding officer, Lieutenant-Colonel Ed Freely, who took a great interest in my project even when he had rather more pressing matters to deal with. I am also pleased to recognise Colonel Tim Collins, who played a big part in my army life. He led by example and that is something I have always tried to emulate.

Once again I am deeply indebted to co-writer and friend Philip Gomm. He would claim to have done little more than dot the 'i's and cross the 't's of my scribblings, and make sense of my musings. But the truth is rather different. Without him *Task Force Helmand* would have remained no more than a jumble of thoughts inside my head.

I owe much to my agent Andrew Lownie, who spotted at least some small worth in my experiences and went out to bat on my behalf. That the irrepressible Kerri Sharp and her team at Simon & Schuster – including Sue Stephens and Rory Scarfe – decided to stick with me for a second book was humbling. That Martin Soames, with his top legal mind, did the same, was deeply reassuring.

There are a few others whose names I would like to mention: Alan Rook, James Hogan, Enid, Helen. They all played their parts in bringing this project to fruition.

I must also pay tribute to Charlie Eckert. He has very graciously allowed me to use many of his photos and they, as much as my words, provide a vivid insight into life – and death – in southern Afghanistan.

If ever I had any doubts about the wisdom of returning to Helmand in 2008, they were dispelled by the enthusiasm, friendship, and professionalism I found amongst the men I went with – the men of 1 R IRISH, and those waifs and strays from other regiments who were thrown our way. Their resilience and good humour in the most testing of circumstances was second to none. I hope they regard this book as much their story as it is mine.

Faugh-a-Ballagh

Chagcharan
Ⓐ ●

R.C South Boundary

W R

D A Y K O N D I

to Kabul

Ghazni
● Ⓐ

G H A Z N I

R. Helmand

O R U Z G A N

● Tarin Kowt
Ⓐ

Z A B O L

Kajaki
●

Qalat
●

Sangin
●

Ⓐ ● Kandahar

K A N D A H A R

Ⓐ
● Quetta

Kabul ■

The area shown

A N

CENTRAL HELMAND

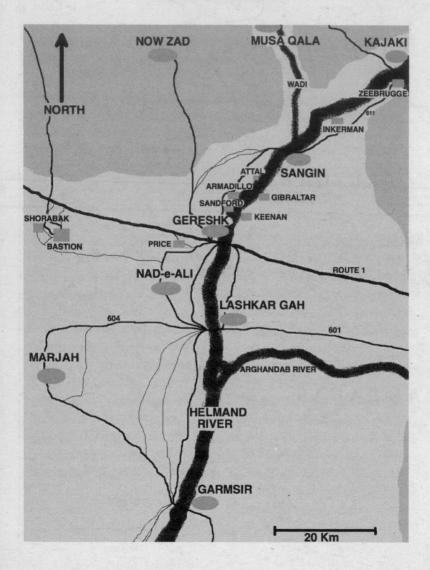

KAJAKI

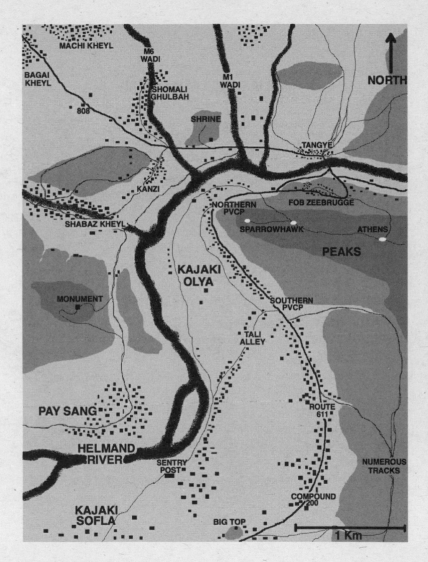

MARJAH AND LASHKAR GAH

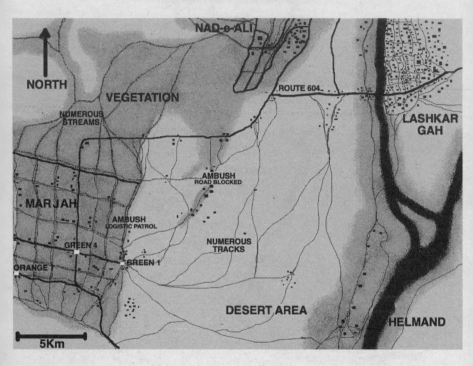

ATTAL

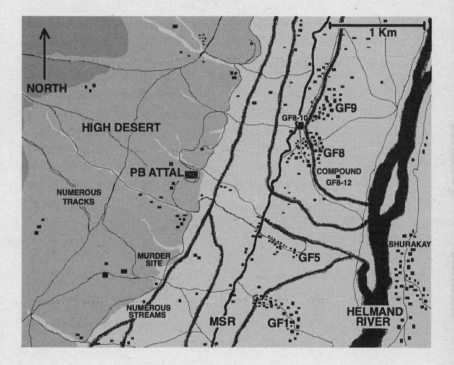

PREFACE

The day before I returned to Afghanistan in 2008 I signed the contract that led to the publication of *An Ordinary Soldier*. At that stage I had no thoughts about writing a second book. Indeed I was focused only on doing my duty and coming home safely, though I suppose in my heart I imagined that, whilst not exactly easy, this second tour of Helmand couldn't put me in any more danger than my 2006 experiences. Not for the first time in my life I was proved horribly wrong.

Whilst I had been away, the war in Afghanistan had changed. The enemy was still coming at us with bullets, but also increasingly too with bombs – roadside bombs, IEDs. And the changing tactics of the Taliban, combined with an unswerving hostility towards us, made them a formidable enemy.

I was extremely fortunate. I did emerge unscathed. Many did not; killed or seriously injured by the onslaught. Upon my return, as after the tour two years earlier, I started to write, but this time I wasn't doing so for myself. I was writing to honour others; attempting to record the bravery and commitment of those who were there with me. For even where I criticise, I realise most of those fighting alongside me – from so many nations – were volunteer soldiers, in Afghanistan to try and do some good, and that alone deserves respect. Once again I was reminded, as if I needed to be, that if others are imperfect then so most definitely am I. *Task Force Helmand* is not the definitive history of this period in southern Afghanistan. It is merely a series of snapshots, the views of just one man. I would welcome the chance to read the thoughts of others who were there – whatever their opinions of the campaign, whatever their opinions of me – because only through the telling will the memory of those who didn't come home live on.

Doug Beattie
June 2009

PROLOGUE

SHABIA

AN AFGHAN FATHER

11 MAY 2008

I looked down into the eyes of the Afghan girl sitting at my feet in the dust. She stared straight back at me, intently studying my face, the huge brown orbs of her eyes betraying nothing of what she was feeling, not a hint. Not fear. Not anger. Not pain. And yet how could they be so expressionless? For she must have been in absolute agony. There were at least three penetration wounds to her young, fragile body, caused by fragments of an 81mm mortar shell exploding close to where she had been playing, the chunks of red-hot metal effortlessly puncturing, tearing and slicing into her innocence. Her thick, dark hair singed by the bits of white phosphorus spat from the detonating weapon; on one side of her head a patch of it had been burned back to the scalp. And the round that had done the damage – a smoke bomb – had been ours. British. Fired from our camp, Forward Operating Base (FOB) Zeebrugge, as part of an attempt to cover the patrol's tentative movements through Kajaki Olya, a village to the south of the dam at Kajaki. It wasn't that I had pulled the proverbial trigger. For

Heaven's sake, I hadn't even asked for smoke cover – with two kilometres to go we were still too far from the enemy positions to need it. There was no immediate threat, none I could determine anyway. But someone had thought otherwise. I had heard the mortars being fired from the FOB. Stood and watched as they detonated around an area known as Big Top, a recognised Taliban stronghold. At that point I didn't know why the smoke rounds had been used, and cared even less. I put the incident out of my mind. For all of sixty seconds.

As we moved off again, the message came through that a motorcycle was careering towards us. It had been spotted by the men of 2 PARA up on the high ground overlooking Kajaki Olya and the route we were heading along known to us as Tali Alley. Earlier some radio chatter had been picked up from the enemy positions, the bravado and excitement of men hyping themselves up for action. But given their distance from us there wasn't much to fear. A sniper would be doing well to hit anything beyond a thousand metres, RPGs self-detonate at 900 metres, and as for Kalashnikovs they are all but useless beyond 600 metres. No, I wasn't unduly concerned about the enemy shooting at us, not yet. But the motorbike, now that was a worry. The hairs on the back of my neck stood up. I could feel my heart quicken. I raised my rifle to cover the bike's arrival. So did the others. Nervousness permeated the patrol. It could easily have been a suicide bomber, or perhaps Talibs racing to get to an ambush point to pick us off as we approached a bottleneck in the narrow, claustrophobic streets that lay ahead. But it wasn't either of these things, though in a way, now, looking back, I wish it had been. The battered Honda 150 first came to a stop close to Will Haighton at the head of the patrol. Three people were crammed on to it.

'Boss, there's a wounded girl on this bike.'

'Send it on to us and secure your area.'

I watched as the motorbike loomed larger, charting its precarious course over the rutted ground. It became clear these people were the other sort of Afghans. Ordinary people caught up in a conflict not of their making or choosing, villagers who were getting it from both sides, whose lives were being disrupted and endangered by both the insurgents and ISAF forces. They didn't want trouble, yet they couldn't avoid it. It didn't matter that they didn't go looking for it, because it came to them.

Riding the motorcycle, struggling with the handlebars, was an elderly man, probably in his sixties, and on his face was etched an array of feelings: panic, urgency, desperation, incomprehension. Behind him was another man, somewhat younger, his arms clasped around the waist of the first. And there, sandwiched between them, barely visible, was the girl, her tiny frame all but hidden by the bulk of the adult bodies and the flowing robes billowing about them. They came to a juddering halt, stopped by some of the Afghan National Army (ANA) soldiers we Brits were patrolling with, mentoring. When the troops realised there was not about to be a suicide attack they quickly became indifferent to what was now under their noses. There was the briefest exchange of words and then one of the soldiers turned and pointed towards me, as if to say, 'Take your problem over there, to him – he'll sort you out.' The rider, the older man, dismounted and heaved the precious bundle into his arms, cradling her to his chest as gently as he could. She put her hands around his neck, and then this latest casualty of war, this collateral damage, was brought towards me as if she were an offering. The old man didn't pick Doug Beattie out for any other reason than because I'd been identified to him as the person in authority. Of course he couldn't have known the effect seeing the suffering of a child would have on me. Couldn't have known I had just become a grandfather. Couldn't have known there was a new grandson waiting for me to return home from this far-off place, a grandson I had yet to see. But to me it was as if he was aware of all these things, as if he wanted me to share his pain in the most gut-wrenching way, as if he wanted to say, 'Are you pleased with what you have done? Is it all worth it, whatever you think you are achieving in our country?'

My interpreter explained what had happened. The child and some friends had been playing near a group of buildings where we knew the enemy often put sentries to watch for our arrival. That was when the smoke had been put down, perhaps as a warning to the Taliban that we were on our way and if they resisted the smoke would be replaced by high-explosive rounds.

As the interpreter recounted the events, I glanced again at the girl and couldn't help other than be utterly moved. She was absolutely beautiful. Her youth and angelic features combined to suck me in. Her skin was olive, and her clothes were clean and well kept. Her small bright lips were pursed, but she didn't speak a word. The more I looked, the more I was dragged into her world; and the more I despaired at what I saw. Only her feet – bare and broken – gave a clue as to the hardships of an Afghan childhood. Those and her wounds. I inspected them. They were oozing blood and must have been so painful. They certainly required urgent medical attention, but I didn't think they were life-threatening. I asked the company commander for permission to bring forward the ambulance, a Vector vehicle, and Rory the doctor, from the Afghan police checkpoint back down the road where they'd been waiting. Readily he agreed.

The girl remained silent as we waited for the help to arrive, but continued to fix me with her mesmerising eyes. The doctor didn't have far to come, just a couple of kilometres; it would only take a matter of minutes. Yet as she sat there, as I stood there, time dragging interminably, I was overcome with guilt. And horror. And sadness. And frustration. I wanted her gone. Not just so she could get the treatment I was unable to give, but so I could escape her gaze and everything it meant to me. I wanted someone else to take responsibility for her. To break the spell she had cast over me.

When the ambulance arrived I helped lift her into the back of it, then half-closed the doors; an attempt to give her a little privacy from the prying eyes of the Afghan troops who had gathered round to see the next scene of the tragedy unfold. The girl was as light as a feather, fragile beyond belief. As Rory started to tend her injuries I moved away to send the nine-liner, the medical incident report, back to the ops room at the FOB. When I returned, Rory was still treating her, yet still she displayed a courage way beyond her years. There was no screaming, no crying. So much dignity from someone so young.

And then, finally, she spoke.

Just a single word, but with it, at last, came the fright. In a pitiful, pleading voice that was barely audible, she asked for water. And she didn't get it, couldn't have it because of her injuries. The one simple thing she had requested from me and I couldn't deliver even that.

Rory closed the doors of the Vector completely, ready for the short drive to a piece of open ground that had been designated the landing site for the helicopter that would airlift her to the regional capital Lashkar Gah for surgery. Just ten minutes after meeting her, I was shut out of her life. The girl's grandfather, the man who had ridden the motorcycle, went with them. The father stayed with me and gave some details about his daughter that I could usefully radio back for passing on to the surgeons who'd be treating her. I was desperate to show him I had some humanity, had some feeling for his predicament, and was not going to wash my hands of what had happened. I told him I would meet him the next day at the checkpoint, when I'd be able to give him an update on the girl's condition. I told him not to worry; she'd be OK for sure. I'd come across a lot worse.

Hollow words from a fool of a man who knew no better.

I never saw the girl again.

And nor did her father.

Because within hours of being hurt, after being transferred to a squalid Afghan hospital, she succumbed to her injuries and died.

Not that anyone told me. The next day I went back to the police checkpoint as arranged with the father. I didn't have much to tell him other than the name of the hospital and a phone number for it. But he didn't show up. It seemed strange but I didn't read much into it. There could have been a hundred reasons to explain his absence. Perhaps he had other children at home he couldn't leave. Maybe he had already received word she was OK. It might have been that the grandfather was now back home and explaining how well the operation had gone. In fact the reason he did not turn up was because he was preparing to bury his daughter; something I only discovered twenty-four hours later when I was reading an email in the ops room at Zeebrugge that perhaps I should-n't have. I was more shocked than I imagined possible. It seemed clear the company commander was not intending to pass the news on to the men. Maybe he was nervous about eroding morale. Maybe it was because we just happened to have a journalist from *Time* magazine visiting us and he didn't want a bad press, an article based around the death of a beau-tiful child rather than the upbeat piece that was eventually published. Most likely he didn't want the mortar men to think themselves responsible. For indeed they weren't. What had happened was an accident. The action wasn't malicious. A judgement call had been made with the best of intentions, no matter that I didn't agree with it. It's just that war is not an exact science. And when things go awry, people die. Often the wrong people. Innocent people. Not that knowing that makes it any easier to deal with.

I would later hear how the father's misery and anger was com-pounded by the refusal of the British authorities to pay him the compensation he asked for, a figure based on the size of the dowry he was likely to have received when she married. The excuse for not paying it? Well, yes, the girl had been killed at the hands of the British, but it had been as part of operational duties, her death had been 'incidental', she was a casualty of conflict. If the man wanted to appeal the decision then there was due process to follow, a journey to Lashkar Gah to be made, a form to be filled out. It made me embarrassed. And ashamed; of myself and of the army and of my country. Even if there was a procedural reason for not paying the man, even if the rules were the rules, did no one have a degree of compassion? An ounce of foresight? How were we going to win the battle to bring the civilians on side – let alone the fight against the Taliban – if we killed one of their number and offered nothing to ease the pain in terms they understood? It was heartless. It was wrong. And it was certainly no way to wage a campaign against an enemy ready to exploit any of our mistakes to turn the 26 million people of Afghanistan against us. Christ, as if things weren't going to be tough enough for us without things like this taking place. Here I was, at the start of my second six-month tour of duty of the country, and already I felt crushed by the weight of this experience.

Oh, and if anyone is interested, the name of the little girl – the one with the huge brown eyes, the one whose innocence was cut out of her by fragments of a British shell, the one whose future we were supposed to be protecting – was Shabia. Her father told me that. She was just seven years old.

PART ONE

THE BEGINNING: KAJAKI

ONE

LOYALTIES AND DISLOYALTIES

MARGARET BEATTIE, A SOLDIER'S WIFE

JUNE 2007

I parked the car outside the house, turned off the engine and took a deep breath. And then another. Margaret would be inside waiting, anxious to know what the CO had said to me; and then what I had said to him. Walking up the path and opening the front door I tried to picture the scene; my wife in the kitchen, washing up, or preparing supper, or reading the paper, a mug of coffee on the table. And whatever she was doing, there would be a look of concern on her face as I entered, worry that Colonel Mike McGovern had asked me to remain in the army. And worry that I'd said yes and agreed to stay in, even though I had done my quarter of a century. Even though I had already made a commitment to my family to leave. Even though the date of that leaving was just three weeks away and Margaret and I had already put the plans in motion to make a go of it in Civvie Street. We had found a new place to live, back in Northern Ireland. Both of us had got new jobs. She would be thinking, hoping, 'Surely, surely, this time, Dougie won't go back on his word? He wouldn't dare. We're so close to the end now . . .' But still there would be doubt in her mind.

Down the hall I went, through to the back of the house. And there she was, at the sink. She heard my footsteps and turned to face me. Out it came.

'So what did he say?'

No Hello, darling, no Sit down and I will make you a cuppa. Just straight to the point. She tried to make her tone light and breezy, the question innocent, but I could sense the fear behind it. I blurted out my reply.

'I'm staying in, love. Only for another eighteen months. Just to help train the battalion to go back to Afghanistan.'

'I knew it. I knew you couldn't leave.' The anger started to well up, replacing the fear. 'And will you be going with them? To Afghanistan?'

She would already have known what was coming but she went through the motions all the same, perhaps wanting to hear how I was going to explain it away. It broke my heart to tell her, but I did it anyway. I'd become practised at it.

'I can't not go, love. The CO wants my help. Anyway, soldiering is what I do best.' Feeble answer. I was on the back foot.

'So what about me? What about Leigh and Luke? Don't we need you? Don't we deserve a bit of your time now? After all these years? After the promise you made?' The anger and bitterness were rising quickly now, the words coming fast and furious. 'Why do you always choose the army over me, why can't I be first for once? Why do you always feel it is up to you to sort out the world? You've done your bit, God knows you have. Why not leave it to someone else now?'

On matters of fact she was right every time. I had served my country, fought my wars, won my battles, been awarded the medals. I had done everything required of me by the army and yet here I was, at the very moment I should finally have been devoting myself to those who loved me, turning my back on them and returning to my other family, 1st Battalion the Royal Irish Regiment.

'You're always talking about loyalty and disloyalty. But where exactly do your loyalties lie? With me or with them?'

This time she didn't wait for my response. Before I could speak she barged past, giving me her parting shot as she went: 'You go back to your men, then. Risk your bloody neck again. But just don't expect me to be here when you return. If you return.'

The door of the living room slammed shut behind her.

I walked to the sink and looked out of the window, out across the lawn. I stayed there for perhaps a quarter of an hour, mulling over everything she had said. And everything I should have said. For if she had been minded to hear it there would have been more bad news. Although the deployment wouldn't take place until March 2008, the training would start almost immediately and that too would take me far from home. In just ten days I would have to go to Germany for a fortnight. Then in August it would be off to Kenya for six weeks. For those who think a six-month tour of duty is just that, then think again. With the training, the preparation, the new skills that have to be learned, a soldier being sent on operations can be away for anywhere between nine and ten months in a single twelve-month period. For Margaret, these extra commitments would mean more time apart; more frustration; more heartache. For once I could see her going through with her promise to pack her bags. Why should she put up with my whims? After all she had endured during the length of our marriage? An old friend of mine, Major Ken Topping, used to tell me, 'Three-quarters of the world is covered by water. The rest is covered by 1 R IRISH.' And the previous five years had gone a long way to proving him right. During that time I had been on four operational tours: Iraq, Northern Ireland, Bosnia and Afghanistan. Indeed I had only been back from Afghanistan for half a year. Yet here I was preparing to go again when I should have been looking forward to a new life without the stresses and strains, not to mention the dangers, of the military existence. If only the CO hadn't asked to see me. Hadn't asked me to stay on. But the reality was Colonel McGovern had played a blinder. How could I, a man of forty-two, walk away from so many young soldiers who might need my help; might be able to draw on some of the experience I had gained? How could I say no to training and leading teenagers, some barely older than my own sixteen-year-old son, who were being thrown into a vicious conflict with the Taliban? How would I ever be able to face a mother or father, wife or girlfriend, of one of those men if they didn't come home alive and I hadn't been there perhaps to save them? So of course I said yes to Mike, as I'm sure he thought I would. Said yes to the regiment that had embraced me. Yes to a unit with a history stretching back to 1689 when an Irish regiment was first raised to fight on behalf of the Crown against the Jacobite army of King James. Yes to the regiment that had taken me in as a nervous, callow youth, and had been loyal to me ever since. Now I was demonstrating my loyalty to it. Over years, decades, centuries, the predecessor regiments to 1 R IRISH had come and gone, been disbanded or amalgamated. It was now the last Irish regiment of the line and I was amongst its number. I revelled in it.

5 March 1811
'By jabbers boys, Oi've got the cuckoo!' cried Sergeant Masterson. The first ever French standard – complete with imperial eagle – had been captured in battle and now lay in the hands of the 87th Irish Foot (Royal Irish Fusiliers). Because of the men's gallantry that day at Barossa, the regiment would for ever onwards wear the eagle on their dress uniforms, and even now, 200 years on as near as damn it, the battle cry of Faugh-a-Ballagh, *Gaelic for Clear the Way, which the men screamed as they launched their assault and put the enemy to the sword, remains the regimental motto.*

It can be hard to explain to someone, even the wife of a soldier, just how much it means to belong to a brotherhood in which men are prepared to fight, and ultimately die, for their comrades and to protect, maybe even enhance a little, the reputation of the unit. The hardships endured and heroism displayed by those who have gone before are an inspiration to every new generation of soldiers. Though they also instil fear. Fear of failure. Fear of not being up to the job. Fear of blotting an exemplary copybook written in the blood of those who gave everything they had at places like the Crimea, the beaches of Normandy, the hills of Korea, and Jhansi in India, where three VCs were won before breakfast. Yet overwhelmingly it was pride that had made me yet again turn my back on my wife, son and daughter. I belonged to something special. I mattered. I was needed. And of course I was doing something I loved. Even as I told Margaret about my decision, and she prepared to unpack the boxes she had already filled for the next stage of our lives, I tried to duck out of taking the blame for my choice. She knew I was a soldier, didn't she? I was a soldier when she had married me, for God's sake. Surely I had a right to expect her to understand my reasoning? But really, who was I kidding? Because just as much as she should have acknowledged my obligations and motivations then surely I should have seen her point of view too? Felt some sympathy for her arguments which, when distilled, amounted to the simple, not unreasonable, desire to spend some time with the man whom, despite every trial and tribulation he had put her through, she still loved. Quite rightly she wanted to spend the rest of her days as one half of a married couple, not as a widow.

At the battle of Waterloo the 27th Royal Inniskilling Fusiliers were at the very heart of the fighting. So much so that the Duke of Wellington said of them, 'They held the centre of my line'. But not without suffering terrible casualties. Of 15 officers present at the battle,

14 were killed. And of the 670 members of the other ranks, 498 died or were injured. Their plight resulted in a neighbouring regiment suggesting their own officers help out the Irish. It was of course an offer that was politely declined with the excuse, 'Sergeants like the opportunity to command companies'.

And it wasn't as if I had many of my nine lives left. During my time in Garmsir, in southern Helmand, in 2006, I had survived by the skin of my teeth. Almost every day I was in a situation where I could have been killed, yet for whatever reason fate conspired to keep me alive whilst others around me were being shot, burned, and blown up, left maimed, scarred and disfigured, both physically and mentally. Some would lose limbs. More than a few would lose their lives. I was lucky to have made it out of there. Almost every step of the way I had been terrified. I'd prayed to God, made pacts with the devil, done anything that might keep me safe and allow me to return to a loving family, and a future. And guess what? It had worked. Despite everything, I had made it out of that Helmand hell. Lady Luck had been on my side. And how was I repaying her? By turning my back on everything I once craved. By giving it all up for the sake of a bunch of hairy-arsed blokes and some dusty old history. The good lady must have been bloody furious.

1 July 1916
On this, the first day of the Battle of the Somme, the men of the 36th Ulster Division were the only division of X Corps to achieve their objective. But because of the heavy losses they sustained (some 5,500 officers and men killed, wounded or missing on that day and the next) and the inability of the flanking divisions to keep up, they were forced to withdraw, losing all the ground they had gained during those initial grim hours. One of the stories told of that bloody battle was of the request by the soldiers to be allowed to wear their heavily symbolic orange sashes, which was traditional at that time of year, into action.

The top brass refused. It was a strange sight then to see, only a short time later, that some of the men emerged from their fortifications wearing greatcoats despite the warmth of a summer's day in France. Once out of the trenches however, the coats were cast aside to reveal the sashes hidden underneath. Unencumbered by their unseasonal attire the troops advanced towards the German lines and, in the case of so many, towards their deaths. And it wasn't only Protestants who paid the ultimate price for King and Country. During World War One thousands of Irish Catholics also fought and died. They served with units like the old Royal Irish Regiment, the Connaught Rangers and the Dublin Fusiliers. Together they comprised the 16th Irish Division – man and boy they were volunteers. Even today the Royal Irish Regiment recruits from both sides of the geographical divide in Ireland and both sides of the religious divide too.

I finally left the kitchen and followed Margaret into the sitting room. She was sitting there sullen and silent. I slumped down into my armchair. Outside, the glow of the early-evening sunshine bathed the house. Yet the warmth of its rays could do nothing to thaw the icy atmosphere between us. Neither of us could work out how to start the conversation, what to say. In a way there was nothing to say, because it had all been said before.

In total, through its own endeavours and those of its antecedent regiments – the Ulster Rifles and the Irish Fusiliers and so on and so forth – the Royal Irish has stacked up a pile of battle honours, 152 to be exact, a selection of which are emblazoned on the regimental and Queen's colours. Amongst these honours is the emblem of the Conspicuous Gallantry Cross, the Royal Irish being the only regiment to receive such a distinction due to the sacrifices made by those who served in it during 'The Troubles' in Northern Ireland.

The odd thing is that if I had not accepted Colonel McGovern's offer to stay on and put my life on the line yet again, and in so doing crushed my wife's latest hopes and dreams, then my time with 1 R IRISH would have ended in rather a damp squib. Because, though the regiment was my family, in a way we had become, if not quite estranged, then certainly distant over the past few years. It was just one of those things. You know how it is; things change, circumstances alter, events happen, and you drift apart from loved ones. Same with the army. Having been RSM to Colonel Tim Collins in Iraq in 2003 there weren't many places left for me to go, at least not within the battalion. Which is why I became something of an itinerant, drifting from job to job and place to place. I spent eight months in Sarajevo as the RSM to an assortment of soldiers from twenty-two nations; six months in Edinburgh as RSM to a non-deployable HQ unit; a year and a half at the Infantry Training Centre in Catterick. By the end I had been commissioned as a late-entry officer, the rank slides of a captain now sitting on my epaulettes. But during none of that time was I serving with my own kind. I was on attachment here, seconded there, posted somewhere else, but always as an individual. Even when I was sent to Afghanistan in 2006, it was to fill a small hole, not as part of a regimental deployment, the need being for a single man rather than a complete battalion. Then when I got back from Afghanistan I was almost straight away on terminal leave, preparing to put the army behind me. There had been no great send-off, no fanfare, no rousing finale with my band of brothers. I was going to slink away with hardly anyone noticing. Which is perhaps why I volunteered for Helmand 2008. Because I was after the last hurrah, the chance to fight alongside men I had not really seen since the Gulf. If I am being honest, maybe I wanted to go out with a bang; like the career criminal determined to do one last job. Thank God, Mike had given me the chance. Sure, things would be tough, not just the tour, but the training beforehand. It didn't matter though. I couldn't wait to get stuck in. I was ready for anything. I was going home.

*

Except home had changed. When I last left the battalion it was based in Inverness. It had since moved and set up camp at Tern Hill in Shropshire, not far from the town of Market Drayton. The CO had also just changed. Whilst Mike McGovern had been the one who had urged me to stay on, the new boss was Colonel Ed Freely and he was the one left to deal with the consequences of Beattie being brought back.

Entering the base, I felt like the new boy at school. I had to collect a pass for my car, complete an arrival certificate and then officially report for duty. During the four years I was gone, a lot of familiar faces had departed, and many new ones had arrived. I am sure that on my return there were plenty in the battalion who took one look at me and thought, 'Who the fuck is he?' It was strange to see what had become of people during my time away. Some soldiers I'd thought would never amount to anything were now in positions of authority. Others I imagined would rise like meteors, languished in the ranks. Amongst those I did recognise – and certainly a soldier deserving of the position he held – was Major Hughie Benson, even more of an old-timer than me. He was the battalion quartermaster, the man who made sure we had the right weapons, ammunition, clothing, vehicles and accommodation to carry out our orders. He organised things, fixed things, moved things. He was a logistical *tour de force*. In the coming months he would have to ensure 600 men got to Kenya. And got back. Went on various exercises to Salisbury Plain, Lydd and Hythe in Kent, and Thetford in Norfolk. And got back. And finally deployed to Afghanistan. And got back. There were a hundred balls to juggle. Occasionally he dropped one, but that still meant ninety-nine were in the air. And on top of all this he and his team managed to find the time to have a brew with me. Suddenly it was like I'd never left.

Just prior to arriving at Tern Hill I did a couple of weeks in Germany. The aim was to give us – I was there with another couple of captains from the regiment – a taste of how the

Americans went about mentoring the Afghan National Army. Also on the course were the French (who wouldn't go anywhere there was fighting), the Italians (who didn't know how to fight) and the Canadians (whose government didn't want to fight, even though their troops were good at it). Stereotypes one and all, but that was the way our allies were regarded by the average British soldier.

The American instructors were good men, and they were good at teaching drills. 1) Do this. 2) Do that. 3) Do the other. Yet they did not always understand why it was – or was not – necessary to carry out those drills. There was no flexibility in what they taught. No understanding that a plan doesn't survive first contact with the enemy, but needs to be adapted, amended as situations develop. There was no obvious comprehension of current Taliban tactics – the use, for example, of command wires to detonate IEDs, or line-of-sight remote-controlled devices – which left their standard operating procedures for carrying out duties like setting up vehicle checkpoints all but obsolete. And the trainers didn't respond well under interrogation. When their rationale was questioned the stock answer was 'This is the drill'. Then they would make a reference to a particular page, paragraph and sub-paragraph in the US Army manual. All well and good for the classroom but I became increasingly worried their techniques would not stand up to scrutiny in the heat of battle. Of course we didn't have to adopt their way of doing things. We could put a big cross through anything we didn't like. The trouble was the Afghans were receiving their basic training from the Americans, and what we had a choice of adopting, the Afghans did not. At least though, we now had some idea of the pitfalls that awaited us.

Back at Tern Hill I learned more of the way the CO worked, though I already had a pretty fair idea as our paths had crossed in the past. I'd first come across him when he was a young officer in the late eighties and early nineties. Later I was his company sergeant-major (CSM) in Kosovo during

NATO's initial deployment there in 1999, and then in Canada and Kenya in 2000. Now the one in charge, he took it as given that his own officers would be fit, aggressive, disciplined, hard-drinking. What he was really after was a spark of intelligence in those immediately below him. He didn't stand on ceremony. He wanted to hear ideas. If they were worthy, he would adopt them. If not, he'd tell you to fuck off.

In fact in the middle of September 2007, after just a few weeks of me being back 'home', we all fucked off – to Kenya. With barely time to acclimatise after arrival the boys were pushed out of the gate and into the bush on exercise. It was stiflingly hot, the landscape was dry and dusty with little or no shade, and water was a rare commodity. All things we'd also find in Afghanistan. For six weeks the battalion carried out exercises in such evocatively named places as Impala Farm, Lawyer Downs, Archer's Post and Dol Dol. Between excursions the men would return to our base, the Nanyuki Show Ground, and get the chance to indulge in a few beers both on and off camp. Before the trip they had been briefed on the dangers they might face, not from any sort of enemy but rather from the local environment. They had been warned about the appalling state of the roads; the poverty; the chances of being mugged; and the risk of contracting HIV if they succumbed to the charms of the local hookers who plied for trade in the bars the men hung out in.

My job wasn't to rough it in the bush, though. Me, I had to plan the adventure training the boys would get the chance to do right at the end of the trip; trekking up Mount Kenya, canoeing and white-water rafting on crocodile-infested waters, mountain biking and rock-climbing. Of course we could have come straight home at the end of the exercise, but Colonel Ed was determined his men should get the most out of the trip, not least because it would be good for morale.

In preparation for the adventure training, whilst out scouting locations, I managed to get a night on the town in Nairobi with a bunch of other lads. We succeeded in finding a watering hole where the Rugby World Cup was being shown on the telly and settled in for a marathon session during which we saw three games and had a couple of drinks; or rather, a few drinks; or rather, several drinks; or rather, rather too many drinks. Which is why when the shooting started we didn't necessarily take it as seriously as we might have done. The owner of a 'matatu'– a minibus-type taxi – who had got into a dispute with some of his fellow drivers just outside the bar we were in, pulled out an AK47, as you do, and started blasting away at his erstwhile colleagues. Everyone dived for cover – except us. In our inebriated state it seemed a much greater priority to avoid spilling our beer than avoid getting shot. The disturbance soon petered out (perhaps the gunman ran out of ammo, or maybe a fare came along looking for a ride) and we resumed our sporting evening, ending up as drunk as monkeys.

The holiday activities in place, I also found myself having to plan more training for our return to the UK. It is an over-simplification to view your average soldier as a 'yes man' who does no more than eat, shit and shoot. The number of skills they have to master, and the levels of competence they have to achieve, are breathtaking. Being physically fit and learning how to fire a rifle is not the half of it. Back at Tern Hill the men were taught about satellite communications. They received extra first-aid training (at the end of which they would be at a level close to that of a paramedic). They learned to drive a variety of vehicles, from the ageing Snatch Land Rovers to the new Jackals, the replacement for the WMIK. And they were introduced to the latest weapons systems, including the 40mm Heckler & Koch grenade machine gun (GMG) and the 9mm Sig Sauer pistol. Most importantly they were expected to get to grips with all things Afghan – the basics of the language, the politics, the culture, the environment, the history. Not bad for young lads who might have left school at sixteen without a qualification to their name and before joining up might never have travelled further than to the local pub or off-licence.

Everyone would also have to understand how 1 R IRISH was going to slot into the much-bigger organisational structure of 16 Air Assault Brigade, as a part of which we were going to Afghanistan. Our role in Helmand would be to act as the Operational Mentoring and Liaison Team (OMLT) battlegroup. We would need to amend our structure to fit in with the way the 3/205 'Hero' Brigade of the Afghan National Army did things, for it was them we'd be working with.

Essentially our battalion needed to provide five companies. One, to be known as Ranger Company, would go to Sangin to support 2 PARA. Numbering some 120 men, it was at regular company strength. The others would be OMLT companies, numbered one to four, each consisting of about thirty-six men and responsible for mentoring a battalion (*kandak*) of Afghan troops.

The only trouble seemed to be that we didn't have enough of our own men to form the last company, OMLT 4. So I was given the job – didn't I have enough on my plate? – of cobbling it together, getting it trained up and then handing it over to someone else to command. Me? I would be second-in-command. My disappointment at this was tinged with realism. Why would they put me, a long-in-the-tooth late-entry officer, in charge of a company? No, that job would go to someone younger.

All this immediate and medium-term preparation meant that whilst in Kenya I didn't get out on the ground with the lads as much as I would have liked; though I made an effort to visit them in the bush to see how the exercise was going. One of those I spoke to was Ranger Justin Cupples. He had come a long way to join 1 R IRISH. Born in Miami, his family later moved to County Cavan in the Irish Republic, where he met his Lithuanian wife Vilma. During the Iraq War in 2003, he served with the US Navy, before later deciding to join us. Aged twenty-eight, he had only just arrived at the battalion.

'How are you finding it?' I asked him.

His terse answer seemed to sum it all up: 'Fuck!'

He looked shattered, but then that was the point of the exercise. It was about hard work. Hard work that I prayed would keep him and the others alive. Of course not everything was hard work, at least not for me. There had been the excursion to the sports bar. And then there was the evening I was transported back in time.

The building was an isolated remnant of a long-gone era that stubbornly refused to crawl off and die. In the fading light and dancing shadows, the Muthaiga Club in Nairobi gave off an air of being exactly what it was, a former gathering place and haven for colonials who had come, seen and conquered Kenya.

In the second or so it took me to cross the club's threshold I found myself teleported back almost a hundred years, from a time of colour to a past defined in black and white. A dark Kenyan, head held high, not least because of the high-necked, starched ivory jacket he was wearing, beckoned us in, a tray in one hand, a crisp towel thrown over his arm.

'Will you take drinks outside or at the bar, sir?' His strong voice drove home his polished, formal English.

On the walls there were scores of monochrome photographs, a social history of an anti-social, élitist period. They portrayed the heyday of the British in Kenya. There were white men amongst their crops. White men at their lodges. White men on safari. White men standing proudly by their slaughtered prey, one foot on yet another big-game trophy. Black people were in the photos too, but always standing in the background, at the sides. They were almost incidental to the pictures, never the focal points. This was the white master with the black servant. Further on, through reception, there were a series of rooms; the reading room, the smoking room, the bar, the restaurant where members could eat and talk: the younger ones extolling hope for the future, the older ones wondering where it all went wrong. You could almost read their thoughts: 'If only it had stayed British.'

I was there with a handful of Royal Irish colleagues, including Ed Freely; our invite to supper, extended by an informal dining club the Muthaiga was home to. We were ushered through the public areas to a side room, where a long single table had been set out for the select gathering. I looked around at the others in the room. The battalion members apart, there was someone else I knew, another military man who by the most bizarre coincidence was my very first CO, Brigadier Adrian Naughton (now retired), who way back in 1983 had been in command when I was sent to Berlin after basic training. Tall and strong, the only thing that seemed to have changed was his hair; once dark brown, it had become liberally streaked with grey. That, and the fact he now lived in Africa.

The others at the table, I didn't know. There was the Irish honorary consul, a short jovial man who wore the look of someone who had attended too many such gatherings but thoroughly enjoyed every one of them and had learned plenty along the way. Then there was a plantation owner. Extrovertly dressed in what can only be described as a Hawaiian shirt, he had piloted his own plane to Nairobi to attend, blaming his late arrival on bad weather over Uganda. Making up the numbers was a pair of wonderfully engaging Germans. I never discovered exactly what they did, but they seemed to be rather too well informed about goings-on to be mere civilians. Given our location the guest list seemed absurdly appropriate.

In such interesting company, the conversation flowed as freely as the wine. We talked of the past and the future, and particularly of a war dominating our present. To the casual observer it was as if Kenya was again playing host to foreign imperialists, except this time the target of their attention was an Asian country and not an African one.

Towards the end of the evening, the floor show began. Our hosts regaled us with a series of skits and songs, before finally the Germans put on a short play of their own. Dressed as slaves, they had the waiting staff act as the colonial masters. In my inebriated state I wasn't sure quite what they were trying to prove or what the message was. I'm not convinced it would have been much clearer if I had been sober, yet it all added to the surreal nature of the occasion. The last act of colonial remembrance took place as we departed: a piper and bugler playing us off the premises.

Life was good.

'Mike, I hope these guys are up to living in the field for weeks on end without their vehicles for comfort? I don't want any J1 [discipline] issues here.'

It was early November and we were back in Shropshire, our Kenyan excursion behind us. The adjutant looked up at me. He was the one responsible for filling posts within the battalion, and with OMLT 4 there were plenty of gaps to plug. We needed almost forty men – yet at that stage there were just three. Myself, Sergeant-Major Brummie Hagans, so named because he had joined up in the early 1990s at our Birmingham recruiting office, and James Cartwright, a Gurkha officer. With not enough men from 1 R IRISH to form the team, Mike was having to trawl around the army to find spare soldiers who were both available and had the right specialist weapon skills – the .50-cal heavy machine gun, the 81mm mortar, Javelin anti-tank missiles. Amongst those he had just scavenged were troops from the TA, the Royal Anglians and the Royal Engineers. Then there were the three he'd just told me about from the 2nd Battalion Royal Regiment of Scotland (2 SCOTS). They were part of the motor-transport (MT) platoon. Great guys, I was sure, but from experience I feared they were likely to be in MT for a reason – injury, age, unsuitability for rifle companies.

'They're good lads, Doug. I've been assured as to their quality.'

I wanted to believe Mike but I was worried that with the tour fast approaching he was in the business of putting bums on seats, without necessarily having the luxury of being able to confirm their suitability. Up against it, I didn't doubt he would have told me anything I wanted to hear just to get rid of me and move on to the next problem.

'All right, Mike, but I don't want to find out any of them are even older than me!'

I couldn't believe they would be. I was a stately forty-two, and the men coming my way were all lance-corporals, a rank normally attained before soldiers turn thirty. Which explains why I was so depressed by the arrival of Lance-Corporal William Brown, who was not a day under forty-six. Forty-six, for fuck's sake!*

Then a few days later Mike gave me a list of more names. They were men no longer needed by Ranger Company. I scanned through them, studying the different disciplines each soldier was expert in. I could find a place for every one. Yet when I sent for them, only four turned up. Of those four, only two had actually been on the list in the first place. Of the other two, one had discipline problems and the other had been downgraded and wouldn't even be allowed to deploy to Afghanistan. I was absolutely furious and I said so to both Mike and the officer commanding Ranger Company, who it turned out, had amended the list after I'd been shown it.

---

* As it would turn out, William Brown and his colleagues from 2 SCOTS proved to be absolute stars; versatile, brave and uncomplaining. But at that moment I was in despair, fearing OMLT 4 would quickly come to resemble a group of British Legion veterans on a coach tour.

My fury got me absolutely nowhere. I was told to make do.

It was nearly the end of 2007 and whilst the other OMLTs had been training together since October, I had barely assembled my team. And I wasn't going to be able to spend any proper time with them now before the end of January because straight after two weeks' Christmas leave I was tasked with putting the whole battalion through a live-firing exercise on the south coast. For the first time we carried out a black-light, night-fighting drill. This involved live firing in total darkness. What made it possible was the use of night-vision goggles and laser-light modules attached to the front of the rifles. When the module was activated, an infrared light marked whatever the weapon was aimed at, and that target was visible when viewed through the goggles.

Another aspect of the exercise involved simulating the treatment of battlefield casualties, particularly those who had fallen victim to landmines and improvised explosive devices (IEDs). For added reality we employed the services of a bunch of amputees, recruited from an organisation called Amputees in Action, which had found a real niche in the market – providing extras who had lost limbs through accidents and disease to the film industry. *Saving Private Ryan*, *Atonement*, *Gladiator*, *Shaun of the Dead*, *Phantom of the Opera*; those on the company's books had been in them all. As in the movies, we added a bit of theatrical make-up and the amputees looked just as if they had . . . errrr . . . lost limbs. The effect was fantastic. I hoped this was as realistic as it would ever get for most of the men, including me. But bitter personal experience suggested otherwise.

The exercise was worth doing, indeed it had to be done as a prerequisite to deployment, but only on its completion was I at last released from other duties to devote myself to OMLT 4. It was already the end of January. It was at this stage we welcomed OMLT 4's new boss, Major Rob Armstrong, Royal Artillery. As with so many others his was not a new face to me (that's what came of having been round the block as many times as I had). In a twist of fate, the man I was going to be second-in-command to, had been one of my officer cadets when I was an instructor at Sandhurst. Slightly short and always kitted out in the latest gear, Rob had a great sense of humour, mixed with a good dose of humility. He was strong, fit and understood the infantry mentality even though he was a gunner. He was also happy to ask advice. Yet it was still a difficult period as he took over control from me, the older, supposedly wiser, man, who had been his tutor when he was still wet behind the ears. He also had to get to know the rest of the people in the battalion from Ed Freely downwards. To cap it all, we were about to go away on another exercise, this time on Salisbury Plain, with the rest of the new Task Force Helmand, 16 Air Assault Brigade.

The period on the plain was the first time everyone in OMLT 4 had really come together. The exercise was scheduled to run for two weeks and we desperately needed every last minute of it. The first seven days were all about us. There was some mandatory training, including a refresher session on the tactical satellite (TacSat) radio and helicopter familiarisation sessions – learning (or relearning) amongst other things the quickest way to get us all into an aircraft, and the quickest way to get us all out again. But apart from that, we could do whatever we wanted. At last we began to make some progress.

But then came week two. On paper this too had seemed exactly what we needed; a fast-flowing, brigade-level exercise involving all units acting out their roles in a succession of scenarios we might expect to find in Afghanistan. For added authenticity the MoD had arranged to fly over 100 ANA soldiers so we could get first-hand experience of how they thought and fought. It would be invaluable. Just one problem. They didn't show up. Issues with their bloody passports, would you believe? Truth be told, they didn't have any pass-ports, and apparently the Home Office officials who were going to turn a blind eye to this minor hiccup got cold feet and decided rules were rules and this lot weren't coming any-where near our shores.

Which then created another problem. Who was going to mimic the role of the ANA? Brigade's answer? Pass the prob-lem down the chain of command to 1 R IRISH HQ. HQ's answer? Give the job of playing the ANA to OMLT 4.

If I had been furious when the Ranger Company OC had offered me his cast-offs, I was now livid. I went ballistic. The other three OMLTs would complete their training at the expense of OMLT 4; and we were already several months behind in terms of familiarisation and preparation. I thought the situation a disgrace. Throughout my career I had regarded the way the British Army practised for war as methodical and rigorous, beyond reproach. Yet in this instance it was a fuck-ing shambles. And I said so.

Woe betide those making the decisions, if their lack of fore-thought and backbone subsequently cost the lives of one of my men. After the fiasco on the plain the only other training OMLT 4 managed to secure was an advanced close-quarter battle course which finished just forty-eight hours before we were due to fly out to Afghanistan. At least it gave us another, much-needed, opportunity to get to know each other and work together for a while. It was in effect the only real train-ing OMLT 4 ever had, though even this was arranged by the team itself, without any input from the battalion. The ques-tion was, would it be enough?

We were due to fly out early on 16 March, the day after St Patrick's Day. The patron saint of Ireland is usually celebrated on the 17th, but as this coincided with part of the Easter calendar – Holy Week, which takes precedence over all saints' days – it was brought forward a couple of days.

What better send-off. First thing in the morning the men were woken by gunfire, tea and whiskey, before they received their shamrocks. Then everyone headed for their respective messes – along with ex-members of the regiment – to down excessive amounts of Guinness, and eat Irish stew, pigs' trotters, wheaten bread and anything else vaguely connected with the Emerald Isle.

But I wasn't part of it. I could have taken Margaret along but it wasn't what I wanted, what she wanted. Those last hours before departure could have been the last I ever spent with my wife. And I didn't want her last memories to be of us getting increasingly drunk. Nor did I want my colleagues making claims on the limited time we had together until God knew when. So I went home and spent the evening with Margaret in Catterick. We hugged a lot and talked very little. What conversation there was included making provisions for the worst. Where was the will? What sort of funeral would I want? How did I want to be remembered? We didn't dwell on the worst, but we covered it. If I was to die, then whilst my wife might mourn my passing, she would not agonise over the formalities of my departure to the Ever After, nor struggle with the practical problems death throws up. I went upstairs to get changed. I took off my civilian clothes and dressed in my combats, then came back down. We kissed and I walked out of the door and down the path, my kit slung over my back. Once, twice, I glanced over my shoulder at Margaret and the life I was leaving behind. There was sadness, but also excitement. My latest adventure awaited. In those few steps between my wife and the car, I went again from being hers to being theirs.

TWO

A DEFEATED ARMY

UNKNOWN US GENERAL

17 MARCH 2008

'Enjoy your stay at Club Helmand.'

It was our welcome to Camp Bastion, the main British base in the province, indeed the whole of Afghanistan.

'Good luck, guys, only six months to go.'

The ribbing was from those who had done their time and were getting the hell out.

'I'll have a beer for you when I get back.'

As we arrived, they were ready to depart; ready to board the C130 Hercules we had just disembarked from and start their transit back to the UK. They would be doing our journey in reverse. For them a short forty-minute hop to Kandahar Airfield on the Herc and then a much longer flight to Brize Norton, family and home.

The grief coming our way was exactly what we would have doled out had we been in their position. For time immemorial, concentrating on the woes of others has been the soldier's way of dealing with the grind of military life. We might have had it bad, goes the thinking, but those poor sods are going to get it worse.

Yet for every two or three giving us lip, there would be another standing silent, a haunted, exhausted look visible on his face even through the darkness of the early hours. He would be the one who had actually done the fighting, the one who hadn't been stuck in camp, but probably now wished he had. He'd be the one who had seen people injured and killed, lost friends; the one who had not only witnessed lives taken, but taken lives himself.

Of the roughly 7,800 troops in Afghanistan at that time (most of them in Helmand), maybe only a third were out in the field, and of those perhaps only half saw regular combat. A smaller proportion still would have been fighting for their lives on an almost daily basis at forward operating bases and patrol bases across the province. This last group didn't need to say who they were, you'd know anyway from the introspective, reflective expression they wore – the thousand-yard stare, as the Americans call it. Their recent past was also betrayed by their hollow cheeks and emaciated bodies. Uniforms would hang limply where once, not so long ago, they had been filled out. It wasn't unusual for those on the very front line to lose a fifth of their body weight, and it showed. No British soldier starved in Afghanistan, but the circumstances meant a sizeable number didn't get the right combination of calories and nutrients required to stay healthy. No, it was impossible to mistake those who had been grinding away at the Taliban on a bloody and sustained basis, for anyone else. It couldn't have been clearer had they been standing there with sandwich boards proclaiming their exploits.

The physical deprivations they would recover from. But what about the psychological toll? I knew – whether they did or not – that in some the seeds of post-traumatic stress disorder would already have been sown. In 2006 it had happened to me and a number of my colleagues. In a few days the body fat would start to come back, the tans they sported would make them look healthy, and as they mixed once again with family and friends smiles would appear to replace the frowns. Yet for a significant number a serious disease would be growing inside them, already starting to erode their mental health. I would have spent time worrying for their futures, except I was already too busy worrying about mine.

I suppose when I agreed to stay on in the army in 2007, there was always the slim chance my deployment would not go ahead, the faintest of chances the British would be long gone from Afghanistan. As if. We were still there, up to our necks in trouble.

We had first entered the country in November 2001, following the attack on the Twin Towers, the objective being to drive out the Taliban leadership harbouring Al-Qaeda. That was done in pretty short order. Except that wasn't the end of our presence in Afghanistan. Far from it. Under a United Nations mandate the International Security Assistance Force (ISAF) was established to support the transitional government. Later ISAF came under NATO control, and steadily it extended its influence away from the Afghan capital Kabul, furthering the writ of the Karzai administration. In 2006, ISAF deployed troops to the south of the country, which included Helmand province. And that's where the Brits had been ever since, in ever greater numbers.* Christ, even Prince Harry had been doing his bit. Luckily for him, he was now back home, safe and sound. Me, I'd only just arrived.

We walked further from the plane. Across the apron, past a handful of the shipping containers you seem to find anywhere in the world where the British Army has rapidly and recently deployed, and closer to the line of waiting buses ready to cart

---

* By early 2008 there were around 43,000 coalition troops from thirty-eight nations in Afghanistan.

us off to our small corner of the vast area of Afghan desert Bastion now consumed. Located north-west of the provincial capital Lashkar Gah, and just south of the main road, known as Route One, that loops around Afghanistan, the camp's immediate surroundings were a great expanse of nothingness, a moonscape. In fact the complete lack of settlements, geological features and vegetation helped increase security as the absence of cover was a serious deterrent to anyone intent on attacking the site. Ringed all the same by fences and watchtowers, Bastion One held around 4,000 troops, many of whom never got beyond the wire, engrossed as they were in their own jobs and support trades. For those dealing with logistics, communications, vehicles, rations, medical services, guard duty, Bastion was Afghanistan. Other than for the heat and the dust it could have been anywhere in the world. And the camp was being expanded further. Bastion Two was under construction and would be home to 2,000 members of the US Marine Expeditionary Unit (MEU) who were coming to play in Helmand.

We were shepherded on to the buses for the final leg of the journey, to be reunited with our kit and taken to transit accommodation. Driving down the dusty roads I couldn't help but wonder just how long Bastion would be needed or indeed remain standing? Things seemed to have taken on an air of at least semi-permanence since my last tour. Would it, finally abandoned, in the decades and centuries to follow, form part of the tourist trail just as the forts of Alexander the Great had done in the 1960s and '70s , before thirty years of war had put paid to foreign visitors (other than those with guns)? 'This is where the British and Americans were based during that vicious war of the early twenty-first century. As you will notice it lies mostly in ruins now, but over there, just visible sticking out of the sand, is the top of the monument built to remember the campaign dead.' Already there back in 2006, I wondered how many names would eventually be on it?

The soulless nature of the place was only reinforced by the unending rows of regimented tents, but I was gladdened by at least one thing – I was done with flying. I have always hated being airborne. There are those who get a thrill out of it. Not me. I regard it as no more than a means to an end. Something to be endured, not enjoyed. It didn't matter whether I was in a helicopter, on a Herc or even in the relative luxury of the VC10 that had got us as far as Kandahar. After eleven hours on board the plane, squeezed into a seat with almost a complete absence of legroom, surrounded by ninety-six men from 1 R IRISH – most of who seemed to have the most God-awful hangovers as a result of too many toasts in honour of St Patrick – plus about the same number again from other regiments and corps, it was a blessing to finally walk down the steps and regain some feeling in my feet.

But the relief was short-lived because my stay at Kandahar was a brief one, just ninety minutes. Off one plane and quickly on to another for the leap into Helmand. The Herc was too small to take us all so some people had to hang around for a while. Not me, though. My name was right at the top of the list of those to leave on the first shuttle. If it hadn't been 02:00 hrs those left behind could have ventured out of the makeshift arrivals-and-departures lounge, and explored the boardwalk, an incongruous parade of fast-food outlets – Burger King, Pizza Hut, Tim Hortons' coffee shop, plus a souvenir shop for fuck's sake – built by the Americans to create a home from home. Unsurprisingly this was not how we did things. New arrivals wouldn't find such a High Street at Bastion, the shopping opportunities limited to the British Forces' equivalent of the corner shop, the NAAFI, which sold such staples as ice-lollies, flip-flops and hot-dogs.

What they would discover waiting for them instead was an intense series of introductory briefings, mainly explaining the most recent assessments of security, the latest examples of enemy tactics and techniques, changes to the political environment and the current workings of our ISAF colleagues. Unfortunately it was the very first session that was to stick in the mind, and for all the wrong reasons.

The sergeant-major stood in front of us and recounted a conversation he'd only just had with a US general visiting Bastion ahead of the imminent arrival of the marines. As the American officer was being shown around, he offered his thoughts on the modern British soldier in Afghanistan.

'You know what, Sergeant-Major,' the unnamed three-star had said. 'I served in Vietnam and witnessed first the collapse of military discipline and then the collapse of our campaign. I saw in the way men dressed, in the ways they carried themselves, all the signs of a defeated army. And now as I walk about here, I see it again. A defeated army.'

The general had gone on to explain more about what he found so upsetting. His beef was that the men had got sideburns, moustaches and beards, their hair was long and unkempt, no two people seemed to dress the same. Where was the discipline? he wanted to know.

I couldn't believe what I was hearing. What on earth had the general been thinking of? It was an astonishing thing for one commander to say to another from a different nation. It was contemptuous, arrogant. And just as bad, here was the sergeant-major passing these supposed pearls of wisdom on to us in a vain attempt to get us to brush our hair, press our trousers and polish our boots. Neither he nor the general seemed to grasp the realities of going to war, nor the motivations of British soldiers.

What every soldier who goes off to fight wants is the freedom to do the job without getting bogged down in the petty and bureaucratic. For months, maybe years he will have knuckled down and acquiesced to the mundane, repetitive aspects of military life found in the barracks. Yet when it comes to putting his life on the line a soldier wants to be treated as an adult. He wants to wear kit that is comfortable and practical. He wants to concentrate on the serious business of guns, bullets and bombs, not razors, scissors and irons. And any commander worthy of the title will recognise this and cut his men some slack. If the warrant officer standing in front of me seriously believed the first thing 1 R IRISH wanted to hear about after arriving in a war zone was the dress code then he had judged the mood badly wrong.

And he also seemed ignorant of another basic fact of life in Afghanistan.

In Afghan society, a beard is viewed as a sign of age and authority. It gives men credibility and commands respect. What is the point of British troops with faces as smooth as babies' bottoms trying to deal with village and tribal elders, resplendent with their masses of facial hair, when custom dictates they won't have a cat in hell's chance of being taken seriously?

What we were being told was bollocks. I knew it. The men knew it. Shame the sergeant-major didn't. For the next two days we tried to put that shit out of our minds, as a string of different personnel, all rather more on the money than the first bloke, acquainted us with the very latest situation in Helmand. Having been up to our necks in briefings, the tide finally turned and the time came for us to move once more. All of 500 metres.

Just half a kilometre to the west of Bastion lies Camp Shorabak, the home of the 3,800-strong Afghan National Army brigade we had the job of mentoring. Our own – again temporary – quarters were in a camp within a camp. Tombstone had originally been set up by the Americans to house its own ANA facilitators, but now we would be sharing it too.

We would be living in Nissen-type huts, about ten of them. Several were for sleeping, but others acted as washhouses, the cookhouse, ops room and medical centre. There was also a quartermaster's building, TV room, gym and communal area the teams could use for planning. The OMLTs we were replacing comprised men of 2 YORKS. They would be with us for a few days to give us a hand-over.

I dumped my kit on a cot bed just through the door of the hut given over to housing officers. Beside the bed stood a small fridge now being used as a bedside table, its useful days as somewhere to keep things cool long behind it. I also spread out some of my stuff on the neighbouring bed after being told its regular occupant was somewhere up-country. Taking in my new surroundings and the men who were filling it, I was again struck by the contrast between those who had been at the sharp end and those who'd been camp-bound. The latter looked fresh, fit, relaxed. The former looked wrecked. Their kit was dusty and dirty. A few were unloading ammunition from magazines, putting the bullets into their upturned helmets ready to be clipped up again. They also had an array of grenades; smoke, high-explosive, many displaying the dents and scrapes they'd received from being knocked about in environments far less cushy than the one I was now in.

To some I nodded in acknowledgement, others were too engrossed in what they were doing to notice my arrival. One or two came over and shook my hand. From those who wanted to talk I gleaned every scrap of information I could. Where had they been? What had they done? How had they found it? Were the Afghan soldiers up to scratch? No good waiting to enquire later. These men would soon be gone, as would the critical detail they carried in their heads. This process of picking brains was extended and formalised the next day when 2 YORKS outlined the specific mentoring problems they had encountered and what they had done to overcome them. It was invaluable stuff, and at last it seemed to everyone as if we had done as much preparation as we usefully could. We had got to that point where everyone was just itching to get out on the ground, to get going – to get soldiering.

On 22 March it looked as if we might get our chance. OMLT 4 was being moved to Gereshk to replace the existing mentoring team there which was coming to the end of its tour. It would be our first deployment in Afghanistan as part of what the Ministry of Defence called Operation Herrick 8 or plain H8.

Just as Tombstone was American, so too was FOB Price. You could tell that by the Stars and Stripes that flew sneeringly above the base. In full sight of the local population, this wasn't the way to win friends and influence people but there wasn't much I was going to be able to do about it because once again we were squatters in a US facility. Also calling the FOB home were some Estonians and Czechs, a group of British territorials mentoring the Afghan National Police (ANP), and a complete battlegroup of Danes. The Danish presence was no surprise, given that this part of Helmand was their area of responsibility. Amongst the firepower located at Price was a GMLRS battery – a GPS-guided rocket system known as the seventy-kilometre sniper – which had the range and accuracy to fire 200lb high-explosive warheads right across the province in aid of all coalition forces.

It didn't take long before Taff, one of those mentoring the ANP, had a question for me.

'Doug, do you know a runt of a guy called Ranger Getty?'

'Yes, sure I do, why?'

'Well, the first and last time I met him was when I dragged him out of a hole in Sierra Leone when we went in to rescue your men held hostage by the West Side Boys.* He was a

---

* In August 2000 eleven men of 1 R IRISH were captured in the jungle of Sierra Leone by a militia group called the West Side Boys. Five of the hostages were released a few days later but the other six remained in captivity for two weeks until they were freed in a combined SAS/Parachute Regiment rescue mission. One of the rescuers, Brad Tinnion, was killed during the operation.

scrawny kid and I lifted him out with one hand. My first thought was "Fuck me, they've starved him half to death," then later someone told me he always looked like that!'

I laughed. Taff was right. Corporal Getty, as he now was, didn't look like your typical soldier. Small and thin, with ginger hair, he had actually turned out just fine and had got over his African adventure. He was also in Afghanistan, working as a joint tactical air controller (JTAC) calling in air-strikes in support of the brigade.

Whilst my team – one of two command elements in Gereshk – spent most of the time at Price, other members of OMLT 4 were spread around the town and the local vicinity, doing pretty routine stuff, getting out on patrol, extending our footprint about the place. As for enemy activity, there was relatively little of it. Our arrival coincided with the build-up to the poppy-harvesting season in May. Things were also quiet because of the good work done first by 3 Commando Brigade and then 52 Brigade, whose men had managed to drive many of the Taliban northwards along the Upper Gereshk Valley. The effects on the town were striking. If Lashkar Gah fulfils the role of administrative capital of the province, then Gereshk, some thirty kilometres east of Bastion and Shorabak, sitting on the main orbital highway, is the commercial centre and it seemed to be thriving, the market constantly teeming with people. For brief moments it was possible to believe the enemy posed no threat at all.

Which wasn't to say we didn't have dramas, occasionally self-inflicted.

Late one night, after sixteen hours in the ops room, I gratefully turned in to catch a few hours' sleep before it all started again. But within thirty minutes of getting my head down I was shaken awake by the watch-keeper. A small fire had broken out at one of our other bases, a checkpoint on the opposite – east – side of the Helmand River to the town. Initial reports suggested it had been put out and no serious damage had been done. I went back to bed. Two hours later I was shaken awake again. A different picture was emerging. Over the radio Captain James Cartwright, who was in charge of the OMLT team at the checkpoint, gave me more details.

The fire had originated in an accommodation room, a candle setting light to a mosquito net. The blaze quickly spread to clothing and bedding and before anyone could do much about it the whole room was ablaze. Ammunition started to explode and kit, including weapons, body armour and helmets, was burned beyond recognition. The fire was eventually put out by the valiant efforts of some of the men, but not before the equipment – and the room – were lost.

So how did our blaze begin? It turned out that because of the lack of any electricity at the checkpoint, neither from the mains nor a generator, one of the men had been reading his book by the light of a candle. Falling asleep without putting it out, the candle burned right down and set alight first the box it was sitting on and then the netting, a slight breeze from the open door quickly fanning the flames. Apart from the small matter of not putting the candle out, the soldier wasn't doing anything wrong. The use of candles is a well-practised procedure in the army and troops are advised to carry at least two for such situations where there is no power or light. Thankfully there were no injuries or deaths this time, but it could have been very different. In the early 1990s in Londonderry four men of the Ulster Defence Regiment weren't so lucky. They perished when their barrack room caught fire. It is bad enough losing men in action, without good people being claimed by accidents.

Our stay in Gereshk was due to last for six weeks, but after only half that time we were pulled out. It was decided by the Afghan commander of the ANA brigade, General Mohaiyoden, that the *kandak* we were mentoring needed a break. They had been in Gereshk for five months even before we arrived, without any leave or time off. They would be pulled back to

Shorabak to enter a training cycle and OMLT 4 would go with them.

I was bitterly disappointed. If things had been quiet in Gereshk, they were going to be a whole lot quieter at the main camp. The last thing I wanted was to be stuck in the middle of the desert, teaching men the principles of soldiering, rather than having the chance to help them put such skills into practice. More galling still was that others from the regiment were doing what I – and indeed the other men of OMLT 4 – craved. It was frustrating to come so far and now be so close to the action, and yet not have the chance to make a contribution. It wasn't about being gung-ho or having a death-wish. Nor indeed a blood lust. The motivation was to do what I had spent a lifetime being trained for, to test my abilities again, to share the dangers and hardships faced by the rest of 1 R IRISH. Anyway, hadn't I volunteered to stay on so perhaps I could help some of the younger members of the regiment when the shit hit the fan? I wasn't going to be able to do that, stuck in camp. There was also the selfish element. This was my last chance of frontline soldiering. My last tour. My swan-song. I was desperate to make it something to remember. But how? Orders are orders and mine were to stay at Shorabak. At least Margaret would be happy. By the middle of April I had just about resigned myself to my fate – which is when the battalion CO, Ed Freely, came riding to my rescue.

General Mohaiyoden had again been shifting pawns about on his giant chessboard. After a rather convoluted series of moves, some Afghan soldiers from Kandak 1, just returning from R & R, were tasked with going to Kajaki. The problem was their mentors were with the rest of the *kandak* in Sangin. So some replacements were needed. It was decided eight men from OMLT 4 could do the job. But who would be leading them? There was a near stampede of officers volunteering to go, me included. Not that I fancied my chances, given that I was 2IC. But to my astonishment Colonel Ed gave me the nod. I have no idea why. Who knows, perhaps he felt sorry for an old–timer. Whatever the reason I wasn't going to query it. I had got what I wanted. I was going back to the front, to Kajaki, an area I was already familiar with. I couldn't wait.

THREE

THE SOPRANOS WITHOUT
THE HUMOUR

MAJOR MIKE SHERVINGTON, 2 PARA

21 APRIL 2008

The Chinook lumbered – no, lurched – into the air. Immediately the nose dipped, and the aircraft started moving forward and upward at the same time. In seconds we were crossing the fences that marked the inner and outer perimeters of first Camp Shorabak and then Camp Tombstone. We might have been airborne but we weren't yet fully on our way. Once we'd hopped over the defences, before heading north, the pilots carried out a lap of the base and surrounding area, looking for any insurgents who had got a little too close for comfort. It was a reminder to those who wished us harm, and might have been watching, that we were serious about protecting ourselves and were not going to let them dominate the ground around the bases. The fly-by was also a good use of British and ISAF resources, saving on valuable fuel, and more importantly airframe flying hours, carrying out more than one task per flight.

As first we careered round the camps and then adopted a

rather more linear flight-path towards Kajaki, I took in my surroundings. I was hard pressed to remember I was sitting in a state-of-the-art helicopter. Every expense had been spared when it came to the aesthetics and comfort of the interior. Me and twenty-two others were sitting in two facing rows of seats, some of which were secured to the floor, whilst others folded away. They were simple in design – little more than strips of red cloth slung between aluminium poles. We were inside what was essentially a long metal tube, more square than round in section, with two sets of giant rotors bolted on top, and four sets of wheels anchored below. The skeleton of the aircraft was mostly invisible, covered as it was from the inside with grey lagging, but I caught glimpses of what was underneath. There were the ribs – spars bolted together – on the outside of which was riveted the metallic skin. Then there were the muscles, tendons and arteries that took the strain and kept the lifeblood of the Chinook pumping – hydraulic cylinders and pistons, oil pipes and water pipes, electrical cables. This was the anatomy of a helicopter.

All around us was a mass of equipment, clipped, tied and hung from an assortment of hooks, netting and webbing. On the floor ran a set of rollers to help shift more quickly whatever the cargo of the day might be. In our case it was much-needed supplies of food, ammunition and vehicle spares destined – as we were – for Forward Operating Base Zeebrugge, where its arrival was eagerly anticipated. I could see boxes with the words D Coy 2 PARA marked on them in bold. Amongst the ordnance were 81mm mortar bombs and Javelin missiles. Strewn on top of all this was our personal kit, bergan after bergan, every one stuffed to overflowing.

As for weapons, each man had his SA80 rifle between his legs, the barrel pointing downwards in case of a round being negligently discharged. This way a bullet would go through the floor rather than up through the motors and rotors keeping us airborne.

A second Chinook, flying some 300 metres to our flank and slightly to the rear, was loaded in a similar way. Our mini air armada was completed by an Apache attack helicopter; its job to go ahead and secure the area around the landing zone ready for when the two lumbering giants arrived. The vulnerability of the cumbersome Chinook had become all too apparent in 2007 when a CH-47 belonging to the Americans was shot down whilst over-flying one of the numerous villages that make up the Kajaki district, leaving its US crew and one British soldier dead. Yet there was little choice but to use these aircraft for moving men and equipment around the hostile Helmand environment. I tried to think of something other than our susceptibility to attack.

Using the light pouring in through the portholes punched in the side of the helicopter's skin – and the picture window created by the lowered ramp at the rear of the fuselage, a loadie crouched down and peering through it looking for the merest hint of enemy activity – I studied the three men of 1 R IRISH I was travelling with. Interspersed amongst the Afghans we were there to mentor, these were the last members of my team. They were all young, relatively inexperienced and, from the expressions on their faces, nervous, probably full of self-doubt.

Directly opposite me was Corporal Chris Kennedy, universally known as 'Colonel'. I was never sure why, but suspected it was because he always had an opinion, always had a better way of doing things, and was happy to express his thoughts as if he were the one in charge. Born in Manchester, Chris was tall and athletic. His brown hair was shaved to a skinhead. A long black tribal tattoo climbed up his left arm and over his shoulder. Big and strong he was the backbone of my team. He retained his Mancunian accent yet had the airs and graces of an Irishman. Chris fitted in well. When we got to Kajaki his job would be to mentor an ANA sergeant and his section of ten men.

Closer to the front of the cabin, and the open door that led to the cockpit, was Will Haighton from Belfast, a lance-corporal who had only just got his stripe. Married with a young daughter, he had been training with the OMLT since December 2007, but mainly with other teams so I didn't know him at all well. However, I did know his brother. Dennis Haighton had been one of my platoon sergeants when I was a company sergeant–major. We had served together in Kenya and Canada and I regarded him as a fine soldier. We had become good friends and I was pleased to have his younger brother with me now. Like Colonel, Will would be mentoring an ANA sergeant and his section.

As would Ranger Andy Muldrew, who sat closest to the ramp. Just twenty, he had only been in the regiment a year or two, and was full of youthful enthusiasm. It would be a tough job mentoring an Afghan NCO probably ten years his senior and who was likely to have a lot of combat experience. Life would have been easier if he – indeed all of us – made up part of a large British battlegroup, just as 5 SCOTS, and 2 and 3 PARA did. Yet the work of the OMLTs was crucial to solving the Afghan problem long-term; training the local security forces to sort out their own mess.

As with Will, I hadn't known Andy long, and was pretty much ignorant of his background other than the fact he came from Dover. Dover, for fuck's sake. Why the hell had he joined an Irish regiment?

Just before deployment I'd asked him. 'Jesus Christ, Andy, why is a man from Kent in the Royal Irish?'

'Because my dad served with the regiment. He got out when the battalion was in Dover.'

'Your dad? You don't mean Dennis Muldrew?' I said in astonishment.

Andy nodded his head.

If ever I felt old, that was the moment. I had been in Dover with Dennis. But as well as now feeling my age, I also felt pride. There had to be something about the character and reputation of the regiment that joining it so often became a family tradition, a tradition underlined by two of those sitting around me in the helicopter – the son of one former colleague and the brother of another.

I shifted my gaze to the rest of the occupants, the Afghans, men of Kandak 1. Like us Irish they too were a disparate group from a variety of backgrounds, cultures and tribes, sheltering under a broad, catch-all umbrella. There were Hazaras, Uzbeks, Tajiks, Pashtuns and more. Amongst the variety of languages they spoke, Dari seemed to be the most common. Few seemed to speak Pashtu, the local tongue in Helmand. In a way they summed up the huge difficulties there'll be in creating a cohesive Afghanistan – in which people recognise the authority of a single president and a Kabul-based central government – from the chaotic, violent federation of clans and families it currently resembles; a federation in which loyalties are decided by blood and honour, rather than party manifestos and votes at the ballot box.

As I studied the faces of these fighters, their ethnic origins became increasingly apparent. Some were distinctly oriental in appearance, their ancestors coming from the Turkmenistan region. Others were more obviously from towards the border with Pakistan. Then there were those who had a European look – several wouldn't have looked out of place on the streets of Rome or Athens or Istanbul.

But what I didn't yet know about the Afghans was their individual stories, their unique backgrounds. To me they were nameless individuals with no personalities. Yet it was critical that I – and the others – discovered what made them tick, and quickly. We would have to fight together as a unit. Often we would be putting our lives in their hands. It was well worth our while understanding their motivations and assessing their abilities.

Whilst my main priority was staying alive, there was also the small matter of professional pride. I wanted the Afghans to prove to the men of 2 PARA whom we'd be working with, that the ANA could do the job; that an Afghan solution to an Afghan problem was possible and not just pie in the sky. And to achieve that I needed to make the Afghans part of my team – and my team part of theirs. At that moment it was still very much them and us. I made a mental note.

We were nearly there.

The journey had not taken long yet the metamorphosis of the landscape had been striking. Some of the change I had glimpsed from the Chinook, the rest I already knew – from my 2006 tour.

First there was the transition from the desert surrounding Shorabak and Tombstone, with its small villages, long, winding tracks, and moon-style landscape, through to the lush, vivid colour of the Green Zone flanking the Helmand River. This fertile land was the territory the Taliban had made its own, building strongholds amongst the smothering foliage, winning over – or intimidating – the locals to gain their support. Further on again, where the Green Zone started to wither away as the river contracted, the sand's dominance was emphatically reasserted. Beyond this came the first hints of the dramatic geography that lay further up-country, gigantic monolithic rock structures jutting forth from the otherwise undulating landscape. Then one peak would become two, two would become four, and so on and so forth until the summits, uninhabited and uninhabitable, merged into vast rows of impenetrable mountain ranges.

But we weren't going that far. A few stages back, where the Helmand River still ran strong, lay Kajaki – and the dam synonymous with it. Looking out of the window I caught a glimpse of the lake feeding the hydroelectric turbines embedded in it.

A minute or so later, having eased ourselves between the ragged cliff faces rising up each side of the raging Helmand

River, we touched down, our great aerial beast settling first on its haunches, then stretching out to its full length on the sand of Helicopter Landing Site (HLS) Broadsword. An instant later and the ramp was fully lowered and we all spilled out – to be greeted by two groups of British soldiers. The first group was the outgoing OMLT. The second was some men from the other half of my team who had arrived the previous day; as we would have done if our helicopter had not been unserviceable.

There was just time for a few nods and smiles in way of greeting before we were dragged back to the Chinook to offload the stores and equipment. In no time at all the first air-craft had been unburdened and was off, making way for its sister ship to land and disgorge its contents, before it too returned to the skies and began the return journey south.

All we then had to do was shift the gear to the FOB des-tined to be our home for the next couple of months. We employed anything with an engine to carry the stuff the last leg of the journey; a pair of quad bikes with trailers, a Pinzgauer (an all-terrain vehicle), even an earthmover with a bucket, from the teeth of which we slung the rucksacks.

I decided to walk, talking to Captain Basim Mohammed, the departing OMLT commander and another Royal Irish officer, who had been at Kajaki for nine weeks. Basim was of Middle Eastern origin and we had first got our hands on him whilst he was at Sandhurst. Briefly he had left 1 R IRISH to try and seek his fortune in the City but this had bored him stupid and he rejoined in time to be deployed to Afghanistan.

His main job in Kajaki had been to extend the ISAF foot-print as far as possible to prevent the enemy forces using indirect fire to target the FOB. It had been a slog, regularly involving eight-hour patrols in forty-degree heat, all of which left the men routinely shattered.

Initially Basim had been working with the men of 40 Commando but 2 PARA, under the command of one Major

Mike Shervington, had taken over from them during the most recent roulement – the regular six-monthly rotation of British forces in which one brigade replaces another.

I asked Basim about the local politics. 'Who is the local governor and chief of police now? Please tell me it's not still Abdul Razik and Haji Faizullah?'

'Exactly. You don't know them, do you?'

Indeed I did – from my time in the region at the back end of 2006 and early 2007. During that period Faizullah had lived, with his men, up a mountain, somewhat nervous of being amongst the people for fear of making himself too easy a target for the Taliban. Back then I had even opened a new police HQ in the nearby village of Tangye but he had refused to use it, though things had recently improved with the ANP finally agreeing to occupy the building.

As for Razik, he was living near by, within the ISAF-controlled area around the dam and the FOB. At the dam itself, helping to guard it, were men from the local Afghan militia. Their commander was a member of the Alozai tribe, as were Razik and Faizullah. All three had family ties to each other, and to the former governor of Helmand, Sher Mohammed Akhundzada, who was now in Kabul, trying to get reappointed to the top job in the province. The political situation was, as Mike Shervington would later describe the labyrinthine political situation, similar to the hit American TV show about the Mob, *The Sopranos* – but without the humour.

I doubted the Afghans at the dam had any great loyalty to the legitimate provincial governor. Their prime allegiance would be to the Alozai, which meant the tribe controlled the whole region around Kajaki. And not just Kajaki, for the Alozai also ran Musa Qala, some forty kilometres to the west. Such was politics, Afghan style.

We turned away from the Helmand River, which we had been following, and hauled ourselves up a steep slope towards the FOB. The men called this final approach to the base the 'travelator' because it seemed to go on for ever. It was absolutely the last thing they needed as they returned from patrolling in searing temperatures. I flipped back my helmet to let some air circulate around my head. It made little difference.

The base itself was a series of buildings the Afghan ruling council, and even the royal family, had once used as a country retreat. Later on the Soviets occupied the site as an R & R facility, and heavily mined the area around it to preserve their privacy and their safety. The weapons had never been removed and continued to lie out of sight in so-called legacy minefields. One of them had already taken a British life, that of Corporal Mark Wright of 3 PARA, who died after stepping on the buried device in 2006. For his bravery trying to help others hurt in the same incident he was posthumously awarded the George Cross. Corporal Wright's rifle and equipment remained unrecovered in the minefield, a stark reminder of the threats the often benign-looking landscape offered up.

Not that it was only the Russians who'd left their mark on the area. As well as the police station I'd helped set up still being in existence, so too was the Joint District Co-ordination Centre (JDCC) I'd established in January 2007 just prior to leaving Afghanistan after my first tour of the country. It stood in the small corner of the base turned over to the OMLT and the Afghans.

As we got to the end of our journey I was pleased to see the remainder of my small 1 R IRISH squad come out to greet me. Leading the charge was Sergeant Jim Carney. Although he was from the Celtic fringe, he was Scottish and not Irish. A Glaswegian serving with 4 SCOTS he was another of those attached to us for the tour.

I had brought him on board because of his uncanny ability to source anything we needed. You name it and Jim would get it. I didn't know how, but he did his best to ensure we were as well equipped as anyone in Helmand. I had no intention of actually taking him out on patrol – not because I had any reservations about his abilities in the field, but because his time was better served back in the camp in a logistical role, protecting our interests, ensuring we never lost out on kit to our colleagues from the Parachute Regiment.

With Jim was Corporal Billy Sirisavana, a typical warm-hearted, easygoing Fijian, who would be my communications expert. Like so many of his countrymen over the years he had joined the British Army and was currently one of twenty-five Fijians serving with the Royal Irish.

Their role model was Trooper Talaiasi Labalaba, who started out as a Royal Irish Ranger and then passed selection for the SAS. He was killed in July 1972 in Oman at a place called Mirbat. With the enemy – several hundred Communist guerrillas – advancing on their position, nine Special Forces soldiers stood their ground, with Labalaba single-handedly manning an artillery piece, a 25-pounder, firing at his foes at point-blank range. Despite suffering a horrendous facial wound he continued to take on the enemy. After being shot again, he succumbed to his injuries. He was posthumously awarded a Mention in Despatches, but it was widely felt he deserved far more. Whatever the debate over his decoration, there was no disagreement about his bravery. He became part of SAS folklore.

Lastly there were Ranger Al Owens – a fellow Portadown man – and Ranger 'Crofty' Croft, who was barely out of training. They would act as force protection. In total that made eight of us from 1 R IRISH to mentor thirty men from the ANA. Together we comprised the third fighting platoon of 2 PARA's D Company.

That night I stood alone on the walls of the camp (they were made of HESCO, large steel mesh cubes, complete with a liner, each filled with earth to form giant building blocks) and looked out north over the Helmand River towards the

village of Tangye just beyond. Out to the west lay the settlements of Kanzi and Shabaz Kheyl that were, nominally at
least, in our hands. Further away still, to the north-west I
could see dim, flickering lights in the villages of Bagai Kheyl
and Machai Kheyl. This was enemy territory; both places
were in the hands of the Taliban. Strange to think. Everything
appeared so peaceful.

Major Mike said it was Kanzi and Shabaz Kheyl that would
be the targets of a charm offensive, a softly-softly approach,
during which we would try and bring a little reconstruction
and development. We'd also operate small field surgeries to
treat the aches and pains of the native population, which hopefully would help us win a degree of trust and respect from the
locals. To help achieve this, Mike was keen to employ the
services of Governor Razik, pushing him out to meet his
people as often as possible to help spread the good word about
ISAF.

When I had spoken with Mike earlier, he had mentioned
two more villages, Kajaki Olya and Kajaki Sofla, both south of
our position. They too saw Taliban activity.

As well as the three platoons of D Company based at the
FOB, there was a strong supporting cast, including an 81mm
mortar team (comprising three barrels, each with a crew of
four). A Fire Support Team (FST) co-ordinated the indirect
fire – not just from the mortars but also from the air and the
British-manned GMLRS based at FOB Edinburgh near
Musa Qala. Then there were men of the Fire Support Group
(FSG) based in observation posts up on Sparrowhawk East,
Sparrowhawk West and Athens – three peaks overlooking
Zeebrugge.

And it didn't stop there. At Zeebrugge there was also Mike's
HQ team; a bunch of engineers; some guys working with the
Unmanned Aerial Vehicle (UAV); and perhaps the most
important people of all – the medics, of which there were
four, led by a doctor, Rory. A medic would accompany each

platoon when they went out on patrol. Or at least they would accompany each of the two British platoons. The Afghan platoon didn't get a medic. Which meant nor did we.

(We should have arrived with our own medic in tow, but at that stage there hadn't been anyone available to us so it was assumed the company we'd be working with would supply one instead. But that's not how D Company saw it. We might have been their third fighting platoon, but in this respect we were expected to be self-sufficient.)

The patrol – the OMLT's first since we had arrived – moved slowly through a landscape all too familiar to me. For it appeared as if very little had changed since 2006, at least not for the better. Tangye remained deserted. Doors and shutters hung precariously from broken hinges, the damage caused by looters intent on emptying the shops and buildings of their contents. Telegraph poles and electricity pylons stood forlornly, the wires that had once been strung between them almost uniformly severed. The ground was littered with the frames of old motorcycles, anything of use long since scavenged. As we broke out of the western side of the village, the landscape opened up to reveal fields of poppies tended by Afghans, the soil irrigated by a network of ditches. Beyond the fields lay Kanzi and here too I could see people; mostly large groups of men. Between them ran small children.

Beside me walked the ANA commander, Captain Sherafadin, an Uzbek from somewhere north of Kabul. He had only been in the Afghan Army for about seven years, but as a man of forty-two he had done a lot of fighting before that. During the 1980s he had fought with the Mujahadin against the Soviets. To leave me in no doubt as to his exploits he pulled out an old Polaroid picture of himself, resplendent in traditional Afghan dress, sitting astride a still-smouldering Russian armoured personnel carrier, with corpses strewn all around. He was clutching an AK47. The weapon, he told me, had been captured from one of his victims and he carried it to this day. He had served alongside the famed General Massoud – the Lion of Panjshir – who the Americans supported against the invaders. Later Sherafadin was with the Northern Alliance when they overthrew the Taliban in 2001. After that he joined the ANA, and was given the rank of captain because of his time as a jihadi. To look at, he didn't seem your typical warrior. He was perhaps 5′9″ tall, with a wispy moustache and olive skin. His features were oriental. He spoke Dari and had only the most basic of Pashtu. But his military pedigree was faultless and he was keen to come out with his troops on patrol, which was more than many of the ANA commanders ever did.

At that moment he and his men – plus my OMLT guys – were picking up the rear, the two PARA platoons leading the way. In front of the Paras a couple of WMIKs were already on a piece of high ground known as Shrine, where they could cover a lot of the open country.

We came to a halt in the welcome shadows cast by some compound walls close to the M1, a dry watercourse that during the rains fed into the Helmand River. We waited to be called forward to interact with the locals. We waited. And we waited. And we waited. Nothing.

Mike Shervington was with the WMIKs on Shrine, with one of the PARA platoons that had the job of clearing the immediate area of mines. They stuck out like a pair of bulldog's bollocks, so after ninety minutes of not much going on, the inevitable finally happened. Temptation had got too much for the Taliban and the bollocks got shot at. The fire wasn't particularly heavy and not very accurate. Which might have been a blessing for those on Shrine, but was a pain in the arse for us because most of the rounds flew straight over the top of the hill and landed close by.

Mike's response was swift. With the enemy some 800 metres away, the GPMGs opened up. So did mortars from inside Zeebrugge. Then finally the GMLRS was brought into the fray too, firing a mission of three rockets. I didn't agree with Mike's tactics – I thought we should have moved in on foot to beat back the enemy instead of trying to dominate the ground by indirect fire – but I couldn't fault the weaponry we had available or his resolve to use it.

The TiC (Troops in Contact) petered out after an hour and a half and so did our patrol. Though that didn't mean the working day was done. Back at Zeebrugge we made for our little corner of the camp. The men of the OMLT were based in two main buildings, both semi-derelict. One housed the makeshift ops room, store and accommodation for me and Jim Carney; the other provided somewhere to kip for the rest of my team. Neither had any water, and only occasional electricity. Inside them each man marked out his territory as best he could, creating enough space to put his cot (with mosquito net), personal kit and weapon. The blocks were relatively cool during the day, yet at night they resembled furnaces.

There was also a pair of outbuildings. The first was divided in half, the OMLT ammunition on one side and the Afghan ammo on the other. The second building had been hastily converted to hold both a toilet and an improvised shower, the water for the latter stored in bags left to warm up in the sun during the day.

As some of the heat finally dissipated, we chatted to a group of the Afghans. Amongst them were Sergeant Shar Poor and Raz Mohammed. Poor was nicknamed the Russian. A giant man, he had Western features, and was probably the result of a union – forced or otherwise – between a Soviet soldier and his native mother. Mohammed was a sniper and he proudly carried his Draganov rifle everywhere he went. He was a Pashtun, though his hair was tinged slightly blond and he had deep green eyes. It was an odd combination, one I hadn't seen before. I could only guess at his heritage.

One of our big tasks was to convert our allies away from the

Kalashnikovs they favoured using, to American M16A2s, a rifle many Afghans, even though they were fighting on our side, tended to regard as the weapon of the infidel. We were going to have to be careful how we sold this particular baby to clearly sceptical customers.

Much of the debate – about the rifles, and indeed everything else – took place whilst we were drinking tea together. There would be round after round of chai, green tea infused with spices, and sweetened with mountains of sugar.

We also tended to eat with the Afghans. Whilst breakfast and evening meals were cooked by a couple of chefs on the PARA side of the camp, we would usually carry our food over to the ANA, making a point of exhibiting comradely behaviour towards them. This perceived aloofness was something our British colleagues didn't always understand and it left us in a difficult position. We hadn't gone native, yet although we were under the orders of our British masters, it was the Afghans we were supposed to be mentoring and working with on a daily basis.

Routine is important to soldiers when they are on tour. It becomes comforting and gives them something to measure time against. And there in Kajaki, life was starting to assume some sort of pattern. Every other day we would go out on long, exhausting patrols lasting anything up to thirteen hours. Yet we didn't seem to be taking the fight to the enemy, tending instead to remain within relatively safe areas. And when the Taliban did raise their heads we'd only respond with a torrent of indirect fire rather than boots and bayonets. On the positive side, Razik the Governor was continuing to get out and about as Mike had intended. No end of *shura*s – local councils – were held between village elders, the British and the Governor. Mike took every opportunity to big-up the importance of the man. Which might have been good for building bridges, but left me and the other OMLT guys with very little to do other than carry out the static tasks we increasingly seemed to be set with the ANA. It was frustrating for me. And for the Afghans. They wanted to fight the Taliban and prove their worth, yet they were being used in a PR role. It was important the Afghans were seen guaranteeing the safety of the *shura*s; important but not something that did much for their morale. Surely something was going to break the monotony?

It wasn't just legacy mines that threatened the unwary in and around Kajaki. So too did the IEDs planted much more recently by the Taliban. As if to underline the danger, shortly before our arrival, two members of 40 Commando had been killed on the 611 South – the main road running from the dam down towards Sangin and the rest of Helmand province – when their Land Rover had detonated such a weapon. And intelligence showed the enemy was continuing to use such tactics in the hope of striking lucky again. Which was why, towards the end of May, Mike slightly changed his priorities and placed more emphasis on clearing the territory to the south of Zeebrugge.

Our patrol had left camp early, at 05:30 hrs, whilst the rising sun, hinting at the glaring brightness which lay ahead, stained the sky pink. We headed down the 611, shielded from enemy eyes in Kajaki Olya and Kajaki Sofla by the high ground on top of which sat the OPs Sparrowhawk and Athens.

With the two PARA platoons in front of us, we continued on until we reached a vehicle checkpoint manned by the ANP. Then the real work began. With Two Platoon now pushing off the road to the west and moving parallel to the main route between it and the Helmand River, One Platoon started searching for IEDs on the 611. There was no quick way of doing it. Slowly, ever so slowly, men walked forward sweeping the area ahead of them with metal detectors. At the merest hint of anything suspicious it was then down on to their belt buckles, first gently dusting away loose sand and dirt with bare hands, then prodding the ground with bayonets, feeling for enemy devices. Every so often the WMIKs would push forward along the latest section of the road to have been made safe, before stopping again to cover the ground ever further south.

With their grandstand view, the troops up on Sparrowhawk provided a running commentary on the radio about what was happening around us. They paid particular attention to a group of houses and compounds sitting on the 611 about two kilometres away from us that had been labelled Big Top. Marking the point where Kajaki Olya, controlled by the government and ISAF, ended and the Taliban-held Kajaki Sofla began, it was regarded as the hub of insurgent activity in the southern part of our area of operations.

The patrol passed a junction where a track spurred off and headed out into the Green Zone. It was a route well trodden by both the Taliban and civilians alike. The Paras had named it Reg Alley. The Afghans called it Kajaki Street. The OMLT, Tali Alley. And just south of this junction was where the Paras found their first home-made mine; some ordnance roughly equivalent in size to a 105mm shell had been dug into the road at a point where a vehicle was likely to pass over it. Attached to the base of the device, via some wires, was a pressure pad, which when depressed would set off the IED. It was an IED like this that killed the two commandos.

The Taliban were smart enough to ensure locals didn't become victims. They issued warnings that devices had been planted and advised villagers to stay on either one side of the track or the other. Or off it altogether. The more sophisticated mines relied on an ISAF or Afghan security forces' vehicle depressing pressure pads on alternate sides of the road. As the locals never used anything more sophisticated than motorbikes, they were physically incapable of setting them off.

Not more than fifteen metres on, a similar weapon was discovered. Making them safe was down to bomb-disposal teams who would fly in from Camp Bastion or perhaps Sangin. But, first, news of the discoveries had to be passed on up the chain of command. A long chain at that. The guys on the ground spoke to the ops room at Zeebrugge. Zeebrugge spoke to battlegroup HQ in Sangin. Sangin spoke to the Brigade HQ in Lashkar Gah. It needed to go this high because there were only so many Explosive Ordnance Disposal Detachment (EODD) teams to go round. It was Brigade's job to prioritise. Luckily for us, that day we appeared to be near the top of the list, yet it was still going to take them a couple of hours to reach Kajaki.

So Mike said the patrol should move on. But not too far. Our destination was to be 'flanker', one of several imaginary lines — so-called report lines — on the map, dreamed up by Mike as points of reference for our advance, all named after a different position in the rugby team. Flanker ran through two compounds that had been given the numbers 161 and 162. Each and every compound in our area had been allocated a unique number on our charts to try and distinguish one set of very similar-looking mud walls from another. There were several hundred of them in all.

We had now been on the go for six hours and the sun was almost at its zenith in the clear sky. With it so high, there was now next-to-no shade. As we waited to move, the ANA soldiers kept darting off the road to find streams from which to quench their thirst. It wasn't something British soldiers were inclined to do, no matter how parched. The chances of catching diarrhoea and vomiting in Afghanistan were high enough even without supping from rivers, streams and ditches.

Then Mike came on the VHF radio. 'Amber 21 Alpha, you are to push through "10" [One Platoon] and take over the task of clearing the road.'

'Roger, out.'

A few minutes later and we were up at the front. Unfortunately the Afghans didn't have official permission to use the specialised clearance equipment (because it was still labelled 'secret'), which put the responsibility squarely on the shoulders of the OMLT. It was Andy and Colonel who took up the reins. Full of concentration, heads bowed, sweat quickly forming on their brows, then dripping down their faces and into the dust, they started to inch forward, Al and Crofty a few metres behind, GPMGs at the ready, looking out for any activity in the compounds, tree-lines and ditches we passed. We couldn't have been more exposed. Getting ever nearer to enemy territory at a snail's pace, right out in the open. For the two guys at the front it took an immense amount of guts to keep their minds on the task, fighting an almost irresistible urge to look up and scan the surrounding area for the Taliban, but knowing a moment's lapse of concentration could see them blown to bits. In situations like this you almost want to be shot at, want something to break the tension and give you an excuse to engage the enemy. But nobody did shoot at us, so we continued forward, carrying out our drills as we went, the mental stress remaining high. Completely knackered, we finally reached flanker.

'All call signs, this is Zero Alpha,' said Mike. 'What is your water supply like at the moment?'

'10, we're down to about half a litre each, perhaps an hour in this heat,' was the response from One Platoon. Two Platoon was in a similar situation.

I pressed the transmit button. 'Amber 21 Alpha, we've probably got four hours' worth of water.'

I wasn't referring to the OMLT supplies; we had little more left than our Para colleagues. I was talking about the Afghans. They had the advantage of using the *ad hoc* water sources they came across and my assessment was they had several more hours of work left in them. Which meant so did my men.

'Roger, 10 and 20. I will get the CSM on the quad to deliver some water.'

Not that there would be any for the ANA soldiers. None of them carried water bottles and – quite rightly – the CSM refused to let the Afghans drink directly from the jerrycan. But the OMLT wouldn't be getting any, either. It was about perceptions and I didn't want those we were mentoring to think we were receiving some advantage they were not. I needed the Afghans to see we were in this together. There would be no special favours for us.

Anyway, there was no time to sit and wait for supplies because we had just got new marching orders from Mike.

'I want you to push on to "second row".'

The new instructions would put us ever closer to Big Top and the enemy-held positions we knew were there. During the patrol the local pattern of life had seemed pretty normal. Children playing in Kajaki Olya, men tending their crops. But now the civilians were markedly absent. Those we did see ahead of us were heading away south. There was also a lot of movement of people and vehicles around Big Top. It looked ominous. But suddenly it seemed there were more immediate issues closer to home.

'Boss, I've got something!' called Colonel over his personal role radio (PRR).

'So have I,' said Will, who had replaced Andy on the metal detector a little earlier.

'All right, fellas, do your confirmation and let me know what you have.'

I left the guys to it and reported the situation to Mike. Ten minutes later and Colonel confirmed he had found a shell. Will described a pressure pad wrapped in clear polythene, buried under some loose earth.

I passed news of the finds back to the ops room. 'Zero. This is Amber 21 Alpha. IED grid PR41 AQ96327525. Roger so far.'

When I had completed my messages I heard from Mike, reminding us to clearly mark where we'd made our discoveries. The hard work done, it would have been a tragedy if they had still caused casualties.

From his position a hundred metres or so back, Mike had been watching our steady progress with interest. He had also heard the EODD team was only forty minutes away. He wanted to make the most of them when they arrived, so we got the order to push on further still, first to second row and then 'prop'. By now Andy had returned to the front, having taken over from Colonel. Behind them I could see the mental and physical effort was taking a toll on Al and Crofty. Every time the lead pair stopped – which was often – the boys would sink to the ground, bring their GPMGs into covering positions and then wearily rest their heads against the metal.

I chivvied them along. 'Stay alert, guys. Good work.'

Not easy after nine hours on the go.

Bang. Whoosh. Bang.

It was the unmistakable sound of an RPG being fired and then detonating to the east of the road. It was followed up by the noise of AK47s and PKMs. The fire was accurate, sustained and heavy. A torrent of rounds churned up the hard earth. All around me people dived for cover. Me, I found myself with Andy sprinting for some dry trenches just off the road.

'Zero, Zero Alpha, this is Amber 21 Alpha. Contact Big Top. Wait. Out.'

From where we were lying I could just make out the main firing point in a line of trees just to the west of Big Top. As if for confirmation another RPG shot out of the tree-line and airburst just behind us. The open ground we had been stand-ing on just seconds earlier was being gouged by an incredible amount of bullets. It seemed as if there wasn't a square metre of soil left untouched. Not far ahead of us, on the other side of the killing field, Colonel, Al and Will had taken up a posi-tion at the side of compound 200. They had seen what we'd seen and Al was answering back with his GPMG. Will loosed off a few 40mm grenades from the underslung launcher on his rifle. Looking over my shoulder I could see that Captain Sherafadin had gathered together a section of his men and was moving towards the enemy position. I couldn't fault their enthusiasm but I had a terrible feeling they would start an assault with no sort of plan. I had to get to them.

'Zero Alpha, we have enemy to the . . .'

My sitrep was cut short as .50-calibre rounds fired from Sparrowhawk flew over my head and made me duck.

I tried again. 'Zero Alpha, we have an enemy position to the west of Big Top in the area of grid 656744. We also have enemy just south of Big Top at compound 219.'

Mike responded. 'We will use 81mm to suppress both positions. GMLRS on standby. Keep down.'

Immediately I heard the response I did the opposite. I was up and running – across the open ground I had just been so keen to escape. The thought of one of the heavy-calibre rounds finding its target made me sick, a constant reminder provided by the whiz and crack of bullets overhead. There is much speculation about what motivates soldiers to face danger when all they want to do is bury themselves in the dirt – inspiring speeches, thoughts of Queen and country; the reality is these count for very little. What really drives troops on is a sense of duty – to their mates. There is a desire to share whatever danger the other lads are enduring. But that doesn't mean the fear goes away. It remains. And the trouble with fear is that it can just as easily paralyse as galvanise.

I slithered into some sort of cover behind the Afghans.

I had to make the ANA aware of what was coming next. They seemed oblivious to any bigger picture and were casually blasting away at the enemy positions. I reached the captain, hauling the interpreter after me. The officer had spotted a piece of elevated ground further south that he believed would be a great place from which to put down fire on Big Top. I checked with Mike. He gave the OK, and in turn I gave the thumbs-up to the Afghan. Without pausing for breath, he was off with two of his sections. Their journey was not one to be relished – a sprint across thirty metres of open ground, under heavy fire, before reaching the relative safety of another compound hidden from enemy view by the dead ground it nestled in.

But whilst it was the ANA at the forefront of the contact, we were still mere pawns in Mike's battle. We were at his beck and call. Yet I was pleased the Afghans had already shown that when the two-way range was opened they were up for the fight.

As for the Paras, Two Platoon in the Green Zone was engaging Talibs to the west of Big Top. Meanwhile One Platoon was being ordered forward by Mike together with the CSM – a Dubliner – who was bringing up more ammo and water. I was nervous for them, though. I didn't want them to move too hastily into the open ground where we had been caught when the shooting started. So I sent Andy back with his Afghan section to secure the trench system we had first dived headlong into to escape that initial onslaught.

I was now with Colonel and Crofty, plus Sherafadin and about ten of his men, just below the high ground the Afghans wanted to use as a fire position. By this stage, 81mm mortar rounds, originating from Zeebrugge, were regularly landing on and around the target. The fire was generally first class. Accurate and deep, it gave us confidence.

What we needed next though was the cover of the GMLRS rockets landing to move up the high banking. Within seconds of me explaining to the Afghans what we were going to do, three rockets duly arrived, tearing into the enemy positions. The Afghans didn't need telling twice and we scrambled up to the vantage point. Big Top was a mere 400 metres away. The ANA's enthusiasm hadn't waned, yet their technique of getting to their feet and then randomly spraying rounds towards the enemy was questionable. What I wanted was for them to be down on the floor, controlling their rate of fire and concentrating on its accuracy. In the heat of battle, struggling to communicate through an interpreter who was fighting his own war to get himself heard above the clatter of weapons, this was not an easy message to convey. It seemed as if a hands-on approach might work better. I watched as Colonel manhandled a PKM machine gunner to a better position and then gestured wildly at one of his colleagues to come over and help feed the ammunition belt through the weapon.

Despite the Afghans' shortcomings Big Top had taken a real pasting, what with all the small-arms fire (SAF), the mortars, the .50-cals and the GMLRS. If we were going to take the enemy position this was the time to do it.

But instead Mike came over the radio, telling us to withdraw from the top of the high ground and out of view of the enemy position. 'CAS [Close Air Support] inbound and advice is you are too close.'

The aircraft on their way to us were French Mirages. The general view in theatre was that the French were not to be trusted. Better keep a good distance between the intended point of impact and your position – this advice coming from the JTAC with Mike was unambiguous. We slipped and slithered off the hill and back to the safety of the building in its lee. Even so, I was disappointed we were not to push home our advantage. We had put the enemy through it, but were now withdrawing, the natural consequence being that the area would remain in Taliban hands. We had cleared and held the 611 as far south as prop and had got within a stone's throw of the Taliban hub for exerting influence and control over Kajaki Sofla and Kajaki Olya. But were turning back. What a shame. I was convinced we could have completed the job with no more than the platoon of Afghans.*

---

* I believed Mike wanted to go for Big Top that day but that he was held back by orders from on high. ISAF would not get that far south again until August as part of the project to deliver a new turbine to the Kajaki dam during which a full battalion of Paras and another from the ANA took Big Top. Talk about a sledgehammer to crack a nut.

FOUR

COMPOUND 808

CORPORAL CHRIS 'COLONEL' KENNEDY, 1 R IRISH

11 JUNE 2008

'Casualty! Casualty!'

The scream came over my PRR and my heart skipped a beat.

The voice was distinctive, even above the din of battle. It was Colonel's. But what I didn't know, because he hadn't told me, was just who was hurt. He sounded under considerable duress, but was that because he was injured himself or struggling to help one of the Afghans with him?

Rolling on to my side, enemy fire raining down from at least four positions, I desperately fumbled for the pressel switch on the PRR that would allow me to transmit via the VHF radio set on my back. 'Zero. Zero Alpha. This is Amber 21 Alpha. I have a casualty. No further details. Over.'

The message went both to Major Grant Hayward, who was out on the ground with us, and back to the ops room at Zeebrugge.

I peered in the direction in which I had last seen Colonel – entering compound 808. Over the PRR: 'Colonel, this is Boss, send details.'

Even amongst the cacophony of noise, the ominous sound of silence emanating from the radio stood out. It sent a shiver down my spine. Shit.

I tried again. 'Colonel, Boss. Over.'

Still nothing.

I tried over the VHF set. 'Amber 21 Charlie, this is Alpha, over.'

The deafening silence continued. Now my brain was in overdrive. What had happened? Was Colonel wounded? Was he so busy fighting for his life behind those mud walls that he couldn't respond?

I looked around. In all directions there were British and Afghan troops. Andy and his ANA section just to the south at compound 628. Out to the west a platoon of Paras. Will and his Afghan section were close by, too. Then there was the veritable army of acronyms all itching to join in the fight.

On top of Shrine was a pair of WMIKs manned by the FSG (fire support group).

Grant and the FST (fire support team) were at compound 627.

The MFC (mortar fire controller) was preparing to cover us with high explosive rounds and smoke fired from Zeebrugge.

The FOO (forward observation officer) was keying up the GMLRS.

And the JTAC was frantically requesting CAS.

Yet all these letters, all this firepower, was of little use if we couldn't find out what had happened to Colonel and the six Afghans with him, and what help he actually needed. My head was spinning. There was too much going on. Whilst doing my best to make contact with my colleagues, I was still being fired at, bullets raking the ground around me. In my ear I could hear Grant outlining some sort of plan, whilst the Paras, plus Andy and his Afghans, were all sending their own sitreps. For good measure there were repeated yells from the four ANA soldiers alongside me, asking for advice. And on top of it all there was still more chatter from the teams on the peaks, reporting on enemy movement they could see in the distance, but which – for now at least – was not my problem. No, my problem lay 150 metres away with Colonel.

Trying to banish the multitude of voices all demanding to be heard, I pushed myself up out of the dusty hollow I'd created with my body as I squirmed, trying to keep as low as possible. First I got on to my hands and knees, and then on to my feet. Really I wanted to disappear into the ground, get out of trouble, yet I had to do the opposite, get up and move, and in so doing reveal myself to the enemy. I stumbled forward, then broke into a run, hunched over, my head and neck telescoped as far into my shoulders as I could get them. Come on, Beattie, you bastard. Fucking move. Pumped up with adrenalin I might have been, but my limbs quickly started aching from the exertion of my stooped style, my feet alternately fighting for traction in the dust and sand, then jarring badly against rocks and the baked earth. My brain, working at a phenomenal rate, shouted orders to my body. 'Keep going. Keep going. Faster. Faster. Don't stop.' And yet – even though I was covering the ground as fast as I could – the compound didn't seem to be getting any closer. It was as if I was progressing in ultra-slow motion. And all the time I wondered what I would find when, if, I finally reached my goal.

Things in Kajaki had changed over the previous few weeks. Major Shervington and the majority of his men had been pulled out to join the main effort in Sangin. Mike's replacement was Grant Hayward with patrols platoon. Cobbled together (wasn't everything in this war?) with the rump of Mike's men they created X Company. A smaller force than the outgoing D Company, it also had a more limited mission, the order now from Colonel Joe O'Sullivan, the boss of 2 PARA, to contain the Taliban, rather than confront them and expand the ISAF mandate. Yet Grant arrived full of vigour and was keen to flex his muscles. I saw in Grant a different side to 2 PARA. Not softer – he was just as up for a fight as Mike was – but more aware of the bigger picture and the efforts being made by soldiers other than those from the Parachute Regiment. It wasn't that Mike spared no thought for the contribution of the Afghans (he held weekly chai sessions with the ANA and offered some of his men up to help the Afghan sniper team) but I sensed he would essentially measure success in Kajaki in terms of how 2 PARA behaved and what they did or didn't do. I had even sat in on a briefing where a Para officer asked if, after completing his patrol, he should leave a calling card, a so-called 'death card' for the enemy to find. A sort of '2 PARA woz 'ere' message. It was all a bit over-the-top, a bit American. Not wrong, just symptomatic of their mindset, perfect for certain circumstances, not necessarily right for these. To Mike's credit, his answer was 'No'.

Grant was less overtly gung-ho and, from the OMLT point of view, his opinions on how the ANA could and should be used were encouraging. He also had some fresh ideas about how patrols should be carried out. He was keen to keep the physical burden on the troops down to a minimum. To that end he ensured kit was not humped around unnecessarily and arranged vehicles to transport men to and from the specific areas they'd been ordered to patrol. It meant men were fresher, and had more time on task, chatting to the locals, making their presence felt, collecting intelligence. (Regular intelligence-gathering was a key part of his strategy.) He was also keen to continue Mike's work of mapping the area, right down to the smallest of compounds, giving each walled settlement a history; 528, that's where we were ambushed last week; 406, that's where enemy snipers have been located. Etc. Etc. Combined with a log detailing the general pattern of life in the surrounding villages, it all went towards creating a better understanding of the environment and importantly it was something to be handed over to whichever poor sods arrived next.

There was one thing I thought Grant was misguided on, however.

Like Mike, he embraced the Governor and the Chief of Police, charmed by their stories of how they were both involved in liberating the dam during the struggle against the Russians. Their exploits gave them great kudos amongst the ISAF forces, the US non-military contractors in Kajaki and indeed some of the local population. However, theirs wasn't the only version of events doing the rounds. Another one suggested our heroes had not taken control of the dam by storming the camp and clearing the main Russian stronghold, wiping out many of the enemy in the process, but had instead walked in unopposed when the Soviets left. (The supposed site of the Russians' last stand, a large two-tiered block of offices and accommodation, stood derelict and ignored at the edge of Zeebrugge, scrub trees and bushes growing up around it.)

I continued to have reservations about both men and was concerned by their close ties with Sher Mohammed Akhundzada. If the Brits weren't keen on Akhundzada regaining the governor's job – which they weren't, given the strength of the province's illegal drug trade – then the pair's loyalties to him weren't necessarily going to make our job of working with them any easier. I was worried also that details of ISAF operations were being passed on to the Taliban by men – under Faizullah's control – in the ANP. Not that there had been much to tell recently, as we continued to be restrained by our orders – and on paper this meant not taking the fight to the enemy as often as we would have liked. This was now having an impact on the local population. The Afghans who had returned to the village of Kajaki Olya having heard it had become part of the ISAF-controlled zone were leaving again. We could not provide the security we had promised and so the Taliban came and went with impunity, coercing the residents and using the settlement for their own purposes. The situation in Kanzi was similar. A thriving community when I had first arrived, it had become a ghost town, the last inhabitants departing after the poppy harvest had been gathered in.

By now, the only occupied village within ISAF control was Shabaz Kheyl, but even there the population had shrunk, fed up with being pushed and pulled between the two opposing forces. We would patrol through the streets, singing the praises of the internationally supported Kabul government, only for the Taliban to emerge almost as soon as we'd disappeared round the corner, to give completely the opposite message. The trouble was, we didn't want the village to become the front line, because that in itself would force the rest of the residents to leave. Some of those who had already been displaced had fled to the hills, whilst others had moved further into Taliban territory where at least they could take their produce to market without getting caught up in the fighting. A few remained within spitting distance of the village, living in makeshift mud huts or under canvas, together with their animals, just a few hundred metres from their former homes. The real answer was for us to take on the Taliban further north and west of Kajaki, well away from the dwindling civilian population, but the boundary set for us lay only just beyond Shabaz Kheyl and the people living there. Grant's only option for making a difference was to test the boundary and then push beyond it as far as he dared in the hope that this would entice the Taliban to raise their heads, only to then take a beating. If successful it would create a buffer between enemy-held territory and the last remaining populated village we controlled. As for the bait in the trap? Well, that was the ANA, and by association the OMLT. Us.

It was early June and I sat on a bench at the back of the briefing room to receive yet another patrol brief. It was something I had been doing pretty much day in, day out, for five weeks.

The room wasn't big and it was crammed full with all those commanders involved in the mission. With the help of a large map Grant went through the plan.

We would leave the FOB and head north towards yet another pair of deserted settlements and search and clear some compounds. This wasn't a completely random objective, as it was believed the enemy had dug a series of tunnels connecting the various walled complexes so they could move unseen between them and get into good firing positions from which to target our base. Only a few nights previously a number of Chinese 107mm rockets had come scudding in our direction only to fall short and detonate harmlessly on the mountainside below. Even so, it showed the Taliban had noted we weren't patrolling as deeply as previously and had taken the initiative to mount an attack which although unsuccessful could easily cause casualties the next time they tried it. Once we had cleared the compounds we would turn west in the direction of Kanzi, recently the scene of more enemy activity. The aim was to detect and make safe any IEDs they might have planted.

Simple.

Then the CSM went through the admin side of the patrol – dress, rations, weapons, ammo, water, what to do with prisoners of war, what the medical drills were. It was basic stuff, much of it I'd heard often before, yet for the sake of the utmost clarity it is gone through before every outing.

The last thing to be done was synchronise watches. As tradition dictated, the FOO took the lead, the army being run on artillery time, a throwback to the Great War.

Briefing over, I went to find Captain Sherafadin and pass on the good news. I found him sitting, bare-chested, outside his building, next to the radio he used to keep in touch with the ANA HQ in Shorabak, underneath a small lean-to he had made for himself. He wasn't alone. With him was the Russian, the pair of them sipping tea, a fly-infested sugar bowl between them. As I approached, the Russian stood up and gave me the limp handshake characteristic of Afghan greetings. He handed me a cup of chai and gestured for me to sit down in his place. I asked him to go and find me an interpreter. The Russian sloped off.

As for Sherafadin, he wasn't as jovial as usual or as eager to do the mission as he might have been. There had been some infighting amongst the ANA and this was blunting his enthusiasm for the job. A replacement section commander, a sergeant with the entirely inappropriate name of Mohamid Ali, was causing friction in the unit and he had his own clear views on how the mentoring process should work.

Our role, as set down in the manual, was to advise and support the ANA and act as a link between them and coalition forces. It was also to ensure the Afghan officers made the decisions, commanded the men, were first into battle. How else would the Afghans learn and gain the experience needed to one day run the country themselves? Of course the reality didn't quite match the theory. More often than not, the OMLT members would be forced to lead by example, demonstrating the theory, and that invariably meant being at the front, closest to the enemy, rather than at the back. Still, the goal remained consistent – encourage the Afghans to fight their own battles. Which is not how Mohamid Ali saw it. In his mind he was there to follow British orders, not to come up with any of his own. In the end it all became too much for Sherafadin, who, through his working relationship with me, was now damaged goods as far as the sergeant was concerned. Which is why he decided to sit out this particular patrol and let his NCOs get on with it. Given that he had taken part in every operation we had so far conducted, which was in itself unusual for an Afghan officer, I wasn't going to make an issue of it. As for Ali, well at least he was being mentored by Colonel, who was by far the most experienced member of my team, so I was hopeful the Afghan would knuckle down and come to accept the rules.

Giving orders to 'Colonel' in Kajaki Olya.

'Colonel' (right) with Pete, who shared my 'contact' in Kenya with the taxi driver.

An ANA soldier in action.

ANA troops at prayer.

Briefing an ANA commander before a patrol. Sometimes diplomacy doesn't work.

Congratulating the same ANA commander after the patrol. The Afghan flag on my arm was worn to show solidarity with our ANA allies.

British and Afghan troops assault compounds in Shomali Ghulbah.

The view from the top of the Kajaki dam, with the turbine house below.

Brown-out as a Chinook lands covered by an Apache attack helicopter.

Weighed down with standard equipment, only the helmets are missing. Brummie is on the left.

Brummie's WMIK after a mine strike in Garmsir. He was lucky to survive.

'Junior' Stewart with Afghan pals and a new M16A2.

105mm artillery pieces firing in support of British patrols in contact.

Marjah, moments after the suicide bomber struck.

A TacSat antenna being pointed towards a satellite in order to establish
communication.

The last photo taken before we departed Marjah. Jon (far left) was killed just weeks later.

Attending the wedding of my daughter Leigh while back in the UK on R & R in July 2008.

When the time came for the section commanders to hear what they would be doing, at least Ali seemed to listen, for a few minutes anyway, which by my reckoning was pretty standard for the majority of Afghans, who uniformly gave the impression of having the attention span of five-year-olds. I handed out maps marked with our objectives. On our arrival in Kajaki this would have been a waste of time as the ANA didn't know one end of a map from another (which was strange given that they had been receiving mentoring for eighteen months by that stage and map-reading was high on the list of priorities. I suspected the Afghans were just playing dumb to avoid taking responsibility). A bit of intensive training had gone some way to alleviating the problem. My mini-brief complete, I asked for questions. There were several. Not about the upcoming task but about kit. The Afghans constantly believed they were being short-changed when it came to equipment and they could never resist having a dig, pushing to find out when they might get what they clearly regarded as rightfully theirs.

'Captain, we need PRRs.'

'We must have camel packs for water.'

'More food, we have not got enough rations.'

And so it went on. Compasses, head torches, pouches, better transport; the shopping list got longer every bloody day, but it was not in my gift to give them any of these things. I answered each request with a weary shrug of the shoulders, a practised look of sadness and regret painted on my face. Usually I got a smile in return. The Afghans understood I couldn't deliver what they wanted, yet they felt obliged to ask just the same. I suppose, in a country of such hardship and deprivation, where everything is a struggle, sitting back and politely waiting for something to happen wasn't an option. If you didn't ask you were never going to get. And yet, with me, ninety-nine times out of a hundred they were left disappointed. I suspected it was a feeling they were used to.

My interrogation complete, the section commanders shot off. I sent Billy Sirisavana after them to gauge their mood. Billy, the Fijian, had managed to build up a fantastic rapport with the Afghans – perhaps his swarthy complexion made him appear more one of them than one of us. He had been teaching them English and I was confident he would find out if there was anything troubling them before we set off. This was pretty crucial, because I didn't want to be in charge of a group of gun-toting Afghans if they were disillusioned, even rebellious, and I did not have any inkling of it. Billy had delivered for me before, though what he uncovered was not always palatable. On one occasion an ANA soldier had been caught stealing a cot bed from one of the Paras and was brutally beaten with a stick by Sherafadin before being made to march up and down the main road in the heat of the day with all his equipment on. Billy revealed that even before the captain had meted out his own punishment, the NCOs had battered the man behind closed doors. It only reinforced my opinion of the unforgiving, brutal, summary justice Afghans were capable of. Yet it was not my place to intervene. Perhaps after the punishment had finished I would go and have a quiet word with Sherafadin and tell him of other ways of instilling discipline. But the last thing I wanted was for him to lose face in public and have his authority undermined. It was important that the Afghans were in no doubt there was a chain of command and at the end of it sat their own commander, not me.

Even when no malice was intended, and the Afghans were merely joshing about, things could get out of hand. Such as the time a young Afghan soldier had to be airlifted out of Kajaki, suffering from a broken pelvis. My initial thought was that he had been paid a little too much attention during 'All Man Thursday', the ANA's day of recreation, when they would chill out, listen to music, sing songs and dance, and on occasion indulge in a bit of homosexuality – not all of it between consenting adults. There was a distinct pecking order. It was the younger soldiers who had to watch themselves. Rank, as they say, has its privileges. In the case of the man with the broken bones, only later did Billy discover that, rather than being the recipient of too much loving, he had in fact fallen victim to the Russian's attempts to prove his physical prowess. Seizing the soldier and whirling him above his head, the Russian then promptly dropped the hapless bloke on to a rock, fracturing his hip. It was surprising what Billy could find out.

That night I sat with the men watching a DVD – Peter Kay doing his stand-up routine – in our makeshift recreation room. We had already eaten the evening meal. Pasta. Again. Often the Afghans would ask us to join them for dinner. I was happy to go and sit with them, indeed I usually did, but the threat of a dose of the shits would normally dissuade me from sharing their food – usually rice and beans with flat bread. Like our rations, it was pretty bland.

As the credits rolled on the DVD, before I could get my head down, there were still plenty of things that needed doing. I had to make sure the ANA sentries were in position on the western perimeter of the camp. I had to make sure the OMLT was doing its share of guard duties with 2 PARA. Then I had to do a turn in the ops room, listening to the radio, absorbing information about the situation elsewhere in Helmand. Every now and then there would be mention of my Royal Irish colleagues. A Company of 1 R IRISH was in Sangin, mentoring the ANA and – together with Ranger Company – supporting 2 PARA. Very early on they had suffered a big setback when the company commander, Major Simon Shirley, was seriously injured by an IED. Pictures of the aftermath of the attack, including the badly damaged Land Rover he had been in at the time, quickly winged their way from email inbox to inbox. It was sobering stuff and made me pleased to be on foot, not vehicle-bound.

Meanwhile men from B Coy 1 R IRISH were mentoring the ANA's Kandak 2 in an area known as battlegroup east centred around the town of Musa Qala. The main British contingent there was 5 SCOTS.

Finally, though, even I ran out of things to do and it was time to try and catch a few hours' sleep, though I hated going to bed. It allowed too much time to think. About my own situation. About my family. And yet every time I hit the sack it meant I was one day closer to the end of the tour, one day closer to going home. I finished writing a 'bluey' (an army letter, so called because the paper is blue) to Margaret, then lay down on my back, listening to my iPod. I knew that even when I managed to get to sleep, there was little chance of it being deep and uninterrupted, contaminated as it would be by nightmares, disturbed by gunfire. Four hours was the norm. I closed my eyes.

We formed up at the top of the hill, besides the ops room and the travelator, everyone trying to find some last-minute piece of shade before the work began. I stood almost at the front of the patrol, just behind the lead section – which included Andy and the Russian – and just in front of Colonel with Mohamid Ali and his men. With them were two combat engineers who, amongst their other duties, had found themselves working to shore up the rickety wooden bridge over the Helmand River that sat almost directly beneath the camp. Today they were coming with us. We'd be using their skills to give us quick access to compounds we didn't like the look of, not through the front door, which might be mined or watched by the enemy inside, but via holes in the walls blown out with bar mines (lengths of HE shaped like short planks, wrapped in green, heavy-duty plastic). The last group of OMLT and ANA soldiers was Sergeant Gullam's section, mentored by Will. Only then came the Paras.

Before leaving, Grant carried out a radio check, making

sure everyone could be heard on the VHF system. I also checked all of the OMLT could hear each other on their PRRs. We were ready to go. Grant gave the thumbs-up and we moved off, the Russian first, Andy close behind making sure the Afghan moved at a realistic pace and was headed in the right direction. Not that much could go wrong in the first few hundred metres. The only way out was down the hill, passing first the old jail, then the Governor's compound, before striding through the main gate, manned by the ANP and the local militia, and into the unknown. Quickly we were on the wooden bridge and into Tangye. We had only been going for five minutes or so, but already the ANA had stopped at the ANP checkpoint to guzzle some of their water as if they had been on patrol for hours.

Breaking formation without an order was something a British unit would rarely do. As for the Afghans, it seemed to be their standard operating procedure, darting back and forth from the road to have a drink, scavenge amongst the ruins, or even pray. You could get annoyed with them, but what was the point? You'd be hard pressed to change their behaviour, so it was best to let them get on with it and hope they quickly got bored. Glancing back I could see the men of 2 PARA studying our tactics with something little short of consternation on their faces. Oh well, that's how it went. It was the Afghan way. Besides, the measure of these men wasn't to be found in the method of their marching. It would be in the way they fought. And, when I heard a burst of automatic fire resonate through Tangye, I thought their chance to demonstrate their skills might have arrived sooner than I'd anticipated. It wasn't the enemy, though; rather, an ANA soldier who had accidentally fired his M16, having been one of those converted on to the weapon away from the AK47. As the M16 can only be put on single-shot or a three-round burst, the ANA always patrolled with their rifles on the latter setting. But the M16's safety catch can only be applied when the weapon is made ready. Unfortunately the Afghan cocked his gun but didn't apply the catch. So when he then managed to pull the trigger, the inevitable happened. Luckily he only shot the ground and not one of us. I would speak to him about it later.

On we went. Towards our target, south of the village of Khalawak. As we left the road and started crossing open ground the formation changed, with Andy and Colonel's sections to the front and Will to the rear. I was somewhere in the middle, making sure we always had at least one foot on the ground – meaning that whenever soldiers are pushing forward, there are others who have gone firm, covering the movement, scanning for enemy activity. It was slow, methodical stuff, but eventually we made it to the compounds we were set to clear. First the OMLT mentor would scan the entrance with a metal detector, searching for IEDs. If there was any doubt about what might be found inside then we'd use the bar mines to create a brand-new door. Entrance chosen, in would go the ANA.

For what seemed like an age the painstaking clearances went on, largely without incident. Though all the time we were aware of possible trouble brewing to the west. With their commanding views, the men positioned on the peaks saw what they believed to be the enemy reinforcing their positions around the villages of Bagai Kheyl and Machai Kheyl. It was vital to have the 2 PARA guys on the case. Concentrating on the job in hand, and down in the dips and folds of the plain, it would have been all too easy for us to miss the bigger picture and remain blissfully unaware of impending doom. It took three hours but at last our work – at least the first part of it – was done. Time for the second bit. In the days running up to the patrol we had received intelligence that the enemy had laid IEDs in the area close to the north-eastern tip of Kanzi, close to a wadi they were known to use as a route in and out of the area. Grant had decided the second phase would involve checking for these booby traps and for good measure pushing for a reaction from the enemy spotted from the peaks.

His voice came over the radio. 'Amber 21 Alpha, you are to move into Kanzi and clear the area south of Shomali Ghulbah. You are not to proceed past compounds 638 and 644, over.'

The formal part of the message over, Grant sent a warning. 'Just be careful. We think there might be IEDs in that area. Don't take any unnecessary risks. If in doubt, just pull out.'

I appreciated the sentiment. I sent Colonel on his way. As he went he met a number of locals, some of whom warned him off one particular compound. They also insisted Shomali Ghulbah was empty, other than for occasional use by the Taliban. The info duly noted and passed back up the chain of command, Colonel got on with the job. For both commander and subordinate these are the most difficult of times. Colonel had his orders yet it takes a real strength of character, real bravery, to advance in the knowledge that at any stage – after any step – injury and death might await, and despite all the training you've had it might not save you from the enemy's bullets or bombs. Going into battle involves a whole set of unknowns. You can reduce their impact. Prepare for them. But you can't eliminate them. It is the randomness of war that is truly frightening. Why do some people live and some die? More often than not it isn't about skill or experience, but simply good and bad luck. Some people's cards have been marked. Others have not. Trying to rationalise it only makes things harder to deal with, because there is no rationale. It is about fate. And one's fate can turn on the most insignificant of events. That is what is truly frightening. Knowing your destiny is out of your hands.

And just as Colonel would have felt the strain every time he turned a corner, entered a compound, raised his head above the safety of some shelter, so did I watching him do it. It was me who had given him his orders and, with every step he took, my heart was in my mouth, wondering what would happen next. Had I made the right decision? Had I taken into account all the relevant factors? Had I sent him to do something I wouldn't have done myself? Had I – please God, no – sent him to his death? Because if I'd fucked up, then that would be the consequence: death or injury. No less.

I can only liken it to a football manager standing on the touchline, merely an observer as the team he has picked goes off to carry out his game-plan. If he gets it right, then the glory is his. Get it wrong and there is little he can do other than stand and watch as the disaster unfolds. That's the definition of impotence. Only, in the manager's case he'll walk away with nothing more than a bruised ego, whilst a military commander ends up having to write a letter of condolence to the bereaved.

For sixty minutes Colonel led by example. For sixty minutes the enemy let him get on with it. Safe and sound. Yet diabolically this was the wrong result. What was wanted, what Grant had been hoping, was for the Taliban to show their hand and engage, so he could get stuck in. Bluntly, the bait had not been taken. Yet still I saw an opportunity. Why not push the ANA on that little bit further, finally flush out the enemy and let everyone see exactly what the Afghans were capable of. Let them see the ANA putting their lives on the line for their own country.

'Zero Alpha, this is Amber 21 Alpha. I think I could move forward and clear compound 650.'

There was silence. I could picture Grant contemplating the scenario, assessing risk versus reward. Weighing up the info he had received about enemy activity. In the end my offer proved too tempting.

'OK, Doug, 650 and no further.'

I walked over to Colonel.

'OK, big man,' I said, poking him in the arm. 'Get your section and go and clear 650. Take the engineers with you.'

I tried to sound relaxed and nonchalant, hiding the nervousness I always felt when putting my men in danger. I doubted Colonel was fooled; yet he agreed without hesitation.

'Roger, Boss,' was all he said before mustering his section of ANA, briefing Mohamid Ali and setting off.

To the others, I explained Colonel's task and their role in covering his back. I watched as, inch by inch, Colonel advanced towards and reached 650. Then the engineers did their job. They laid the bar mine and – boom – there was a huge explosion that sent dust and debris billowing into the sky. As it drifted on the almost imperceptible breeze, the ANA poured in through the hole the device had created.

'Compound 650 clear,' relayed Colonel.

I moved in behind them and headed for the western wall and a fissure in it. I couldn't resist looking through it. Following the course of the 611 – not a dwelling, but the major route through the area – another compound dominated the immediate landscape. 808. An imposing set of walls and buildings, isolated and formidable, it overlooked, indeed overshadowed, the highway, its only immediate neighbours two further compounds, 807 and 809.

There was no question that 808 was outside the bubble Grant had been given, yet I also understood he was keen to stretch our authority around the FOB. What is the SAS motto? 'Who Dares Wins.' Not as corny as it sounds. And not an attitude unique to the special forces. For Grant to win in the Kajaki area of operation, he was going to have to take a gamble. For me to prove the worth of the ANA, so was I.

'I think I can now clear 808 with little difficulty from this position.'

I could again sense Grant weighing up the odds. His hesitation meant he was tempted. A few seconds later he gave in.

'Roger, Doug, clear 808.'

I squatted down next to Colonel.

'Boss, you want me to go for it?' There was an eagerness in his voice.

'No, Colonel, I don't want you to "go for it". I want you to clear the compound. Very carefully.'

Back came a smile. The smile of a child in a sweet shop. Together we deliberated on the best way to achieve the task; Colonel would go forward with half of his Afghan section plus the two engineers. I would be a bound behind them with the other half. We viewed the ground and broke it up into chunks, identifying milestones, assessing distances, working out extraction routes, identifying possible threats. Was the enemy lying in wait? Were there mines? Throughout our deliberations Mohamid Ali sat and said nothing. He didn't want to lead. Indeed he didn't look as if he wanted to do the operation at all.

Colonel and his team set off, following a bund line (a fold in the ground) that ran east to west. I moved too, perhaps forty metres behind, along the same route. No rush.

One hundred metres to go.

The Afghan soldiers with me scanned the ground around us, the RPG operator peering through its sight, lining up possible target after possible target, panning from one to the next.

Sixty metres to go.

Colonel at the front. Mohamid Ali at the back.

Forty metres.

Colonel could now clearly see the main entrance to the compound, a set of red metal double-doors, one half-open with debris lying in front of it, a small pump house to the left of them. To the right-hand side of the doors there was another wall, much lower, which would give the men some shelter whilst the engineers were dispatched to blow their way in.

Twenty metres.

I was sending sitreps back to Grant so Colonel didn't have to.

Ten metres.

It was all going perfectly.

'Almost there, Boss.'

'Roger, mate, be careful.'

Whoosh. Bang. Crack. Bang. Zip. Bang. Thud.

A veil of enemy fire came down from positions to the north, at least four of them. Instinctively I ducked, only to have to quickly raise my head again to try and decipher what was happening to my men. I was in time to see two RPGs explode, one against the compound wall, the other immediately in front of Colonel and three Afghans. They were all flung to the ground. Fuck it. Fuck it. Fuck it.

'Contact. Wait. Out!'

My message was academic. Grant could clearly see, and hear, what was going on. As could Andy. And the FST. And the FSG.

Enemy fire clattered around me too, some of it furrowing the dirt, other high-velocity rounds spilling over my head. I needed to get forward and on to the raised ground I had spotted and do what I had promised – give some covering fire. I scrambled away from the protective fold of the landscape and towards the knoll, accompanied by my small group of ANA. Crawling into position they immediately opened up with their assortment of PKMs, M16s and RPGs. From their various locations, the other Brits were on the case too. There was now a real spider's web of shooting going on. If the lines of bullets and grenades had been traced on a plan, the result would not have resembled parallel, ordered, two-way traffic, but rather a crazy crisscrossing of deadly lead, more closely mimicking the chaos of a busy Beijing intersection during rush hour.

I felt like a novice in his first firefight. I tried giving another sitrep detailing where the Taliban were but my words didn't add much to the sum of human knowledge. The pressure was getting to me, the message garbled, my mind on other things. I had not seen Colonel or the others since the RPG round had detonated.

Then came the scream over the radio.
'Casualty! Casualty!'

I burst through the red doors of compound 808 and collapsed on to the floor, flat on my face, my rifle skidding out of my hand. I had run no more than 150 metres, yet it was as if I had just completed a marathon. In a suit of armour. In 45-degree heat. Well, the temperature bit was accurate. I was soaked to the skin from sweat; my heart about to break through my ribs and jump out of my chest. Yet my first emotion was one of relief. Pushing myself up out of the dust I saw Colonel and the Afghans. They must have dragged themselves through the open door, whilst I was dodging rounds up on the hill. Colonel appeared unharmed. Not so the ANA soldier he was leant over. The Afghan was a bloody mess. His clothes, old-fashioned US Army fatigues, torn ragged. He had borne the brunt of the RPG explosions I witnessed a few minutes earlier. His right foot was at a perverse angle, a bone, greyish white and splintered, protruded through the skin of his ankle, the boot in shreds. There were numerous other shrapnel wounds to the front of his body, injuries also to his right arm and the right side of his face. The man lay motionless, though conscious, as Colonel did what he could for him, showing more support and concern than his countrymen. The rest of the ANA contingent was crouched in the lee of the wall, not even returning fire, Mohamid Ali amongst them. I was disgusted. Only the engineers were busy trying to do something, fashioning a makeshift stretcher out of some wooden staves they'd found amongst the wreckage of the compound.

(Just as the Afghans weren't allocated medics, nor were they provided with the fold-away rigid stretchers the Brits normally carried and – given the OMLT presence on this patrol was only six men, and we were already weighed down with water, radios, weapons and ammo – we didn't have them either. Hence the need for *Blue Peter*-style improvisation.)

'You doing OK, Colonel?'

'I'm all right, but he needs some help,' he said, gesturing down at the injured man.

I looked again more closely.

And winced.

I had seen some traumatic, bloody things before and just about dealt with them. But this was almost my undoing. Much of the shrapnel had hit the casualty in the groin. Several pieces had peppered his scrotum. Another piece of metal had almost severed his dick and it remained firmly embedded in the member. Ouch. I felt myself crossing my legs. As Colonel tried to attend to the wound, the patient became increasingly animated, perhaps more embarrassed by the intimate attentions of two British soldiers than concerned he might lose his beloved organ. I tried to take stock of our situation and, bizarrely, for a moment felt almost calm. The noise of battle reverberated through the compound: small-arms fire and RPGs still hitting the perimeter; HE mortar rounds striking the enemy positions no more than 400 metres away; so too, massive bullets from the .50-cal., its slow, heavy bursts easily distinguishable from the other form of weaponry. I sent the nine-liner medical report back to Zeebrugge so they could arrange an incident response team (IRT) helicopter for the casualty. It was going to need the specialist skills of the surgeons back at Camp Bastion to save the casualty's pride and joy, indeed his life. Colonel had done as much as he could, using field dressings and some black masking tape the engineers usefully had in their kit, some of which they had also employed to complete the stretcher, the poles they had found now threaded through two zipped-up ANA combat jackets.

As I sat, trying to come up with an extraction plan, I studied my surroundings again. It was clear 808 had taken a battering, probably repeatedly. There was barely a patch of ground within it that remained un-scarred, cratered and pummelled by ordnance during previous skirmishes. In front of me, in the middle of the compound, was the largest crater of all. Perhaps fifteen metres wide, it was half-full of water, probably from the underground watercourse known to traverse the Kajaki area. The western wall was badly damaged. Part of the northern wall was demolished. Elsewhere, there were numerous puncture marks of varying sizes. The place had more holes than a teabag. It was clear that 808 had been regularly fought over, probably not just during this campaign but in previous wars and conflicts. Which suddenly reminded me we had not been able to give the place a proper sweep for mines. The Taliban liked nothing better than booby-trapping places in which ISAF soldiers would – sooner or later – end up. Shit. There was not much I could do about it now other than try only to step on those bits of sand that had already carried my weight. I hoped others would be as conscientious. Suddenly Grant's voice spat in my ear to say that in a couple of minutes there would be a GMLRS strike on the Taliban positions, together with a smoke mission from the mortar teams. These would be our cue to get the hell out of there, back to the relative safety of compound 650, some 400 metres away.

'Doug, when the GMLRS hit I want you to move.'

All we had to do was be ready when the bombardment started. I explained the plan to Colonel. The wounded soldier was heaved, none too ceremoniously, on to the stretcher. Four of his colleagues were pressed into service to carry him when the moment came. The engineers would lead the way; followed by the stretcher party, then Colonel, me and the rest of the ANA. As the seconds ticked by I could see the Afghans itching to leave, those tasked with moving the injured man hovering over him like a pack of wild animals desperate to pounce on their prey and rip it to pieces.

Given that it was me who had pushed for the ANA to clear 808 I was disappointed with the way they had conducted themselves under fire. And yet you can only gain battle experience by experiencing battle. On this occasion they had been found lacking, and big-style, but I hoped it would put them in better stead for the next confrontation with the enemy. More than the men though, I was pretty hacked off with Mohamid Ali. He was a fucking reprobate, an idle man full of his own self-importance. If I could have got away with it I'd have given him a 5.56mm pill to the head. Of course I couldn't, and anyway, as it stood the enemy might still do the job for me.

I was worried my plan for an orderly withdrawal would quickly turn into a rout, an every-man-for-himself free-for-all.

'OK, stand by, stand by.'

I gave the order verbally through the interpreter then underlined the message with a hand signal that involved me putting my arm in the air and pulling down on an imaginary chain, one of those used to flush old-fashioned toilets where the cistern is above head height. It was an American signal, one you'd spot in war films like *Rambo*, *Platoon* and so on and so forth, and now it was also an Afghan signal, given that most ANA soldiers received their basic training from US forces.

The ground shook under our feet. Just afterwards we heard the crumps – three of them. The seventy-kilometre sniper had struck the enemy positions 250 metres away. I put a boot against the doors and kicked them fully open, then followed it up with a red phosphorous smoke grenade to cover our exit.

'Go, GO. GO!'

The ANA didn't need telling twice, let alone three times. Led by Mohamid Ali, they were off, amongst their number two of the four men I had allocated to make up the stretcher party. Fucking idiots. Thank God the engineers were still with us. They stooped down and each took one of the remaining corners. Struggling through the doors, we went too. Progress was tortuous, not least for the injured Afghan soldier. He was shaken and jarred as those carrying him stumbled and tripped on the uneven surface. More than once, as the bearers lost their footing, he was spilled on to the ground, crying in agony, before being hauled back on to the litter by the orderlies. Behind all this came Colonel and I, firing and manoeuvring as we went. First it was him crouched on one knee, shooting as I ran past him ten paces or so. Next it was me down in the dust, trying to control my breathing, trying to get some sort of half-steady aim at the enemy, before pulling the trigger. As I fired, it would be his turn to come past me. And so it continued. One always leapfrogging the other.

'Moving.'

'Magazine.'

'Stoppage.'

'Back in.'

We provided a running commentary of our progress. We both ran out of ammo in no time at all, Colonel just before me. Slinging his SA80 over his back, he made a grab for the M16 the casualty had valiantly been clutching to his chest despite his injuries. When that was also empty, Colonel chucked it to the ground, sank down and opened up with the only thing he had left, his Sig Sauer 9mm. No matter the enemy was several hundred metres away. And the pistol had an accurate range of perhaps thirty metres. Colonel might have had more chance of inflicting damage on the Taliban by throwing the weapon than firing it. But I could understand what he was up to – it was comfort shooting, a reaction to the nervousness of battle. It didn't really matter to Colonel what he was doing, as long as he was doing something. It was the measure of the man that even when he had a pretty genuine excuse to turn and run, he continued to offer support in the best way he could. Not that my admiration for what he was doing would stop me taking the piss out of him for his actions when we got back to Zeebrugge. If we got back. Come on, you bastards. As I stumbled after the stretcher I looked up and saw a cloud of dust beyond 650. It was converging on the compound from one side as we were making for it from the other. As it got closer I finally saw what was causing it. At its heart was the CSM astride the quad bike used for evacuating casualties. But he was playing a dangerous game. In his brave attempt to reach us he had to pass two or three points where it was feared the Taliban placed IEDs, including a crossroads where the road, the 611, crossed a wadi.

We were now in spitting distance of compound 650. Not that any of us had the energy to gob at it. The stretcher party crashed through the entrance and collapsed to the floor, taking the patient with them, Colonel and I close on their heels, our entry concealed by a cloud of smoke from an 81mm mortar shell that had slowly drifted across the battlefield and then enveloped us.

Reaching the compound I had lost sight of the quad, but through the pall I could still hear its engine; getting closer and closer, before finally the CSM arrived. Not, for him, much time to recover. The patient was manhandled off the stretcher and on to the four-wheeler and that was it; the CSM was gone, careering back the way he had come, back past the danger points, all the way to the foot of Shrine, where Rory and the Pinzgauer were waiting.*

It was 17:30 hrs and the sun was starting to set. There was perhaps an hour of daylight left. I collapsed in a long shadow cast by the compound wall, and tipped back my helmet. I was shattered, but still alive. And so were the rest of the men in the OMLT. And that made up for any shortcomings we'd found with the ANA.

---

* The Afghan was eventually taken to Bastion for treatment. Later he would have been transferred to Shorabak. I didn't see him – or his member – again.

FIVE

JOB DONE

MAJOR GRANT HAYWARD, 2 PARA

21 JUNE 2008

It felt as if I was falling for an eternity.

My leaping-off point on the side of the cliff now several metres above me.

The acceleration had been instant. From nought to bloody fast in the blink of an eye.

And yet despite the speed of my descent the layer of deep blue beneath me wasn't getting much closer. Or did it just seem that way because, so expansive was it, so featureless, there were no reference points from which my brain could calculate how high above it I really was?

And then all of a sudden I hit it feet first; the cold water giving way as my legs broke through, followed by the rest of me. There was a roaring in my ears as I plunged into the now-boiling cauldron, full of twisting currents and explosions of bubbles. I sank further, calm already being restored to the surface as it seamlessly closed in above me. I was slowing fast, the density of the fluid acting as a drag on my progress. I held my breath, knowing that any second I would be pushed back upwards.

And then my head was free.

For a moment I gently trod water, taking in my surroundings. Almost directly overhead, more men were preparing to follow me down. To my right somebody else who had jumped just before me was now scrambling out on to the rocks at the base of the cliff.

I tried to look through the clear water, wondering how deep it was. I could see my toes but nothing beyond them. Given I was now swimming in the vast lake formed by the Kajaki dam, I imagined it would be a long, long way to the bottom.

It was easy to see why Kajaki had become such a favoured R & R haunt for Russian troops. It must have been a wonderful escape from the ravages of the bitter fighting they endured during their extended time in the country between 1979 and 1989, when they finally completed their withdrawal. They had spent a decade – ten long, bloody years – fighting a war that many regarded as the Soviets' Vietnam. I wondered if the British Army would be in Afghanistan as long? Christ, it might just be. We'd already been there seven years – a year longer than the Second World War. And three years longer than the First. And there was no clear exit strategy in sight. For me, it didn't really matter. This really was it. I was determined never to come back to Afghanistan. But the young men serving with me were likely to return two, three, perhaps four or more times in their career – who was to say? I forced myself back beneath the surface of the water, and let the chill numb the depressing thoughts coursing through my brain. Then with little grace I struck out for the shore.

A couple of weeks had now passed since the fiasco of compound 808. Yes, the ANA had been at the vanguard of the fighting, but this had in itself underlined weaknesses; not least amongst some of the Afghan personnel – in particular, Mohamid Ali. On our return to the FOB after the abortive mission, I had shared my annoyance over the sergeant's performance with Captain Sherafadin. I told the senior officer that Ali had to be either removed or much more tightly controlled. Finally, after yet more patrols during which Ali steadfastly refused to pull his weight and do his job, I spoke to Sherafadin again and gave an ultimatum. It was him or us. Either Ali went or his section would be left unmentored. The man was a liability. He was ignoring orders and so putting the lives of his soldiers – and mine – at risk.

Presented with the stark choice, Sherafadin took action. He demoted Ali back to being a mere rifleman. His replacement was Sergeant Rasol. As brave as a lion and good fun with it, the only drawback was that every time I looked at him I didn't see a fearless Afghan patriot, but rather Private Walker, the spiv character in *Dad's Army*. But whatever his facial appearance and mannerisms, he was a massive improvement on the soldier he had taken over from. And what's more he made me laugh.

In Kajaki, things had become relatively benign. We got into a few scrapes with the Taliban but without incurring serious casualties. Not so elsewhere in Helmand. 2 PARA lost six men in three separate incidents in quick succession. In the first, three Paras were killed by a suicide bomber north of Sangin. Soon after, two more died when their patrol came under fire near FOB Gibraltar. And then Sergeant-Major Michael Williams was shot dead during a firefight with the Taliban in the Upper Sangin Valley. He was a good friend of Grant's and, at forty, being one of the older members of the battalion, his death was felt keenly by everyone. It was the 'if it can happen to him, it can happen to anyone' syndrome.

Yet whatever hits we were taking across Helmand, there was still a job to be done and we had to continue getting out and about.

Our skirmishes with the enemy tended to occur when we headed north from the base. All the time we tried to interact with the local population, but this became harder and harder as their numbers continued to shrink.

In the middle of June we conducted a Medcap in Shabaz Kheyl – an operation offering medical treatment to the local population, a sort of field surgery. After the village had been cleared (not of locals, but checked for enemy fighters and ambushes), Rory and his colleagues set up the first-aid post in the open next to the parked-up Pinzgauer they were using to cart about the medical stores. It wasn't long before they were confronted with a queue of Afghans stretching round the block. Obviously word had gone out and many people had travelled great distances to be there. A few had come along simply to witness the spectacle but the vast majority were patients who'd sensed a rare opportunity at last to get their ailments seen to. It was the medical equivalent of the feeding of the 5,000. It seemed as if no one wanted to miss out; they all wanted a share of our limited supplies. Most of the work was straightforward. Administering immunisations, handing out tablets, stitching or strapping old wounds that refused to heal. Probably the biggest single complaint was toothache. Afghanistan was clearly a huge untapped market for Colgate.

Waiting patiently in line with the others was an elderly man with a pronounced stoop who supported himself on a gnarled stick. His long, matted beard was almost entirely grey. He must have been about sixty (not bad, given the average Afghan male life expectancy is a meagre forty-four years, and that of a female only a fraction longer) but looked even older. Every so often he shuffled forward with the rest of the line, as the next person was called for treatment. Finally his turn arrived.

'What's the problem?' Rory asked through the interpreter.

'It's my wife. She has a bad back and very sore hips.'

Rory queried whether the woman couldn't herself come along for examination.

'No. That is not the Pashtun way.'

This was true, so Rory continued his once-removed diagnosis.

'When did the pain start?' 'What exactly are the symptoms?' 'When did she last have children?' 'What age is she?'

It was the answer to this final question that dumbfounded Rory and the rest of us standing around, watching and listening.

'She is thirteen years old.'

This wife – this girl – had yet to fully reach puberty, but even so she had been given – more likely sold – to the old man. There must have been an age difference of almost half a century. That was shocking enough in itself, even before you considered her lack of physical maturity. But we shouldn't have been so astonished because this was the way they did things in the rural areas. It wasn't out of the ordinary. This was just the way things were. Had Shabia, the girl killed by the mortar shell, lived, then she too was likely to have ended up in such a relationship, her father exchanging his daughter for a sizeable dowry with which to bolster the family's paltry income. No wonder he had been so keen to secure compensation from the British. Not only had Shabia been his flesh and blood, she was also the prospective source of a big contribution to the finances of her kith and kin.

Yet just because it wasn't exceptional, did it mean what was happening to the thirteen-year-old was right? Not from my perspective. The very fact that what was occurring to children in this blighted country was so routine should have been a clarion-call for change. I thought about the news I'd recently received. That I'd just become a grandfather. Forty-two and me a grandfather. My beautiful daughter having given birth to a beautiful son. Tristan was going to grow up in a loving family, in a society that even at its worst would surely offer him something better than was the norm in Afghanistan? What sort of country was it that routinely snatched from children the innocence of youth long before they'd had the opportunity to fully enjoy it? But then I thought of Shabia. The innocence of youth had been grabbed from her too – much more than that, her very existence had been wrenched away. Not by the natural and societal hardships of her own country and culture, but by us. The invading hordes, by ISAF – the very people supposedly in Helmand to extract her from tyranny. Her future might have been uncomfortable, hard perhaps, unbearable even. But at least she would have had one. Not any more. We had snuffed it out.

I desperately wanted to believe something better would eventually derive from the reasons for her death. Wanted to believe the greater good was being served by our presence. But I wasn't convinced of it. Not by a long shot. The thoughts and the arguments continued to whirl about my head. I was in danger of being sucked under by them. At that moment I wanted to be as far away as possible from that God-forsaken place. Away from the squalid misery of Afghanistan. At home with my grandson. Yet I couldn't. I'd signed on the dotted line, agreed to remain in the army and complete my tour. And that was that. I had made a pact with the devil and it couldn't be broken. There was no escape. Not yet.

Whilst the Medcap might have done wonders for our reputation, we were struggling to achieve anything much militarily. In the main this was because we weren't allowed to. Our sphere of influence consisted predominantly of a bunch of uninhabited villages. With the locals showing no interest in returning, empty they looked set to remain. And quiet with it. The one thing our constant patrolling did go some way to achieving was to keep a lid on the enemy's cockiness, limiting their enthusiasm for getting close enough to the base to mount an attack. We didn't stop their activities, but we certainly suppressed them.

One night Grant ordered the ANA, with the OMLT, to push further south than we had done for a while and assault an enemy position known as compound 261 or Sentry Post.

Unfortunately, to get there, we had to make our way through other unoccupied, semi-derelict compounds. Approaching these was one of the scariest things I have ever done. Not because I was unduly worried about the enemy being present, but because of what they might have left behind – booby traps, roadside bombs, IEDs, take your pick. Exacerbating the problem was a shortage of night-vision equipment. Actually, not a shortage of the kit, but a complete absence of it – at least for the Afghans. I did have some. But that only gave me the dubious privilege of going first.

Step by fearful step I led the patrol towards a point where we at least had a murky view of compound 261. As much as I peered down and strained to see the ground, I really couldn't make out a thing in the almost pitch black. If there had been any degree of ambient light then after a while my eyes would have become accustomed to it. But there was none. Certainly not enough to help spot particular, discreet hazards. A thin trip wire, the tilt-switch of an anti-personnel mine, a bit of ground recently disturbed by bomb-makers and then brushed back into place. No, if any of this were out there, then I couldn't see it. Damn it, where was the light pollution when you needed it?

When we did at last make it to Sentry Post, I was sweating, my hands dripping with perspiration. It had been hot work – even at night the temperature was above twenty degrees – but the most obvious cause of my condition was nerves. It was with profound relief we arrived safely to find the enemy position empty.

Very carefully, we retraced our steps back to camp.

Back behind the wire I held a debrief. It was obvious not much in the way of intelligence had been gleaned from this particular excursion. In answer to the question, 'What did you see?' the replies were uniformly the same.

'Fuck all, Boss, I was too busy trying to watch where I was putting my feet in case I lost a leg or two.'

Uniformly too, the men sounded knackered, the mental stress of trying to avoid getting blown up having taken its toll. Sometimes the very absence of combat can wear a soldier down as much as the ferocity of battle. At least being involved in a fight with the enemy is a release for pent-up emotion and worry. It gets the blood flowing, the adrenalin pumping. But waiting for that first shot, the first explosion, is truly debilitating. It sets the mind racing off in all directions. Repeatedly you run through the 'what if' scenarios. You imagine the worst, and it is all you can do to concentrate on the task at hand. They used to refer to the mental trauma caused by being under constant bombardment as shellshock. Since then the terminology has moved on. Now there is something called combat stress. Yet even this is not quite an accurate description, because it implies your psychological health is only affected once you are in the face of the enemy. Wrong. The anxiety begins long before you are in contact. You only needed to look at me and my men to see that.

Another mission Grant tasked us with was on a slightly bigger scale. Rather than clear a compound, he wanted us to clear a village. Shomali Ghulbah. It had been devoid of residents since OMLT 4 had arrived, yet it was still being used by the Taliban as a point for mounting attacks on British patrols and the FOB. We were to start at compound 650 and move through the settlement until we got to 676 – twenty-seven sets of walls and buildings we had to first breach and then check for signs of enemy activity. It was a long, long day. Some of the compounds we entered through the front door, but most of the time it was a case of using high explosive to make our own alterations to the properties by blowing a new entrance through the perimeter. The engineers accompanying us would take half a bar mine, prop it up against the sun-baked earth with a stick and then light the fuse that ran to the detonator embedded in the explosive. Thirty seconds later there'd be a deafening explosion, as dirt and smoke blossomed out to engulf the soldiers waiting to go in through the newly created opening. Within a second or two of the detonation the engineers, armed with pick-axes, would leap into the cloud of debris and start swinging furiously at any stubborn bits of masonry still doing their best to restrict the flow of ISAF troops into the compound. It didn't take many blows before the hole was sufficiently large for the OMLT and ANA to charge through without impediment, firing as they went. From then on, it was a case of moving to every corner of the compound, checking with metal detectors any areas likely to be locations for booby traps. Once the compound had received the thumbs-up it was on to the next target.

At the end of it though, we looked a sorry state. Covered head to toe in a thin layer of dust, we had taken on a ghostly appearance. My throat was raw – dry from shouting, and all the crap I had inhaled. From our final vantage-point in compound 676 we had a grandstand view of enemy-held Bagai Kheyl and compound 808. Despite the large smattering of pockmarks and shell holes it still stood imperious. It was tactically important and to me symbolically critical. After our ignominious retreat from 808 two weeks earlier, I wondered whether we'd ever be allowed another crack at it.

It began to look as if we wouldn't. We were fast approaching the end of our time in Kajaki, the decision having already been made that the ANA *kandak* we were mentoring could do without our services. The plan was to pull us back to Shorabak and give us another tasking. Already some people had left. Will had been injured in a contact, damaging his leg as he dived from a roof to escape heavy enemy fire, and casevaced out. Colonel had gone off on R & R, as had Andy and Billy. Then Crofty went, too. A couple of replacements had turned up – Sergeant Rab McEwen, a short, stocky man with a dry wit from 4 SCOTS, and Junior Stewart, a Royal Irish ranger I had recommended be busted down from lance-corporal before the tour started – which he was. But even with the new arrivals there were now just four OMLT men available for patrol, with Jim Carney still back at camp doing his good work on the logistics front. The Afghans were in a state of flux, too. Sherafadin had gone, replaced by another captain I suspected wouldn't be as keen as his predecessor to leave the camp. We'd also lost a lot of ANA soldiers on medical grounds – several because of that Afghan curse, dental problems. Typically their teeth were in a bloody awful state. For a while we would dose them up with painkillers, but in the end there was no alternative other than to send them back to Shorabak to get help. Standard treatment would involve the removal of the several teeth – it was never just one – causing all the problems.

Despite the ever-shifting sands of manpower we stuck to our tasks.

And then, lo and behold, for what proved to be our very last patrol in Kajaki, we returned to 808.

From my observation point in compound 627, one of the gun ports the engineers had blown in the wall, I stared across the open, undulating ground towards our goal. The man with the honour of leading the way was Al Owens. Given our shortage of numbers I had been forced to make him a section commander after the departure of Colonel. It would be the young ranger, leading the ANA, who took the fight to the enemy. He hadn't done the right courses to be in this role, he didn't have the time served in the military, but what he did possess – and what made me confident he could pull it off – was several weeks' worth of frontline experience, which was the equivalent of months and years in the classroom. There was also his boundless energy and enthusiasm. Even so, as I watched him move out, still I was nervous.

In their approach to 808, Al and the ANA didn't hang about. In pretty short order they disappeared from view one by one through a hole in the western wall of the compound. A minute or so later, confirmation came through.

'Boss, this is Al. Compound 808 clear.'

He had only just finished his sentence when the enemy decided to remind us of their presence. Clearly our swift occupation of the objective had got their backs up and they were intent on letting us know about it. The response of the Afghans – both those with me, and Al's lot – was the best I had seen since I'd arrived in Kajaki. It was sustained and accurate fire. And soon it was matched by mortars from the FOB and outgoing from the fire support group.

It is important for a commander to be in a position where he can influence a battle, and in this case that meant me going forward to 808. Not for the first time I forced myself to my feet intensely aware I was railing against every sense of self-preservation. What you have to do as the bloke in charge – run towards the danger, not away from it – is very much at odds with what you want to do as a vulnerable, fragile human being made of flesh and blood, i.e. keep flat on the floor, your face buried in the dirt, desperate to prevent the enemy rounds flying about you finding their target. So it was that I dashed between the relative safety of the two compounds. I tried to duck low as I ran. I wanted to believe that by doing so I was actually presenting a much smaller target to the enemy. Of course there was still a good five and a half feet of upright, lumbering soldier for the Taliban to take aim at. My legs aching, my heart pounding, my head throbbing, I covered the last few metres to 808 and made it inside, intact.

Catching my breath, I was all ready to send the initial contact report.

But Al beat me to it. 'Contact. Wait. Out,' he yelled into the mic of his radio.

A pause and he was back on the VHF set, variously giving target indications to the FOO so he could align the GMLRS, to the Javelin missile team, and to the mortar fire controller. He was as cool as a cucumber, and when he had given his orders to those in charge of the remote firepower he turned

back to the ANA, who hung on his every word. From someone so young it was fantastic to see. Al took me to one side to
give me the lay of the land. What he said was clear, concise
and relevant. He told me everything I wanted to know, and
nothing I didn't. And with that he was off again.

By now day was rapidly turning to night. Still Al kept a grip
on the situation, amending the Afghans' arcs of fire as necessary, marking targets, dishing out more orders. And all the
while – despite the weight of fire ranged back at them – the
enemy continued to keep up the pressure. Time and again
there were flashes of blinding light and puffs of grey smoke as
airburst RPGs detonated in the sky around us, sending show-
ers of shrapnel raining down on 808's defenders. I saw Al
jump back as a large-calibre round impacted only inches from
him, yet almost immediately he was back in position, realign-
ing his weapon and re-engaging. Then, for the first time since
we had arrived in Kajaki, the enemy also employed mortars.
They fired at least six. If they had been anywhere near accurate, they'd have been a problem. Luckily they weren't.

We had made our point. We had advanced on 808, and
held it under attack. We had shown the Taliban we were prepared to take the fight to them, that we were able to move
where we wanted, when we wanted. It would also keep them
guessing, make them wonder what we would hit next. And it
was also about numbers. We weren't going to wipe the enemy
out, but every time we killed one of them we knocked their
resolve, put doubt in their minds, undermined morale just a
little bit.

Yet what we couldn't now do was keep 808 indefinitely. We
would have to withdraw. But this time it would be on our
terms.

An F-15 repeatedly swooped in left to right across the
enemy positions some 400 metres away, dropping a series of
500lb bombs on targets Al and I had identified. As the aircraft
pounded the enemy, night finally closed in.

Fighting as it gets dark is a completely different ballgame. Targets start to lose their sharp definition; shrubs, trees, mounds, all suddenly assume human form and find themselves on the receiving end of 5.56mm rounds. Explosions that during the day appear little more than a plume of dust and debris become spectacular, with flame erupting, volcano-like, into the gloom. Then there's the tracer, small bursts of red colour scratched on to the black canvas by the .50-cals, GPMGs and SA80s.

Individual senses are heightened, your imagination starts to run riot. You feel more vulnerable, alone. You start to doubt whether the man who has been fighting at your side all day long is actually still there. And even if he is still there, what if he mistakes you for the enemy? What if you mistake him for the enemy?

I spoke to Al. It was time for him to lead us back to safety. Fire and manoeuvre. Fire and manoeuvre. Steadily, methodically, he organised our withdrawal. Secure once again in the folds of the earth some way back from the compound, we called in the other two sections. Then Grant gave permission for us to return to Zeebrugge. But despite what we had just done, despite the dark, I was reluctant to go. During the fighting the enemy had randomly fired mortars at the village of Shabaz Kheyl. I was worried about the damage they might have done and asked permission to go and check. Grant agreed. To my immense relief the only dead I came across were some animals.

Our final act in Kajaki was to say farewell to the men of X Company, men we had forged strong links with.

Waiting at HLS Lancaster, for our forty-minute hop back to Shorabak, Grant took me to one side. 'Well done, Doug. Job done.'

I was sure he would have liked us to stay on and help carry out the plans he still had for the Kajaki area (indeed X

Company would take several casualties over the coming months, and play a vital role in the delivery of a third turbine to the power station, displaying to best advantage the offensive spirit the Paras are renowned for). But the powers that be had other things in mind for us and it seemed there would be little time for a rest. I clambered on board the helicopter to take my seat. It was 27 June and we had been at Zeebrugge for two months.

The Chinook lurched into the air. Immediately the nose dipped, and the aircraft started moving forward and upward at the same time, quickly leaving the HLS behind. Somewhere not far below would have been 808. It was never likely to have a permanent owner, but as we headed south it was safe in the knowledge that the last boots to have stamped their authority on the place belonged to 1 R IRISH. We had left our mark.*

---

* For the bravery and leadership Ranger Al Owens showed in the capture of compound 808 he was awarded the Military Cross. For his earlier actions at the same compound Corporal Chris 'Colonel' Kennedy received a Joint Force Commander's Commendation.

PART TWO

THE MIDDLE: MARJAH

SIX

A DISASTER WAITING TO HAPPEN

CAPTAIN DOUG BEATTIE, 1 R IRISH

30 JUNE 2008

I couldn't have avoided the gruesome scene even if I'd wanted to.

It was a natural reflex, call it impulse, which made me twist sharply towards the sound of the explosion the moment I heard it. The sort of impulse that means you can't help but turn your head to see who's shouting hello when you're walking down a busy High Street, even when you just know – 100 per cent – they won't be calling after you. The same impulse that means you look up from whatever you're doing when the siren of a police car or an ambulance or a fire engine breaks the peace. And yet I wish I had somehow managed to resist the urge, fought the natural reaction, for what I saw was utterly grotesque. I watched as in almost slow motion a fountain of smoke, bodies, parts of bodies, bits of a military vehicle, spewed into the air. The macabre assortment of debris arced upwards for perhaps thirty or forty metres, before reaching a point where the energy of the explosion was spent and gravity took over as the dominant force. For the briefest of moments, at the point of equilibrium, the detritus of the blast hung in the sky as if weightless, before looping lazily back down towards the ground, to be strewn haphazardly across the dirt and dust.

Jesus Christ.

We had started before dawn – and it had taken ten hours – but we'd finally managed to clear six kilometres of ground between the main 601 east–west highway (which links Kandahar and Lashkar Gah) and the Arghandab River that flows south of the road, pretty much parallel to it. Compound by compound we had made steady progress. The Taliban operated with impunity in the area between the 601 and the river. It wasn't that any of the villages dotted about were regarded as particular enemy strongholds but, because we lacked the manpower to dominate the zone, the Taliban were brazen. They came and went as they liked. Our mission was a rare ISAF foray into this particular bit of territory.

The Afghan soldiers had done most of the grafting. I'd mentored one company together with Jim Carney and Al Owens, and two more Brits (Territorials) who were new to theatre and wanted to see the lay of the land before starting their jobs working with the ANP. With the help of another pair of mentors, Captain Dave Stanley – a Liverpudlian Royal Engineer based in Germany – had guided the other company. The Afghans had been diligent in their task even if at times they seemed to have forgotten the reason for entering compounds was to root out the enemy and not loot whatever they took a shine to.

At one point the ANA became convinced a village we were approaching was occupied by the Taliban. We stopped for two long hours as the Afghan soldiers observed and studied and argued and tried to come up with a plan. Everyone seemed to want to have a say. In the end I got fed up with waiting and led the company forward myself under the watchful eye of

Dave and his men off to the flank.* What we found was not the enemy but a group of old men leading their extended families in tending their fields. The crop wasn't opium poppies – they would already have been harvested – but corn, cucumbers and aubergines. We chatted to the locals for a while. It was confirmed the Taliban were regular visitors and because of a lack of ISAF presence the villagers had little choice other than to provide the insurgents with food and shelter as and when they demanded it.

As we prepared to move on, water was brought out for us to drink. Cold water. Our own supplies had long since run dry, our camel packs drained. It wasn't something to be recommended – the chance of getting the shits was high – but still I sipped some of the liquid I'd been offered. Not merely because I was dying of thirst (though at that moment I could have wrung the sweat from my socks and drunk that) but because I had to – it was an offer I couldn't refuse.

We needed to build relationships with the locals and this hospitality seemed genuine, not merely a case of buttering up the infidel. It would have been impolite and inappropriate to refuse; whatever the consequences for my stomach and bowels. Though if I needed a reminder of what might be in store I only needed look at James Cartwright, who was in charge of our little excursion. Suddenly debilitated by diarrhoea and vomiting, he was no longer commanding the two companies from his vantage point on a block of high ground. As James alternately shitted and puked from the back of the Afghan Ranger pickup he was in, it was left to Brummie Hagans to take control.

---

* In Lashkar Gah, the ANA soldiers we were mentoring came from Kandak 4. Most of them were from Kandahar province and spoke Pashtu – this was in contrast to the men of the other *kandak*s the British were involved with, who were predominantly from the Kabul area and spoke Dari. Only recently posted to Helmand, Kandak 4 was short on equipment, short on operational experience, and short on command and control. It showed.

As the patrol progressed we had been joined by a couple of WMIKs led by Rab McEwen, plus an assortment of ANP vehicles. Eventually we finished our task, but it had taken its toll. Everyone was exhausted, not least Jim Carney. I looked across at the man who in Kajaki had been the camp-bound logistician, but here in Lash was back out on the ground. No longer in the first flush of youth – who was I to talk? – Jim was feeling the heat, but he didn't complain, just got on with the necessary. Anyway, we'd done the job and we'd soon be back at base. Yes, all in all, it had been a good day.

Which was when the explosion shattered the peace.

The two WMIKs, together with Dave and his ANA company, had been some 300 metres behind us as we made our way back to route 601. And it was some 300 metres to our rear that a plume of smoke was now drifting into the sky. Clearly something catastrophic had happened to this group, but because of a gentle rise in the ground I couldn't see exactly who had taken the brunt of the blast.

With the rest of the OMLT I started to run back the way we had just come. At the same time the Afghans with us continued on their merry way, seemingly oblivious to what was going on. I let them go. I didn't have time to do otherwise.

As we moved I tried to get hold of Dave on the VHF set. 'Amber 42, this is Amber 43, over.'

There was no reply.

Jim was more worried about Rab. I could hear him calling for Rab over the PRR. The pair were from the same regiment and good mates. Whatever fatigue Jim had been suffering just moments earlier had now gone, to be replaced with frantic concern for his friend.

We came to a point where we could at last see the aftermath of the explosion. It was shocking. Lying on the track was the charred hulk of a vehicle; twisted and smouldering, it looked as if it had first been crushed by a pair of giant hands, then tossed into a furnace. Around it were human remains. A wave of relief washed over me. Because the bodies were Afghan. The vehicle was Afghan, too. Dave, Rab and the other Brits were unscathed. Thank fuck. It was a strange sensation, feeling some sort of elation that, despite the carnage laid out in front of me, for all the death and destruction, there were no UK casualties. I had feared the absolute worst, but been blessed with the merely bloody terrible.

The bomb had detonated under the cab of the open-backed Ranger as the vehicle passed over it.

The driver, and the commander in the passenger seat, had taken the full force of the explosion as it ripped up through the unarmoured floor of the truck. As the blast expanded outwards it took the driver with it, ejecting him through the windscreen. All four of his limbs were amputated in the process, severed by a combination of shrapnel from the bomb, metal torn from the chassis, the steering wheel and the toughened glass of the window. What was left of him was thrown ten metres clear. If not killed instantly, he was probably dead within seconds of hitting the ground. Certainly he was way beyond help now.

The commander had also been blown clear; his torso, minus both legs and an arm, lay face down some twenty metres from the wreck. There was no sign of movement, but no one had yet got to him to confirm he was dead.

I tried to count the injured. I stopped at seven, and that didn't include the commander – what was left of him. These men had been the ones huddled in the rear of the truck as it rattled along over the bumps, all looking forward to getting back to their camp. Now it was fifty-fifty whether several would ever look forward to anything again. Some had lost whole limbs, others just hands, feet and fingers, most had broken bones and penetration injuries, the wounds ranging from the size of a pea to gaping chasms you could put your fist into.

Dave Stanley told me what happened.

Rab's WMIK had been leading the ANP vehicles steadily northwards when they came to a junction. Rab pulled up short, knowing crossroads were favoured locations for the Taliban to plant roadside bombs. His intention was to clear it or find a way round it, but before he could do either the Afghans charged past, anxious to get home, ignorant of the dangers, or happy to ignore them. It proved to be a dreadful mistake. There was no immediate way of knowing what device had actually done the damage. Was it a landmine? A pressure-pad IED? An IED detonated remotely? The chances were it had been a PPIED but this was by no means certain. Nor were there any guarantees there weren't more bombs around us. We'd have to clear the ground, inch by inch. As most of the men started to tend to those casualties they could safely reach, I ordered a couple of the lads to begin the search for other mines.

'Bloomers, get the ebexes [the name of the search equipment] from the back of your vehicle and start clearing the ground back towards us. Follow the vehicle tracks already on the ground.'

'Roger,' came the reply from Rab's driver.

'Al, I want you to clear towards Bloomers and his vehicle. Don't worry if you overlap – it will give us confirmation the ground is safe.'

As we worked we heard the moans and cries of the injured. They were hard to ignore. The first thought was to rush and help. But what would be the point of that if in so doing we set off another bomb? Became casualties ourselves? We were a small team as it was and there was a real risk we could be overwhelmed by the situation. (It didn't help that half of the Afghans had fucked off northwards and of the half that remained, most seemed disinclined to assist their colleagues; instead they just milled around supposedly securing the area, but not doing a very good job of that either. Not for the first time in Afghanistan I was furious at the Afghans' reluctance to lend a hand.)

Even as we created safe corridors to and from the casualties and the remaining vehicles, we had to be wary of all piling in to administer first aid and so not have enough men protecting our flanks, looking outwards for any sign of enemy fighters creeping in to finish off the job they had so ably started with the bomb. It was all about priorities; and at that moment the overriding priority was to prevent the casualty list getting any longer.

I had told the pair of Territorial lads to go and find, and then secure, a suitable location for the medical helicopter to land. A nine-liner had been sent by Rab, and the IRT was being scrambled to recover the casualties.

They would also take away the dead, one of whom was now confirmed as the vehicle's commander. Matt House – a TA member of 4 PARA from the Lake District, where he was a paramedic and who on this occasion was acting as our medic – had finally managed to reach him. For a moment or two there had been a glimmer of hope as Matt found what he thought were very faint signs of life, but all too soon they evaporated.

'Well, Matt?' I had asked as I watched him kneel beside the body.

'Not a chance,' came the matter-of-fact reply. And with that he turned his attention from the dead to the living.

'Oi!' I yelled at a group of Afghan policemen, pointing at the body on the ground. 'Move him over there and bring the other one, too. Then cover them both up.'

Sixty-five minutes on from the explosion and the helicopters started to arrive, inbound from Bastion. There were three of them; an Apache leading, followed by a Chinook and a Sea King. Because there was no JTAC with us I was unable to talk to the attack helicopter over a secure frequency, which meant I had to risk speaking to the pilot over the VHF in 'hail' that was insecure.

If the Taliban had been monitoring our radio traffic they would have heard me explain to him the exact location of the HLS and the nature of the threat.

Only after speaking to the Apache pilot did I realise I'd fucked up big-style. Knowing I was speaking over an insecure channel I should have used a code to translate the grid references of the HLS into something the Taliban wouldn't have been able to decipher even if they were listening in. But I hadn't done so. Now I had to pray the Taliban weren't laying on another surprise for us.

As the Apache circled slowly overhead, checking for any signs of enemy activity, the Chinook descended towards us, kicking up an all-enveloping storm of dust – a so-called 'brown-out'. As the helicopter settled, the force protection team spilled out of the back to take up position whilst five of the casualties were carried to the aircraft and up the ramp. As we didn't have any stretchers the wounded men had to be manhandled in. It was none too graceful and, for those hurt, all too painful, but there was no other way of doing it. Then, with us turning our backs on the fresh whirlwind of sand, covering our eyes with our hands, the Chinook was up and away. Even before the dust settled the Sea King took its place, whipping up yet another hail of grit. The last of the injured soldiers were dragged on board. Finally, so too were the dead. The pilot, under orders from HQ, had at first refused to accept the bodies, arguing the ANP could take them back to Lash in the rear of their vehicles. But after some rather choice language from me he saw the error of his ways and changed his mind. In less than two minutes the Sea King was also airborne again and turning for home, the Apache close behind. A kind of calm settled again on the landscape. The noise of the helicopters had faded. Gone too were the screams of the injured. It was almost as if nothing had happened – well, except for the stark visual reminders. The dark stains in the sand where the blood had been soaked up; tattered remnants of uniforms; abandoned bits of equipment;

and of course the contorted carcass of the destroyed pickup truck. Some of the Afghans gathered together the larger pieces of clothing and kit, now soaked in fuel, and flung them into the remains of the vehicle. I set it all alight with a red phos grenade. I wanted to make sure nothing was left for the enemy to salvage. Standing back, watching the flames leap, I felt absolutely exhausted. I'd already been shattered at the end of the patrol. Adrenalin had kept me going since the bomb went off, but now the tank was empty. Yet we still needed to get back to the road. Once again we started the trek north, towards the 601. It was an arduous business, made more so because we decided to abandon the track for fear of more IEDs. Instead we travelled cross-country, only to be repeatedly confronted with streams, ditches and dykes. More than once a vehicle got bogged down and we had to haul it out.

It took four more hours, but eventually we arrived back at camp – only to be confronted with news that added insult to injury. The site of the attack was very close to the point where three men, reportedly Territorials from 23 SAS, and Corporal Sarah Bryant from the Intelligence Corps, died when their Snatch Land Rover had been blown up only three weeks earlier. It would have been nice if someone had fucking told us. The information might not have saved the two Afghans who were killed, or prevented so many others being maimed, but then again maybe it might. We could have warned the ANA and ANP that the threat was for real. Or perhaps James would have made a decision not to use vehicles as part of that particular mission. There's no way of knowing, but how can anyone make an informed decision if they are not given the critical facts to make it with?

I took myself off to my cot to calm down and have a few quiet moments to myself. It wasn't easy. The base only measured about 400 metres by 300 metres, and into that space was crammed an exotic mix of people, most, but by no means all, of whom were military.

When I had last been at the camp in 2006 it had been home to the Provincial Reconstruction Team (PRT) and that was about it. Since then it had expanded dramatically – not in terms of square footage, but certainly in the number of occupants. 16 Air Assault Brigade's HQ was there, so too the HQ of 2 SCOTS. Then there was a company of 5 SCOTS maintaining camp security. On top of this came EODD teams, dog sections, medical units, as well as those whose role it was to make the camp work – chefs, electricians, laundry workers, the NAAFI staff. Plus the PRT was still there, carrying out the difficult and dangerous job of trying to get the province back up and running by building new – and repairing old – bridges, roads, schools, sanitation facilities, power plants, administrative offices and hospitals. Add this lot together and you get some 2,000 people.

Oh, and then there was us, OMLT 4.

At this point we totalled more than twenty soldiers. Our quarters were a single tent close to the cookhouse. Twenty-five metres by fifteen metres, it was jam-packed with men and equipment. It served as our store room as well as living accommodation and every bit of available space was taken up with gear; ammunition, weapons, personal kit – you could barely walk down the aisle without tripping over it. Each person had just enough room to put up his cot – with more equipment then stuffed underneath it – and that was about it. With patrols going out day and night, and the almost constant noise of helicopters taking off or landing, plus constantly sweltering temperatures because of the lack of air-conditioning, it was all but impossible to find the luxury of uninterrupted sleep. Even if you could have located a place of peace and quiet, there would never have been enough time to take advantage of it. The pace was relentless, always so much to do and not enough people to do it with. But being busy was no bad thing. It meant nobody dwelt on what had been and gone. The system didn't allow for long periods of contemplation and introspection; there were always fresh problems to deal with, new dangers and issues raising their heads, all of which meant the past was by necessity none too gently shoved aside.

One of the things currently causing anxiety was the patrol base in the town of Marjah, some thirty kilometres west of Lash. Located in a disused school building, and home to six members of the OMLT and ninety ANA soldiers, it was vulnerable to attack, isolated from help and in constant need of re-supply. Its biggest weakness was a lack of power. There wasn't even a generator. Which meant the batteries for essential pieces of equipment like the radios and electronic counter-measures could not be recharged and fresh ones were being routinely ferried in. It had got to the ludicrous point where a re-supply patrol left for the town every three or four days. It was absolute folly. A recipe for disaster. An invitation for trouble. However you looked at it, the situation was madness.

There were only so many road routes into Marjah and, given the regularity of the convoys, it wouldn't need a genius amongst the Taliban to work out our likely movements and plan an ambush. We were setting serious patterns of operation that went against everything we'd been taught. This was basic stuff, applicable to just about any theatre of war. It was a lesson that should have been learned in Iraq and during the three decades British troops spent in Northern Ireland. Either there were a lot of absent-minded people about in Lash or some of those making the decisions were just too young and inexperienced to know better.

I tried to argue what we were doing was wrong, but there didn't seem to be anyone listening.

To me the answer was as clear as the nose on your face. Send in a generator and enough stores to last for, say, a month. That would at least provide a breathing space in which to decide how re-supplies would be carried out in the future. I couldn't understand why helicopters hadn't been employed?

They were being used in less isolated places across Helmand than Marjah, so why not there?

But the answer to that question, the long-term solution, was going to have to be provided by someone else. Because in the short term the latest supply mission had been planned – and I would be on it, as part of a six-strong OMLT together with a platoon from the ANA. Nominally I'd be in command but because this would be my first trip to the town, it was decided Matt would be in the lead WMIK, with me at the rear in another Land Rover driven by Rab and with Lance-Corporal 'Monty' Carson, a South African, acting as gunner. Normally Monty was a clerk, but these were times of need and men rarely stuck to the day job.

Whatever trade you might do in the army, whatever rank you might have, the bottom line is that as a soldier you're expected to fight. Everyone gets given a gun and told sooner or later they might just have to use it. It is in the job description.

We moved out of the base early in the morning and along the 604 (which is what the 601 becomes as it leaves Lashkar Gah heading west), keen to get clear of the town before the daily hustle and bustle was fully under way and we became stuck in it. As we left Lash I settled down in the left-hand seat and took in the surroundings. The picture was similar on both sides of the road. Open desert stretching north and south, uninhabited except for occasional settlements and villages, generally close to or straddling the road, created from clusters of compounds ranging in number from just a handful to forty, fifty and more.

In the larger villages we would pass through checkpoints established by the ANP, now more often than not manned by a sorry-looking bunch of ragamuffins – auxiliary police, community police, local militias, men whose allegiances were most likely to lie with the communities they lived in, rather than to any symbol of government in Lash or Kabul.

Each time we slowed to wend our way through these pockets of habitation I would lock off my general-purpose machine gun (GPMG) on its swivel mount. In such confined areas there would not be the time or space to bring it to bear if we were attacked. Instead I withdrew my Sig Sauer 9mm from the drop holster on my right thigh and held it just below the dashboard out of sight.

With the pistol made ready, I was going against army regulations, but suicide bombers had previously jumped on the bonnets of passing ISAF vehicles then blown themselves up. If any would-be martyr tried it on, he'd be going off to meet seventy-two virgins in paradise without me. I'd make bloody sure of that, rules or no rules.

As we approached the outskirts of Marjah, the road – which had started off wide and metalled, but which was now little more than a rough track – veered southwards. To the right it was bounded by a canal. To the left, by an irrigation ditch. If the enemy opened fire there would be only one option. Full steam ahead. I thought back to Garmsir in 2006 and our hellish time repeatedly travelling up and down the canal road under regular contact. What made the current situation worse was the added threat from IEDs, something that had been rare two years previously but the use of which had since become a standard Taliban tactic.

I had just witnessed the effects of an IED on an open vehicle and I had no desire to meet my maker the same way. 'Matt, I think we will return to Lash via a different route. This place gives me the fucking willies.'

'Roger, Boss, we'll head due east from the school when we leave.'

'All right, mate, let's talk about it when we're there.'

After four hours of travelling we were almost at Green 4, the reference given to the junction on which the school sat. With the town's road network laid out in a regular grid, the easiest way to navigate was to label all the intersections using a system of colours and numbers. Going east out of Marjah you would leave from Green 4, drive through Green 3, 2 and 1 and then hit open countryside. Unfortunately we were still going the other way, into town.

Finally, passing a small market selling fruit and vegetables, plus large bottles of Coke and lurid-coloured fizzy orange that probably had a monopoly on E numbers, we turned into the school compound. Close to the district centre (DC) it sat in the north-eastern corner of the crossroads. No more than a shell of a building, in a horse-shoe shape, it didn't even have a continuous secure perimeter, one side being completely open.

Just across the road lay the ANP regional HQ. Nosing in, the ANA vehicles peeled off to the right, the Afghans heading for the spot where their colleagues were to be found. I followed Matt into the school compound and up to the front of the building to be greeted by Sergeant Jon Mathews, who had set up the PB and commanded it before the arrival of Captain Ben Foster.

Jon was another soldier from 4 SCOTS who was on loan to us for the tour. I had known him for a fair while and had served with him at the Infantry Training Centre in Catterick towards the end of 2005 and into 2006. I liked him a lot. Genuine, diligent, hard-working and kind, he held the respect of his men, never asking them to do something he would not do himself. He wasn't perfect but any failings just seemed to melt away in the face of his warm-heartedness and enthusiasm.

'Jon, Ben, how's it going?' I said as both men came up to meet me.

'Good, sir,' Jon replied. 'Do you want a tour?'

I knew he was keen to show me what he had done to make the best of a bad job.

'Not just now, Jon. I need a shit and a drink. In that order.'

The necessary done, we started to unload the stores. Food,

water, ammo and of course those bloody batteries. I wanted to get it done as quickly as possible, then hightail it out of there before the Taliban could get an unwelcome surprise organised for our departure. With the six of us humping and hauling boxes alongside the OMLT guys from the PB it didn't take long to unpack the wagons and refill some of the now-empty space with what needed to go back to Lash.

Forming up to leave I saw our convoy had swelled by a fifth, an ANA truck having joined us for the return leg of the journey. Unfortunately the head count had actually gone down. It turned out that more than half of the ANA platoon we'd arrived with were staying put in Marjah, leaving just sixteen of them to head back to Lash, plus the half-dozen of us. Not many men spread out amongst several vehicles. It was far from ideal, but we had to go with it.

Situations like this were not unique. The Afghans were notorious for either not telling the OMLT the truth about their plans or altering those plans as they went along. That morning, before leaving Lash, we had stopped off at the ANA HQ to brief them on what the mission entailed and what threats might lie ahead. I had already assessed we'd need a platoon's worth of men to carry out the task and my request had been agreed to. At no point during the briefing was I told many of the men would only have a one-way ticket. If I'd been warned then I would have made other arrangements, taken more soldiers in the first place. As it was, we had been shafted and there was no Plan B. Sod them.

Waving goodbye to Jon and the others we trailed out into the town, heading east, steadily moving from one green spot to another until we were clear of Marjah. After a couple of kilometres we swung north up a track, making for the 604.

We weren't going at Formula One speeds but it was still a reasonable pace, Matt with his WMIK at the front, followed by the ANA Humvee, the two Ranger pickups and the truck acquired at the school. My WMIK was last.

The only time we stopped was to clear any choke points in the road, funnels where there was no choice other than to follow the track because of buildings or geographical features hemming us in from both sides – perfect territory for IEDs, as we had found out from bitter experience.

We were now some three kilometres from the main route. As we drove, I looked out to the north-west. Through the dust, about 1,500 metres away, I could just make out two vehicles racing across the sand. I raised my binoculars to my eyes to try and get a better look at them, but the billowing clouds of Afghan desert and the vibration of the WMIK made it impossible to see any more detail. Yet it seemed to me we were on a collision course, our paths set to converge not that far ahead. I glanced down. All around, running perpendicular to the track and sometimes parallel to it, tying us to our route, were the same sort of irrigation trenches we had been constrained by that morning, heading into town. The trenches had given me the willies then. And now the feeling was back.

A large bang echoed around us, easily distinguishable even above the noise of the WMIK's throbbing diesel engine and the sound of the wind roaring in my ears. I thought I caught sight of a blur flying past me. Then came a second bang and, coinciding with it, to our front, there was an eruption of smoke and dust. The explosion and the impact point confirmed what I thought I had seen. A rocket had been fired at us.

'Matt, I think we have just been engaged with an RPG!'

'Roger, Boss, I will keep going.'

There was nothing else to be done. The attack had come from behind us, so it made sense to keep driving the way we were, to get out of trouble. But after another few hundred metres the convoy halted, my WMIK slewing to the left as Rab braked sharply and turned us slightly away from the direction of travel so it was easier for me to swing the GPMG round and help Monty cover the ground to the rear, just in case our tormentors decided to use the moment to press home their attack.

'Why have we stopped, Matt?' I wasn't keen on being halted and giving men with weapons the opportunity to take another pop.

'Just clearing a VP.'

I looked up the left-hand side of the convoy and easily made out the vulnerable point he was talking about. Up ahead there was a dip where the track crossed a stream. High banking on either side of the route prevented us from finding an easy way to bypass it. I could see Matt, his back to me, walking slowly towards the water, waving his metal detector in front of him, methodically, carefully checking for IEDs. Half of me wanted to shout to him, 'Come on, mate, get a fucking move on! It's my arse sticking out here.' The other half was urging caution – take it easy now, steady, don't miss anything, just do it right.

The ANA had spilled from their vehicles and taken up positions to secure the ground and cover Matt as he went about his work. This at least was good; a bit of initiative from the Afghan sergeant – making a decision and getting on with it.

Five tense minutes (or was it five hours?) later and Matt was happy the route was clear. He jogged back to his WMIK, heaved the metal detector aboard and dragged himself in after it. Then he was on the move again – down to the ford, into it, and out the other side. Same with the Humvee which was following. So too the first of the Ranger pickups. But not so the next pickup. As it nosed in, the front wheels breaking the surface of the water, all hell broke loose. From compounds to the south we'd just driven past, there came a hail of small-arms fire. Then a fusillade of RPGs. One. Two. Three. At least four of them.

Where the fuck to go? I wanted to keep moving ahead,

drive out of the killing zone, but the bloody ANA truck had stopped dead in the water. Shit. We couldn't go forward. We couldn't go back. The banking and the irrigation channels hemmed us in at the sides.

'Rab, Rab. Stop, stop!'

Stamping on the brake and pulling up behind a sliver of cover, he and I both tumbled out of the wagon on to the sun-baked ground as Lance-Corporal Carson swivelled round in his turret and opened up with the GPMG.

'Rab, get into some cover. Monty, keep firing,' I screamed, attempting to make myself heard over the noise coming from the blanket of fire now smothering us. Rounds fizzed and cracked over my head. Others ploughed furrows around me. Stuck at the end of the convoy, closest to the enemy, we were receiving the majority of the unwanted attention. It wasn't a situation I was happy with.

Rab dived for a small earth mound, then raised himself on to one knee and started returning fire with his SA80. I crawled up to the front left wing of the WMIK, trying to put the wheel and a bloody great Michelin tyre between me and at least some of the Taliban fire. Above the din I thought I heard Rab shouting at me, but I couldn't catch what he was saying.

I darted out from behind the wheel to get closer. 'What do you want? I can't fuckin' hear you!'

'Stay in, Boss, they've got your range!'

Cheers, mate. I fell back behind the Land Rover.

What he had seen and I hadn't, were rounds impacting close to my feet, and lines of tracer flying just above the WMIK and hence my head. Not that Rab was getting off scot-free. Five metres away, his position was taking a pasting too. Just as he ducked down to swap his magazine a heavy-calibre bullet slammed into the mound he was crouching behind, sending dirt spewing into the air and into Rab's eyes.

'Keep your fuckin' head down, Rab.'

My head bowed, the rim of my helmet hooded down over my eyes, I kept watching him through the stream of tracer keeping us apart. Some of it flew harmlessly by, just missing the front of the WMIK, whilst other rounds punched into the vehicle's skin, making it rock, and continued to chip away at the lump of ground keeping Rab safe.

Monty was doing sterling work. Fully exposed in the back of the WMIK he was returning fire with a vengeance, concentrating his aim on two compounds to our rear. Not bad for a clerk from the Adjutant-General's Corps. Ever thought of joining the infantry, son?

'Matt, have you got any comms yet?'

From the lead WMIK, Matt came back over the radio, the strain audible in his voice. 'Fuck all.'

I began firing at the compounds to the south with my rifle, allowing Rab to move from his rapidly diminishing hillock and crawl over to where I was now lying prone.

'Listen, Rab, I'm going up to Matt to see what's going on. If you can hold on here, try and get the ANA into some sort of position to begin engaging the enemy.'

Rab nodded his confirmation, lifted himself off his belt buckle and started working his way to the Afghan vehicles, which were all sitting pretty much together in the dip where the stream and track met.

The enemy had now started to put sustained fire down on the other end of the convoy. Matt, who'd been making futile attempts to speak to Lash using the TacSat, waving the antenna desperately about looking for a signal, had now flung the aerial aside and grabbed his rifle instead.

In a crouched run I made my way up the column of vehicles and literally stumbled across a pair of Afghans cowering behind a section of the banking. I grabbed the first by the shirt and yanked him up the incline.

In my best Pashtu I explained what I would like him to do. 'Fuckin' fire, you dickhead!'

As I calmly gave the soldier his orders, his mate scrambled to join us, obviously deciding that, when it came to facing an enraged Beattie, discretion was the better part of valour.

I moved on. Through the stream and past the Ranger pickup sitting forlornly in the water blocking the track, its occupants now being herded together by Rab into some sort of organised unit. Past the Humvee, pausing only momentarily as the ANA fired off a pair of RPGs.

Then I was at the front. From where I saw another vehicle I recognised. Just eighty metres away, sat square across the track at another natural choke point was one of the two cars I'd seen careering across the desert perhaps ten minutes earlier. Just beyond it were more compounds from where the enemy was pouring fire on to the lead WMIK. Not that Matt was taking things lying down. With a clutch of the ANA troops he was matching them round for round, bullets thumping into the body of the pickup and also into the mud walls of the huts the Taliban were sheltering in.

'Matt, what the fuck?'

Buoyed up with adrenalin, trying hard to keep calm and coherent, Matt told me what had happened. 'The vehicle just appeared out of nowhere. Must have been hijacked. The Taliban stopped on the track, got out and did a runner back to those compounds.'

To reiterate their presence another of their RPGs flew over our heads.

We had barely been in Marjah more than forty-five minutes, and then travelling for another ninety, yet in that time the Taliban had organised the ambush. It must have been improvised because they wouldn't have known we were going to return this way – hell, we hadn't known until it was almost time to leave the school. It showed our enemy had good intelligence, was quick-thinking and wasn't afraid to act. They might have been bastards. But they were clever bastards.

We were in a mess.

The vehicles were stuck with no easy way out. There were groups of heavily armed Taliban fighters to the front and the rear and we were a small group of Brits only six strong who had not only to fight ourselves, but also try and get the ANA to do the same. We were in serious danger of being overrun. I wasn't even sure if anyone was aware of our predicament. I dropped on to the ground with Matt as another volley of enemy bullets flew past, too close for comfort.

'Any joy with the TacSat?' I asked him.

'Not a thing. Fuckin' shite,' Matt replied.

'Do Lash know we're in contact?'

'Yes. Managed to get that one call off, but haven't had a thing since.'

The TacSat should have been our most valuable piece of kit – our link to the outside world and the help it offered – yet it was proving to be a right royal pain in the arse. The trouble was, to get a signal, the aerial had to be pointed almost exactly at the satellite, which was in the sky south-west of us at an angle of forty-five degrees. This was the only way we'd be able to establish communications and get to speak to the HQ at Lashkar Gah. It wasn't proving easy.

'Try the OMLT battlegroup ops,' I said to Matt, referring to the operations room back at Camp Tombstone, which was manned twenty-four hours a day.

With that he lifted his frame up off the floor and moved over to where he had dumped the satellite equipment, to try again. Under heavy fire he started to retune the radio. I had to admire his concentration. I stayed where I was for a while longer, firing from my rifle, at the same time trying to take in what was going on.

Over my shoulder I could see Rab had managed to restore order amongst the rear group of Afghan soldiers and five or six of them were now giving decent support to Monty, who was still doggedly firing away with the GPMG. At the head of the convoy the other Afghans with the platoon sergeant had moved slightly to the east to get a better angle to bring fire to bear on the Taliban up ahead.

I looked quizzically at Matt. 'Anything?'

'Nothing, Boss, not even a ping.'

When you get the aerial roughly lined up on the satellite, you hit a button and you are told what signal strength you have. You aim for a hundred, but have a chance with anything over sixty. We didn't have even that. Which meant we were going to have to get out of this on our own.

'OK, mate, what do you suggest?' I asked. I wasn't going to be precious about this. If he had any bright ideas then I was happy to hear them.

'Let's just drive out,' he said before turning back to face the enemy, some of whom had become emboldened enough to try and advance towards us. We sure as fuck needed to do something.

'What will you do with the vehicle blocking the road?'

'I'll just ram the fucker out of the way!'

So that was the plan.

'OK, get mounted up. I'll get everyone else in their vehicles.'

I ran back down the side of the track, using for cover an irrigation ditch that I thought was dry. It quickly became clear it wasn't. With every step, I broke through a thin crust of dried earth, only to find myself wading through several inches of cloying mud hidden beneath, the wet, heavy soil clinging to my desert boots and seeping through the canvas, adding weight to my legs, already leaden from the exertion of the firefight. As I moved I grabbed the Afghan soldiers, this time hauling them off the ground and pushing them back towards their trucks, shouting 'Arocat' as I went, an Afghan word for 'move out'.

We shouldn't have allowed ourselves to get into such a position. In any sort of ambush the key is to keep moving, blast through without stopping. What you don't want to do, what we had ended up doing, is to stop in a killing zone the enemy has chosen precisely because of its advantage to them and extreme danger to you. But the ANA had been taught differently by the Americans. The US way is to pile out of the vehicles and bring as much firepower as possible to bear on the threat. Which is why the ANA Ranger pickup had halted so suddenly in the middle of the stream.

The other mistake was self-inflicted. Our habit had been to separate the WMIKs and put one at the front and one at the rear. Plainly this wasn't effective. If Matt and I had been together we could have worked as a unit, in support of each other, and hopefully kept moving as a pair, encouraging the ANA to stay with us. Instead we were too far apart, with my route forward blocked by the stalled ANA. Keeping together was something I had thought about in training and made a mental note to do once in Afghanistan. Now I made mental note two; implement mental note one if we ever found ourselves in a similar situation – assuming, of course, we got out of this alive.

The ambush was the most dangerous situation I'd found myself in since arriving in Helmand. It was clear there had been a resurgence of Taliban activity around the provincial capital. It seemed as if the Taliban were happy to make this area the new battleground, moving away from traditional scenes of confrontation like Sangin and Musa Qala, which were heavily patrolled by ISAF. So far their decision had been a good one.

Some forty minutes after we had first come under fire I got back to my WMIK. Rab was still doing a great job with the ANA. And so too was Monty with his machine gun. For the entire time he had remained at his GPMG in full view of the enemy.*

---

* Quite rightly Monty Carson received a Mention in Despatches for his part in the engagement.

'Rab, we're leaving.'

'Roger, Boss, let's get to fuck.' There was relief in his voice. Over the PRR I said:

'Matt, fuckin' go!'

'What about the ANA?'

'Just move, mate. If they want out of here they'll follow.'

In the distance — some eighty metres away — I could see Matt's WMIK start to inch forward, him firing from his commander's machine gun, the top gunner firing too. Behind them the Humvee started to go. Then, as they realised their colleagues were pulling out, the few Afghan soldiers who had been slow mounting up scrambled back into their vehicles. Finally it was our turn to roll.

Up ahead, Matt had reached the blockade.

With a wrenching of metal, that was audible even back where we were, he hit the hijacked vehicle — a Toyota four-door saloon — square-on and bulldozed it off the road. Without stopping he roared on past the enemy-held compounds, exchanging fire with them at a range of no more than twenty metres. The ANA were close behind, us bringing up the rear. As we thundered through the Taliban positions I brought my machine gun to bear on a group of the enemy cowering behind a wall. Except they weren't Taliban. At the very last second I hesitated and lifted the barrel away from them. No, they definitely weren't the enemy. They seemed to be the poor sods whose car had just been hijacked. There wasn't much time to study them but they looked as if they could have been from a wedding party (something confirmed later by the interpreter) — yet more innocent Afghans caught up in the fighting. The Taliban might have claimed to represent the ordinary people of the country, but I couldn't imagine this group would be toasting their success. Carjacked by the Taliban, then almost shot dead by the British. It had not been their day.

Back in Lashkar Gah it was clear how lucky we had been.

We did not suffer any casualties but that was more luck than judgement. The vehicles were peppered with holes, the damage done by bullets and flying shards of shrapnel from exploding RPGs. I made my report. There was no doubting the tenacity or strength of the enemy in the Marjah district; certainly their willingness to move forward in the open without obvious regard for the possible arrival of air cover was worrying and underlined their boldness.

My advice was blunt. 'The PB is in a shit location, it achieves fuck-all and it is a disaster waiting to happen. As for re-supply? Don't do another one by road.'

I was confident I would never have to see Marjah again. Surely only fools would ignore the warnings?

SEVEN

BOULEVARDS

THE PILOT OF APACHE 'UGLY 40'

3 JULY 2008

The shooting came from behind us. A burst of perhaps six rounds. From an automatic weapon. Then silence.

In the lead WMIK, we'd only got twenty metres beyond the sodding camp. As for the rest of the convoy, it was still *in* the camp.

I could tell from the sound of the weapon it was one of ours, a GPMG. What the hell had happened? Who the fuck was shooting at whom?

I jumped down from the wagon, sprinted back through the gates of the compound and past the ANA vehicles. There in the front of a Ranger were two Afghan soldiers, clearly badly wounded. Their colleagues were trying to pull them from the vehicle, not exactly tending to them, just attempting to do something.

One appeared to have been hit in the leg and the side of the body, whilst the other had taken a couple of rounds in his chest. Finding out exactly what the chain of events had been would have to wait for a while – first of all, we needed to save these men's lives.

As I tried to get closer to the casualties, their colleagues closed in on me, shouting and pointing, their fury abundantly clear. Amongst them was their leader, the first sergeant. He gave me a verbal tirade, spit raining from his mouth, his appallingly kept teeth plainly visible as he subjected me to the volley of abuse. And all this as his men lay bleeding to death at his feet.

I turned to the interpreter. 'Listen, tell him if he doesn't stop complaining and start helping, his men are going to die.'

'Yes, but he's angry that . . .'

Getting angry myself, I cut the man off. 'Shut the fuck up. You are an interpreter. You are here to interpret what I am saying, not to give me your opinion. I'm not interested.'

'Yes, sir,' he replied, the message received loud and clear. He turned to the sergeant and let loose in Dari.

It seemed to have the desired effect. The NCO became visibly calmer, having recognised his remonstrations weren't getting the wounded treated. One had gone ominously quiet; the second continued to moan, bleeding heavily.

'Tell him to get them in the rear of the pickup and we will drive over to the medical centre.'

A minute later and the convoy was moving forward again, only now we weren't on our way to carry out a standard patrol in the sprawling Babaji district which stretched north from Lash; we were racing back to the ISAF base to get the injured seen to. I sent a sitrep.

'Zero, this is Amber 40 Delta. I am on my way back to your location with two wounded ANA soldiers. I need the medical centre warned and I also need an RMP to meet us at the gate.'

RMP – Royal Military Policeman. There would need to be an investigation. The rounds had come from a British gun and these were only manned by British soldiers. One of my guys was going to have some explaining to do. Ashen-faced, the man in question had already told me – briefly – how he'd cocked the machine gun and it had started to fire automatically. In the military this is known as a runaway gun. He only managed to stop it by grabbing the belt of ammunition as it was sucked through the weapon, breaking the flow of bullets. Discovering why the gun had operated with a mind of its own, or indeed if this really was what had happened – was the soldier telling the truth? – would be down to the police inquiry.

We careered through the already open gates and slithered to a halt outside the medical tent. There to meet us were three medics and a doctor. With a practised professionalism they transferred the patients inside and treatment started. Watching it all was the ANA sergeant. He had been joined by the company commander. They both had faces like thunder. I couldn't really blame them. If two of my men had just been cut up by our Afghan allies, I would have been pretty pissed off too, wanting heads on a plate. This was not the time for me to walk up to them, shrug my shoulders and say 'Inshallah' – 'God's Will', explaining away the shooting as an unfathomable act of divinity. That would have rendered our relationship irreparable and seen me receive a punch in the face. Instead I tried to apologise and promised that the soldier responsible would be harshly dealt with. This seemed to placate them slightly. As did the sight of their men getting the same consideration as would be offered to ISAF forces after a similar event, something that was reinforced by the appearance of an IRT helicopter less than half an hour later to transfer them to Bastion for further treatment.*

Briefed as to the condition of the casualties by the young female doctor on duty, the Afghans, satisfied, headed back to their own camp. There would be no more patrolling with them that day.

---

* The men survived. They spent a couple of weeks recuperating at Bastion, then went on R & R before returning to duty some six weeks later.

I went to speak more fully to the soldier involved. Sitting on some steps near his WMIK, all his kit still on as if he were waiting for his next orders, he was badly shaken. Clearly he hadn't woken up that morning with the intention of shooting his colleagues. He couldn't comprehend what had gone wrong; much less that he might just have killed two of the Afghans he was supposed to be mentoring. I sent him off with one of his mates to get out of his gear and away from the scene. Then I went to his WMIK and studied the GPMG that had done the damage.

It was pretty clear to me how things had gone awry. The pistol grip that should have been locked into the bottom of the weapon, secured with a retaining pin, was hanging beneath the gun, a second pin stopping it falling away completely. Climbing into the back of the Land Rover I saw the first pin lying useless on the metal floor. On a GPMG, if this pin, and hence the grip, are not properly in place then when the weapon is cocked the safety sears cannot engage and the gun will fire immediately without need for the trigger to be pulled. And it will continue firing until either the ammo box attached to the side is empty – in this case that would have been 200 rounds later – or someone manages to grab the belt and snap off the remaining bullets before they can be fed through. What wasn't clear was why the pin hadn't done its job. Before any patrol the weapons are checked, first by the operator and then by the NCO in charge, in this case Colonel. On top of this the young soldier responsible had recently come back from R & R and so just the night before had done some mandatory re-familiarisation on the machine gun. The only silver lining to the shooting was the speed with which the soldier had yanked the rest of the rounds away from the weapon. Better six bullets fired than a couple of hundred. Small consolation for the casualties, though. As for any charges, that was out of my hands – the decision falling to the RMP. I couldn't believe the shooting was anything more than an accident. The trouble is, in the army, accidents have deadly consequences.*

It was all pretty sobering stuff. Yet there wouldn't be much time to think about the incident because soon I had something else to worry about. Apparently the fools hadn't listened. I was going back to Marjah. The next day. On a re-supply. By road.

'You know we should be doing this by helicopter,' I said to James Cartwright, my exasperation all too evident.

'I know, Doug, but they won't give us one.'

'Who won't? Who have you asked?' I pushed him further.

'Well, I spoke to the ops room of 2 SCOTS and they said we are to do it by vehicle, there are no helis available.'

I had no reason to doubt James had fully argued our corner, yet I was still immensely frustrated that my report and recommendations had fallen on deaf ears. Then he spoke some more. It seemed the powers that be might just have had one ear open after all.

'Take as much stuff as they will need in Marjah for a month – after this there won't be another supply run for thirty days.'

Now, this was good news – for those coming after us. However, we were still faced with the not insignificant matter of completing this mission successfully. My sense of foreboding remained.

We started gathering the gear together. There was a lot of it. Perhaps most importantly we now had a generator, one of five allocated to an Afghan Police mentoring team, yet which we had just discovered was sitting unused gathering dust. At least now the base could be self-sustaining when it came to charging up the batteries so vital to its occupants' security.

---

* In March 2009, after a long and thorough investigation, the young soldier was eventually cleared of any wrongdoing and the cause of the incident was put down to a weapon malfunction.

Because of all the prep and the early start scheduled for the following morning – 04:30 hrs – everything was loaded that night. There would be three British vehicles going. One WMIK commanded by me with Jim Carney driving and Al Owens as gunner. Brummie Hagans would command a second WMIK. His driver was Brownie, the 46-year-old lance-corporal seconded to us from 2 SCOTS whom I was so incredulous about when I'd been told about him back in England. Top cover was provided by Junior Stewart. Lastly there was a Snatch Land Rover and that was Matt's. One concession had been made to the danger of the trip – the presence of a couple of communications experts, whose job was to gather intelligence and monitor radio traffic across Helmand. Their real skill lay in their ability to speak Pashtu. Hopefully if the enemy was talking about an ambush we would hear about it before the bullets started to fly.

Weapon-wise I felt we were under-gunned. There was no .50-cal heavy machine gun or GMG, only four 7.62mm-calibre GPMGs (two on each WMIK) and a light machine gun – a Minimi – on the Snatch.

Talk about going to hell in a handcart.

The TacSats were lashed to the bonnets with bungee cords, alongside the HF radio. The HF set would be used until we were about fifteen kilometres beyond Lash and got out of range. Then we would be reliant on the TacSats. In theory, using the TacSats should have been a piece of piss. All we needed were the omni-directional aerials that meant the radios could be used whilst driving as well as when static. Except we didn't have this kit. Which meant the convoy would have to grind to a halt every fifteen minutes or so to allow the operator to fiddle with the unidirectional antenna until he found the satellite low in the southern sky, 'pinged' the set and finally managed to establish comms with someone speaking English. All this could easily take ten minutes. If we weren't careful, we'd spend more time reporting in than actually doing anything.

Loading and securing, attaching and stowing the gear, we talked about the best way of reaching the PB at Marjah. There was a consensus that approaching from the north, hemmed in by the irrigation network, wasn't a great plan – but equally, if we came in across the open desert from the east the Taliban might well spot our movement and organise a welcoming committee for us.

The process Matt, Brummie and I were going through is called combat estimate – a standard set of seven questions that you ask – and then answer – in relation to any plan, course of action (COA), that is suggested. It is a sort of a stress test for military operations. And even when a COA is agreed on, it is not set in stone. It should always be up for debate and if the situation changes then you go back to square one and carry out the assessment again.

We reached a decision.

We would come in from the east because although the expansive vista would allow the Taliban to see us and perhaps prepare an ambush, it would hopefully also allow us to see them before it was too late. This openness, plus the relative lack of water channels, also allowed us more choice over the exact course we would steer to reach Green 4. The abundance of routes meant, short of mining every single road, track and choke point, the Taliban would find it hard to hit us with an IED. This in particular influenced our thoughts.

It might seem strange but combat is rarely the most stressful and nerve-wracking part of soldiering. Coming under fire, getting into a contact, can offer some kind of relief. The danger is suddenly clear, you can fight back, your destiny now more squarely in your own hands. But truly terrifying are the quiet moments before the mayhem, the calm before the storm; the occasions when you are walking or driving through enemy territory, knowing an attack is all but inevitable but not from where or when. Especially an attack from an IED. With every footstep, every rotation of the wheels, you are watching for signs of disturbed ground, culverts running under the road, trip wires or pressure pads, bags or tins or junk lying beside the route, material that might just be rubbish, or might just be a disguised weapon designed to blow you to kingdom come. It takes bucketloads of nerve and a huge helping of willpower just to put one foot in front of another. And then do it again. And again. If there was any other way to do the job, you'd grab it with both hands. But there isn't.

So you try and put the fear out of your mind, take that step, drive another metre, and you concentrate as if your life depends on it – 100 per cent concentration, 100 per cent of the time. There is no opportunity to stop and rest. It is an unremitting process of observe, assess, decide – decide whether there is a threat or not, decide whether to check it out or not, decide whether to gamble your life or not. All this would be exhausting enough if roadside bombs were the only things to be considered, but of course they are not. There are a million and one other issues a commander has to worry about. Are we going the right way? Is the patrol/convoy deployed as it should be? Are we going too fast or too slow? What are the local population doing? Is that man on the motorcycle a farmer going home for his tea or a suicide bomber on his way to the next life?

Maintaining awareness, staying sharp, is exhausting, yet there's no choice, it has to be done. As the saying used to go in Northern Ireland: 'the terrorists only have to be lucky once, we have to be lucky all the time'.

Before turning in we rehearsed the drills we would carry out if the worst happened; if an IED went off, if we were shot at, if we lost comms, if a vehicle broke down. We tried to come up with a response to every scenario.

Sleep that night was fitful. I couldn't shake off thoughts of the ambush three days earlier and how close we had come to disaster. In my mind I was sure we were setting ourselves up for the enemy to have another go. As camp life carried on around me at full pace with apparent disregard for the hour of day or night, I wondered whether I should have protested more about what had gone before, yet I trusted James and Dave Stanley. Both good men, I had to believe they wouldn't be reckless with our lives.

Almost as soon as I managed to get myself to sleep it was time to get up, my internal alarm clock waking me at about 03:00 hrs. Some thirty minutes later I rolled off my sleeping bag – it had been too hot to sleep in it, so I had slept on top – and off the cot, my feet searching for space amongst the thick under-growth of kit that had grown across the floor of the tent.

Quickly dressed, there was no time to shave, just brush my teeth, grab a sandwich and then get to the vehicles to do a comms check. Everything in order, we trundled out of the gates towards the ANA camp. I found what I had expected to find. The Afghan soldiers still sat down to breakfast. No sense of time. No sense of urgency. They asked us to join them. We declined, instead heading back outside to wait. I knew they would be a while. When you are dealing with Afghans you have to resign yourself to their timekeeping. The best you can do is allow for it in your plans.

Eventually even the Afghans could not find another reason to procrastinate further and they traipsed out to their vehicles. A mere twenty men, led by the first sergeant I recognised from our last trip to Marjah, all packed into the same Humvee and two Ranger pickups as before. Adding them to us, it still wasn't going to be much of a patrol in terms of numbers. I thought back to my time just finished in Kajaki and the com-pany-size patrols carried out by 2 PARA with the backup of a FOO, JTAC and MFC. Halcyon days.

Speak to those in charge at the Ministry of Defence and they will tell you how important their duty of care towards the aver-age British soldier is. And rightly so, but as part of the OMLT it was as if we inhabited a twilight zone. We certainly weren't Afghan and yet we weren't quite British in as much as whatever conditions the ANA had to put up with, then so did we.

Heading out of Lash I already had my pistol drawn. It was only as we crossed the Bowlan bridge and left the confines of the town behind that I put it back in its holster. After a while we turned off the 604 and headed due south. At the front, in the lead WMIK, Brummie tried to keep up some momentum, but it became increasingly difficult. (Once more my WMIK was at the back even though I had promised myself not to allow us to get split up again. My poor excuse this time was that as we were on a logistical patrol it was Brummie who made the call on how we set ourselves out – it was his show, not mine. I should have made more of an issue of it, but to my shame I didn't.) Many of the tracks marked on the map didn't exist in reality. And even where they did, there was a tendency for them suddenly to peter out in the middle of a ploughed field. Either that or they'd come to an abrupt end where they ran up against an irrigation ditch with no obvious means of getting over it. With increasing frustration, we tried to box round the obstacles, turning left or right to follow the offending obstruction until we found a bridge or ford. Often our detours only led us to further obstacles. More than once we found ourselves surrounded on three sides by trenches and canals forcing us laboriously to retrace our steps.

Our manoeuvrings had become something of a local spectacle. Word had got round. At every turn there seemed to be another group of locals watching our descent into madness, either looking up from their work in the fields or standing on top of flat compound roofs and walls. We must have looked a sorry sight. The cream of the British and Afghan armies blundering around lost, as if five-year-olds in a maze. Our lack of progress was compounded further by the need to make those damned radio checks back to Lash, using the TacSat now that we were finally beyond the range of the HF set.

The heat was starting to take its toll. The sun had risen fully and was beating down on us with little care for our predicament. If we had managed to build up some sort of head of steam, and make some steady headway, then at least the air flowing past us – albeit hot air – would have taken the sting out of the baking temperatures. But sitting there in the WMIK with uniform, helmet, body armour and webbing on, calculating which turn to take next, was like being a chicken slowly roasting on a spit. Getting out of the vehicle to walk it through a choke point or round an obstacle was becoming a real chore. The fatigue caused by the mental strain, the lack of progress, the long, long hours in the saddle, was wearing us all down and it was about to be our undoing.

'Fuckin' hell, get out, get out!' was all Jim Carney had time to say.

'Get down, Al,' was all I had time to say.

And with that our WMIK lurched violently to the left, off the small bridge we had precariously been negotiating, and began to tumble towards the river below. I should have seen it coming. The crossing, made of logs covered with mud baked hard in the sun, was solidly built, but not nearly wide enough. The edges were bevelled where the earth had crumbled away and did nothing to help the WMIK's tyres find purchase.

In the second or two before we hit the water several metres below, I cursed my luck. I was about to die, not at the hands of the enemy, but by drowning in a foetid Afghan waterway, held under the surface by the weight of the upturned WMIK crushing down on me. Killed in a bloody road traffic accident with not a Talib in sight. That many other soldiers have been killed in similar circumstances over the years because of nothing more than a misjudgement, a lack of concentration, or plain bad luck, was small consolation. In fact it was no sodding consolation at all.

Looking up – or at least what for a moment was up – I saw

Jim clinging on to the steering wheel with all his might. In the back, Al wasn't visible. As an alternative to being pile-driven, head first, into the silt and sediment at the bottom of the channel by the tonnes of metal supposed to protect, not kill, us, he must have thrown himself to the floor of the wagon and clung on (though to God knows what). As I tried to huddle in the footwell, all the unsecured kit flew past me. Ammunition boxes, rucksacks, water bottles, jerrycans; everything. Then we were in the water, a tidal wave spreading out from our point of immersion.

Suddenly we stopped. I was wet, but not yet completely soaked. The vehicle had rotated well past ninety degrees but something had stopped it going right over. My machine gun.

The GPMG was buried in the bottom of the river. Together with the swivel joint and the mounting arm, it was now bearing the full weight of the WMIK.

As I half-crawled, half-fell from the wagon, fully into the water, Jim screamed at me. 'Don't get out! You'll topple it.'

'Shut up, you dick, I'm at the bottom, my weight isn't going to make any difference now. Anyway, too late, I'm out.' There was more than a hint of annoyance in my voice.

I waded through the water, pushing aside the bits of equipment that were bobbing about, then clambered up the bank. Al was already there.

'You OK?' I asked.

He nodded silently, shaken but with no more serious injuries than a few cuts and bruises. Finally Jim abandoned ship too and scrambled ashore, also badly shook up. We stood there like three naughty children (or was it drowned rats?) looking forlornly at the half-submerged Land Rover.

Brummie came running towards us. 'What happened, Boss?'

'Jim fuckin' Carney tried to kill me, that's what.' I was only half-joking.

All worries about our tactical situation had evaporated in

the confusion of the accident. Most of the Afghan soldiers were also standing around, looks of curiosity painted on their faces. Some dropped into the water to try and fish out pieces of kit. Only after some cajoling from Brummie and Matt did they set up a perimeter to watch out for any Taliban whose curiosity might also have been aroused by our misfortune. We were no more than three kilometres from the point of our ambush just days before and now, having coming to realise I was still alive, I wanted to keep it that way.

One thing the Afghans are good at is improvising. With no pulleys or jacks, they succeeded in manhandling the stricken vehicle out of the water, up the bank and back on to dry land. Still on its side when it emerged, they then pushed the WMIK upright, the suspension squealing in protest as it slammed back on to four wheels.

Jim carried out a quick inspection before jumping back into his seat and trying the engine. It fired first time. Sodden men and dripping equipment back on board, off we went again.

We hadn't covered more than a few hundred yards when I noticed something funny about my machine gun. It started to go limp, the barrel drooping, the butt in my shoulder slipping out of place. I pulled back from the weapon and looked at it quizzically – just in time to see the GPMG, together with the swivel joint and mounting arm, fall off and land unceremoniously in the sand.

'Amber 45 Alpha, this is Amber 43. Stop the convoy.'

Brummie brought us all to a halt. I hopped out and walked back to the gun, which lay forlornly on the ground, surrounded by a couple of hundred 7.62mm rounds that had spewed from the ammo box as if a metallic creature had been disembowelled where it fell. I could see the gun had sheared off where the weapon met the arm. All four retaining bolts had failed, irreparably. In the act of saving our lives the gun and the mount had been put under immense strain. Bearing the full weight of the WMIK, the bolts must have suffered metal fatigue and now, after a few heavy jolts on the rutted track, they had given up the fight.

'Would you fuckin' believe it, Jim? Let's just hope we don't need it.'

I grabbed hold of the gun, cradled it in my arms and carried it to the wagon before chucking it in, forcing Al to quickly pick up his feet as it clattered to the floor.

Back in my seat I yanked my SA80 from the rack between Jim and me. It seemed so puny after the GPMG. Like a toy. I felt naked and exposed. Suddenly vulnerable. Just as Afghans regard an AK47 being fired as merely the source of a lot of noise (no matter that bullets are being chucked out, too) so now I saw my rifle as nothing more dangerous or effective than a pea-shooter.

'OK, Brummie, let's go,' I said with no trace of enthusiasm.

It was nearly midday and we had been on the road for a good six hours. The heat was relentless, though it did mean I was drying off quickly after my baptism. As I looked around, I could still see locals busy in their fields, tending the crops and tilling the soil. Mostly they were old men, women and children.

This in itself should have given me cause for concern.

We were now converging on Green 1 from the north, a two-metre-wide irrigation canal bounding us on the right, the west. The only way to cross it was via the bridge at the upcoming junction. Running parallel to the canal on its other side was a similar track to the one we were using, lined with tightly packed compounds that extended all the way down to Green 1.

On our left, the east, were a few more scattered compounds, then fields, and finally, in the middle distance, other settlements.

We were half a kilometre from the intersection. And my sense of foreboding was growing. Those Afghans I had seen out cultivating were quickly disappearing, the women drifting off in ghostly fashion – covered in their full-length burqas they seemed to glide across the landscape. Then came the old men, one of whom was being carried. Was it time for lunch? Or did they know something we didn't?

'Brummie, I have civilians leaving . . .'

I never got the chance to complete the sentence.

With the fury of a tornado, the enemy struck. From the other side of the canal. Extremely close, no more than fifteen metres away, they poured fire on to the two lead vehicles – Brummie's WMIK and Matt's Snatch Land Rover – stopping the patrol dead in its tracks. Then bullets started to rake down the entire length of the column, riddling first the Humvee, then the two Rangers, before finally smacking into us. AK47 rounds pummelled and punctured the skin of the vehicle (so much for Kalashnikovs generating mere noise) as did heavier-calibre rounds, the sound slightly different for each type of bullet that slammed into the bodywork.

We were so close to the enemy that their tracer rounds, some of which weren't just riddling the wagons but also flying over our heads, had not even had the chance to light up by the time they passed by. Glancing over my shoulder I saw red specks starting to appear in the sky as the bases of the bullets finally illuminated way beyond us before they arced over towards the fields only recently vacated by the farmers. It would have been mesmerising to watch had it not been for the little matter of our impending deaths.

As soon as the shooting had started, the ANA bailed out of their vehicles and were either sheltering behind them or in one of the scattered compounds to the left of the track.

I watched as a volley of shots shredded the two offside tyres of the pickup immediately in front of our WMIK. In a second they deflated and the truck was left listing *Titanic*-like to star-board. I was now out of the commander's seat and leaning across the front of the Land Rover, rifle braced against the bonnet. I took one shot – and another – at a quartet of enemy fighters scurrying between a pair of compounds just the other side of the canal. Then I switched the weapon to automatic, loosing off short bursts at more fleeting figures as they darted back and forth, in and out of the shadows of the buildings, the sound of my rifle drowned out by the heavy clatter of Al's GPMG.

In Afghanistan British troops work under the rules of engagement as defined on the so-called Card A. As I tried my damnedest to kill my enemy the wording on the card came into my mind.

Firearms must only be used as a last resort in protection of human life. You are only to open fire against a person if he/she is committing or about to commit an act likely to endanger human life and there is no other way of stopping it.

Well, I was covered there, then. Human life was being endangered. Mine. I fired another burst.

A challenge MUST be given before opening fire unless to do so would increase the risk of death or grave injury to you or any other person other than the attacker(s).

Yep, covered there pretty well too.

I ducked down to release the now-empty magazine and shove a fresh one home. Raising my head again, I caught sight of two more Talibs, in the open, a mere twenty metres away.

Should I give them fair warning? 'Army, stop or I shoot'? Sod that.

I brought my rifle to bear and pulled the trigger. One of the men went down as the rounds hit him, whilst the other scampered away.

If you have to open fire only fire aimed shots, fire no more rounds than are necessary, take all reasonable precautions not to injure anyone other than your target.

Targets? These weren't fucking metal plates with human effigies painted on them, sitting at the bottom of the range. These were fighters whose goal was to wipe us out. I wasn't counting rounds. I was trying to stay alive.

This guidance does not affect your inherent right to self-defence. However in all situations you are to use no more force than absolutely necessary.

Well, sod that too. I changed my aim again and opened up on four men who were setting up an RPG launcher, sending them scattering.

'Al, how's it going?' I screamed as I replaced yet another empty magazine.

'Fuckin' enemy everywhere!'

As I took up from where I'd left off, he seized another 200-round belt of ammo, placed it on the feed tray and slammed down the top cover, locking the rounds in place.

All this time Jim was in the driver's seat, engaging with his rifle, unwilling to get out in case we had to make a quick get-away.

'Keep firing, Jim. I'm going to speak to Brummie and find out what the hell is happening at the front.' I slumped to the floor and grabbed the PRR on my left-hand shoulder, pressing the lower of the two buttons (the other one was to activate the VHF set). 'Brummie, this is Doug.'

Nothing.

'Brummie, Doug,' I tried again.

I hoped the reason he wasn't speaking to me was because he was too busy. The other reason was one I didn't dare think about.

It was hard to be certain but there must have been twenty-five to thirty of the enemy taking us on. Al managed to erode that number, dropping a handful of fighters as they pushed through some trees and bushes. But his success was nearly his undoing. He had become the target for at least two groups of the insurgents and the wall of fire concentrated on him made Al dive to the bottom of the vehicle and try to melt into the metal to escape the fusillade aimed in his direction.

'Move the fuckin' vehicle forward!' I yelled at some ANA

soldiers, gesturing that they should push on and marry up with the rest of the patrol they'd stopped a little way behind.

They stared back with blank faces, one of them pointing at the two flat tyres.

'So what? Just get in the fuckin' vehicle and get it fuckin' moving before I start shooting you, you rag-head bastards.' I didn't know how my tirade would have gone down at the ministry of political correctness and I cared even less. I needed to instil some urgency into these people. Anyway, they didn't have a clue what actual words I was using. And they didn't need to. Because my animated behaviour had made the message pretty bloody obvious even to the Afghans. Reluctantly they started to move back to the truck.

'Get ready, Jim. When the pickup moves, we go too. I want to rejoin Brummie.'

'Roger, Boss, but just keep shooting at those fuckers, they're getting a bit close.'

As if to emphasise the point a handful of rounds crashed into the wing of the WMIK, rocking it visibly.

'Stand by, stand by!'

It turned out I was being a bit premature.

Suddenly we started to receive fire from the east. I threw myself to the ground and tumbled into a culvert cut into the banking. Two RPG rounds exploded close to a group of the ANA soldiers who were now back out of their vehicle, faces pressed into the dirt, praying for deliverance from the relentless crossfire. I had little sympathy for their predicament. Weren't we all stuck in the same bloody crossfire? Where did they think salvation was going to come from? The fate of us all was in our own hands. If we stopped shooting back, stopped fighting, then we would take casualties, guaranteed. The Taliban would advance and finish us off. The only way to respond was to give as good as we were getting. Keep the enemy's heads down and try to move forward.

'Brummie, Doug. We are now taking fire from the east.'

'Roger, Boss. We are pinned down just to the east of Green 1.'

We had to continue with plan A and drive on because there was no other option. I ran forward fifteen metres to the ANA vehicle in front of us and slithered to a halt next to the driver who was still on the floor vainly seeking shelter.

I grabbed him by the lapels. 'Arocat!' I screamed in my best Afghan. 'Arocat!'

I was not sure I had pronounced the word with all the right inflections, but once again I hoped the tone of my delivery would leave the driver in little doubt about what I wanted done. He turned to the tyres then gave me one last imploring look, his brow furrowed with the deepest lines of worry I had seen for a long time.

Laying on my thickest Afghan accent, I tried one last time. 'FUCKIN' AROCAT NOW!'

The driver started to move. Hesitantly, but he moved. I ran back to the WMIK.

'Getting low on ammo, Boss,' Al shouted even as he acquired a new target and started to engage with five-round bursts.

'Boss, they're moving.' This from Jim.

I turned and watched as the Ranger inched forward, the right-hand side resting on the wheel rims.

'OK, Jim, dead slow. I will cover the east. Al, you take the west.'

Still on the track, I half-walked, half-jogged, half-stumbled alongside the WMIK, firing as I went.

'Brummie, can you hold your ground until we reach you? Then we will try and push on to somewhere defendable.'

'Roger, Boss. You are some 300 metres to my rear. Give me a shout when you're at 100 metres and I'll go try and clear Green 1.'

As we moved ahead it was easy to forgive Jim for putting us

in the drink earlier in the day. Concentrating on his driving, moving at a snail's pace, he was resolutely ignoring the incoming fire.

Our concertina of a convoy was contracting once again. As good as his word Brummie had made it over the canal crossing and was holding Green 1, where we now joined him. Unfortunately the enemy seemed to be holding just about everything else. There were Taliban to the south, closing in from the east, and moving down from compounds in the north, where the attack had first started. Four more Talibs were moving along a track westwards, towards a village at Green 2 and hence towards Marjah – unfortunately that was the way we wanted to go, too. Luckily Brummie's top gunner Junior evened things out a little. Joined by Al, Matt and one of the signallers on top of the Snatch with the Minimi, he made sure none reached their destination.

Stationary at Green 1, we needed to set up some sort of perimeter again and I divvied up the tasks. Brummie continued covering the ground to the west. Me, the north. The ANA, the south and east. With us co-ordinated and together for the first time since the ambush began, the rate of Taliban fire seemed to drop off. It gave us the breather we needed to try and speak to Lash again.

Throughout the engagement Brummie and I had been struggling to establish a radio link with the ops room there. We had managed to open a TiC with them but that was about it. Now, with Brownie standing on top of the WMIK, antenna in his hand and arm outstretched, we had continuous comms. We requested helicopter support and were told an Apache would be dispatched. In reply I let them know we didn't have a JTAC and so the link between myself and the pilot would have to be over the VHF radio on hail and in clear.

I sat down beside Brummie, suddenly worn out by the

efforts of the day. The enemy fire had become sporadic but we were still completely surrounded and I wasn't going anywhere until the air cover arrived.

'This just ain't funny, Brummie.'

'I know, Boss. It all got a bit too close for comfort back there.' He bent his leg so I could see the bottom of his boot. There was a neat hole in the sole where a round had entered, narrowly missing flesh and bone. A shout broke my concentration as I marvelled at Brummie's lucky escape.

'Enemy, enemy,' came the cry from Junior and with that he opened up at some more insurgents he had spotted crossing open ground, heading for the village at Green 2. Still in the driver's seat, Jim manoeuvred our WMIK alongside Brummie's so Al could also join in. Between them they didn't give the enemy a chance, killing at least three before they could disappear from view and find safety amongst the network of compounds the village comprised.

By this stage we had been under fire for ninety minutes and I was getting anxious that the AH should appear sometime soon. We still had to get out of this mess. Still get to Marjah. And still get home again.

'Boss, I'm going to give the ops room another call,' said Brummie.

He left the relative safety of the wall of the shop we had parked behind at the junction and went back to the WMIK and the TacSat.

A minute or two later he had some news. 'Boss, the AH is inbound. The pilot wants you to give him a call.'

Brummie had just completed his sentence when Brownie flew off the top of the WMIK and huddled up beside it. Minus the aerial.

'What's up, mate?' Brummie enquired.

Brownie's reply was another illustration of just how serious the situation was – lull or no lull: 'Fuckers just shot the antenna out of my hand.'

His reaction to the near-death experience? 'I need a fag and a cup of tea.'

I tried to raise the helicopter pilot. 'Ugly 40, this is Amber 43. In contact. How copy?'

No answer. I tried again. Still no answer.

I waited a second.

'Amber 43, this is Ugly . . .' The rest of the sentence was drowned out by the deafening, grating sound of hash, white noise, static.

'Ugly 40, this is Amber 43, you are very difficult to me. We are a small British unit working with the Afghan security forces. We are in contact and request support.'

The white noise was there again.

But then suddenly it evaporated and the distinctive voice of the pilot cut through the airwaves, the languid, EasyJet style unmistakably that of an aviator. 'Roger, Amber 43, I have you. Signal strength three. What is your situation?'

I repeated our predicament and told him we were at Green 1.

'Amber 43, we don't have spots marked on our maps. Send grids.'

Fuck. He wanted the exact grid references. And to give him that I needed the code word for that day with which we could translate the reference numbers into letters so our exact location could be transmitted securely even over the open frequency.

'Brummie, what's today's code word?'

'Don't know, Boss.' He shrugged and continued to try and fix the TacSat.

I asked the signallers. They didn't know. Nor did Matt. Or Jim. Bollocks.

Rather sheepishly I spoke to the pilot again. 'Ugly 40, this is 43. Send code word. Over.'

'Boulevards.'

Boulevards? Jesus Christ. How on earth do you spell that?

What was this, *University Challenge*? I turned to my team-mates again.

'Brummie, how do you spell Boulevards?' I asked.

'No idea.'

'Matt? Any idea?'

'Sorry, Boss.'

It was our fault we hadn't discovered the code word before we'd left that morning. But which too-clever-by-half dick had come up with Boulevards? Boulevards, for Heaven's sake – it wasn't even English. KISS. Keep It Simple, Stupid.

'Matt, ask the signaller in the top cover position.'

He did, but the raised eyebrows and the shrug gave away the answer. The signaller asked his mate. Another blank look. If ever there was a ludicrous moment in battle this had to be it. Conducting a spelling test with bullets whizzing past, and everyone failing miserably.

'Jim, over here. Brummie, Matt, come on.'

We had an Apache pilot desperate to help, an enemy still trying to destroy us, the ANA wondering what the hell was going on and my own men looking for a bit of decent leadership. Yet it all looked set to fall apart for lack of a dictionary.

'Bolevards?' Not enough letters.

'Boolevards?' Don't be stupid.

'Boulavards?' Nope, didn't seem right either.

'Boulevards?' Now, that looked better. Worth a try.

'Jim, use B O U L E V A R D S to translate this grid. 08117823.'

Crouched beside a wall, Jim did as I had asked. Thirty seconds later I spoke to the Apache pilot again and with a degree of confidence passed on the co-ordinates as Jim had given them me.

The reply was sobering. 'That grid puts you somewhere in Pakistan. If you want us to help, then you had better get it sorted on the ground.'

We had got it wrong and I couldn't work out why. I was

sure we now had the right spelling of the word and Jim had used it to work out our position in cipher. How hard could it be? I was getting angry now and I was about to take it out on the pilot several hundred feet above us. Who the hell was he to tell me to get things sorted on the ground? Perhaps if he got out of his fucking £30-million bit of fancy kit, put on a pair of boots and picked up a rifle, then he might understand what we were up against, the self-righteous arse.

'Ugly, I am a small unit, under fire from a numerically superior force. I have the ANA with me and trying to control them is like herding cats. Over.'

This was a hollow whinge. It was me who had fucked up by not finding out the code for the day and then, having had to beg for it, had somehow managed to apply it incorrectly.

I didn't have time to start over again, so Brummie took the bull by the horns and broadcast our location to him in clear. Sod anyone listening in. Anyway, anyone within three miles would have known what was going on because of the bloody noise.

This time there was no mistake. Within seconds the Apache was overhead and his presence gave Brummie the confidence to strike out for the Marjah PB even before the aerial assault began. There were still enemy fighters heading west – the way we had to go – but the SAF and RPGs had died down. I hoped the mere sight of the attack helicopter might encourage the enemy to keep their heads down. The convoy was reassembled: Brummie once more at the front, the ANA in the middle and me at the back.

Before setting off I spelled it out to the ANA first sergeant. 'If we get ambushed again, then keep moving. Do not stop. For anything. Got it?'

We hadn't travelled more than 100 metres beyond Green 1 towards the village at Green 2 when the Taliban attacked again, the AH apparently no deterrent. Brummie's wagon was the main target, a grenade detonating just feet from the front nearside, ripping off the commander's door, sending it spinning into the field.

Even as Jim tried to put his foot down, the Afghan vehicles in front of us ground to a halt; despite my orders all of five minutes earlier. The ANA soldiers bailed out and haphazardly started to engage Taliban positions away to the north. We had no choice but to join in. Over the radio I told Brummie to stop. I needed the helicopter to do its stuff. I sent another contact report to the pilot. His response was ferocious, everything I dreamed of.

A flurry of airburst cluster rockets exploded above the treeline to the north, releasing a deadly storm of flachettes – small darts – designed to rip through flesh. It must have been hellish to be on the receiving end of them. I wondered whether to feel sorry for my opponents, but quickly thought better of it. This was not the right time to consider the rights and wrongs of certain military equipment. We were still pinned down and under heavy attack, with a lot of the enemy fire coming from the west, concentrated on Brummie and his crew. The Taliban were trying to kill us and we had to stop them – by whatever means available. The AH pilot came back over the VHF radio, requesting more targets. I told him to wait.

'Brummie, Doug.'

Not a peep.

'Brummie, Doug.'

Still silence.

I was getting angry again. The ANA were lying about, contributing little, Al was doing his best to cover our rear, but now I couldn't get hold of Brummie. I needed him to give me the locations of the enemy at Green 2 for the Apache to engage so we could push forward. It seemed as if we were losing control of the battle.

There are times when your blood boils so much that you go and do something stupid with little consideration for the consequences; be they a night in the cells, an earful from the boss, the cold shoulder from the wife, or in my case, there and then, a bullet between the eyes. The red mist had descended and someone was going to suffer my wrath. I had become blinkered to the dangers around me, my rage overpowering. Was I the only one in this fucking patrol trying to get us out of this mess? I stood up straight in the middle of the road and stormed off towards the head of the column, the ANA on my left, to the south, trading rounds with the enemy to my right, the north. I marched on, oblivious to the airburst RPGs detonating overhead, the bullets impacting at my feet, the rounds whizzing past in front of me and behind me. I reached a beam of intermittent red light, flashing before my eyes, at about head height. I broke through it without hesitation – impossibly managing to find a gap between the tracer – and strode on. It is incomprehensible to me how I didn't get hit. I can only liken it to walking through a room crisscrossed with a spider's web of laser beams, trying to reach the fabulous diamond on the pedestal in the middle that you are intent on stealing. There is no way you can avoid breaking the rays of light and setting off the alarms, yet somehow you do. It was the same with the streams of bullets. I walked through them all, finding spaces that barely existed between the supersonic lumps of lead.

As I progressed, rifle hanging lazily from my right hand, I was screaming blue murder at the Afghans, trying to persuade them in none-too-subtle terms that if they did their jobs then they might just get out of this alive. 'Get up and fight, you bastards!'

Again, I didn't have the translator with me, but there is some oratory that transcends mere language barriers – including me spitting blood. The men cowering around me were not the famous tribal warriors of myth and legend. They were a rabble, intent on letting the OMLT do the dirty work for them. I became more annoyed with each step.

For an instant I remembered my time in Garmsir in 2006 and the actions of Major Shahrukh of the ANP. Repeatedly I would ask him, Why do you never take cover? The reply was simple and consistent. I must show my men I am not afraid, he would say. If they see me crawling around they will hide not fight. But if I stand tall, then so will they.

At the same time as remembering Shahrukh's bravery I tried to forget the fate of a man I quickly learned to respect and admire. His courage was to be the death of him, killed by a Taliban bullet.

I reached the Humvee. For the first time in 100 metres I ducked down behind some cover and tried to take stock. The Apache was still to the north. The Snatch Land Rover just ahead, Matt now out of it, the rest of the crew shooting at the enemy from onboard.

Thirty metres beyond that sat Brummie's WMIK, taking the brunt of the enemy attack, being shot at from three sides. After venting my fury at everyone else it was finally time to tear a strip off myself. Hadn't I promised never to split up the British forces? Never to have one WMIK at the front of a convoy and another at the back, with the Afghans sandwiched in between? And yet here we were in exactly that position, neither crew able to directly support the other. Beattie, you fucking fool . . .

'Brummie, Doug.'

This time there was a reply. 'Doug, send.'

'I still have the AH on the VHF. I need some target indications from you.'

He described a single-storey structure up at the Green 2 junction where a group of the enemy were holed up.

'OK, mate. Stand by. When I call, I want you to hit it with both your GPMGs so the pilot can see exactly which building it is.'

I spoke to the pilot, checking first that he could hear me loud and clear. 'Ugly 40, Amber 43. How copy?'

'Good copy, 43. Send target.'

'Follow the track west from our location for approximately three football-pitch lengths.' I walked him in to the Taliban position, checking he was with me every step of the way. 'Confirm you see a major junction surrounded by compounds, mainly to the north.'

I kept the descriptions short and sharp. 'Enemy in compound immediately to the north-east of the junction. Will mark it with tracer when you are on station.'

Unwilling to hover for danger of becoming an easy target, the Apache was flying a slow, wide circle over Green 2. Before telling Brummie to open up, I waited till the helicopter was to the eastern side of its loop so the crew would get an uninterrupted view of the tracer.

'Fire. Fire. Fire.'

The two machine guns clattered into life, firing long bursts at the compound, every fifth bullet a round of tracer. At 838 metres per second (roughly a mile every two seconds) the bullets descended on the target.

Within moments the Apache pilot was on the net. 'Enemy seen. Five men with long-barrelled weapons, RPGs . . .'

Even as he spoke a burst of fifty 30mm cannon shells came from the helicopter, fired by the co-pilot/gunner sitting at the front of the aircraft, the sound, fast, heavy, unmistakable. The huge-calibre rounds bit deep into everything they hit – masonry, mud, pieces of timber, human flesh and blood. Then came the second burst, this time slightly closer to our position, hacking at the track, the fields and more compounds. Debris, smoke and dust billowed into the air.

'Brummie, how's that?'

'Spot on, Dougie.'

I passed on news of the good work to the pilot, then asked him to keep engaging as we tried to press forward.

I moved back down the track to my own vehicle, this time happy to duck for cover as the ANA – galvanised into action by the Apache's contribution to the battle – unleashed a torrent of fire towards the enemy in the north. It was all I could do to stop our allies pressing home with their new-found bravado and charging into the wilderness intent on murder, instead of getting back into their vehicles.

'Let's go, Brummie. And this time no stopping.'

We moved off, but even as we did the enemy opened up.

Over the VHF: 'Contact. Contact.'

Over the PRR: 'Brummie, we're being hit again from the rear, keep going.'

An RPG exploded just behind our WMIK, sending red-hot shards of metal flying towards us, chasing us down the road. Al dropped to the floor of the wagon to seek some temporary cover. We were opened up on from yet more enemy positions but none seemed to be heavily manned. Mostly a man here and a man there. Possibly just $10 Talibs, hired guns rather than real fanatics. Still, they were firing real guns with real ammo.

'Keep moving, Jim,' I persisted, trying to keep the enemy's heads down with my pea-shooter. Being bounced about by the WMIK's unsteady progress along the rutted road, it was all I could do to get the rounds from the SA80 to land within a country mile of the enemy. I switched from single shot to automatic, hoping weight of fire might make up for the lack of accuracy.

No more rounds than are necessary. Only well-aimed shots.

Yeah, right. The equation was a simple one. To stay alive we had to put down more fire than the opposition did. For the best part of the last two hours they had had the upper hand and now we needed to match them, and more, to get out of there.

'Stoppage, stoppage,' Al screamed, the exasperation all too clear in his voice. 'For fuck's sake, it's jammed. I can't cock it.'

With my machine gun lying U/S at Al's feet, we needed his weapon working, yet it was in serious danger of overheating, if it hadn't just done so.

'Use your rifle, Al, or else keep your head down.'

In the commander's seat I released yet another empty magazine from my gun, pulled a full one from a pouch on the left of my body armour and slammed it home.

'This is my last one, Jim, where's your ammo?'

Without answering and keeping one hand on the wheel he fumbled about in his equipment pouches, finally yanking out two fully bombed mags.

We were making progress. We had got through Green 2 and were well on our way to Green 3 – which was now being secured by men from the school, led by Ben Foster, a captain in the Royal Engineers, who was attached to us for the tour – the telltale signs of battle all around. Broken buildings and broken bodies lined our route, victims of the AH's 30mm cannon. Yet still the enemy didn't relent. It was as if the whole community had turned out to welcome us, except it was lead raining down on us instead of ticker tape. Even as I watched, to my left a small group of enemy fighters disappeared in a sandstorm as a wave of cannon shells scythed through them. Self-designating its own targets, our guardian angel hadn't abandoned us yet.

Up ahead, Brummie finally reached the school. A couple of hundred metres behind him, around us, the shooting was at last dying down. After three kilometres and two and a half hours under fire we were in sight of our goal.

Once again the enemy had shown real tenacity and bravery. Even when the Apache arrived they didn't just melt away but kept up the pressure on us. They regarded Marjah as theirs, home turf, and it didn't bode well for our continued presence in the town. We were not going to be tolerated.*

We swung into the PB. Once within the perimeter we took

---

* Though this intolerance came at a high price. Later battle-damage assessment put the enemy's casualty figures at eighteen killed and six wounded.

up defensive positions, wary that the lull might not be the end of the battle but merely the calm before another storm. But after twenty minutes it looked as if, at least for the moment, the danger had passed. The adrenalin started to seep away. Still sat in the driver's seat of the WMIK Jim looked absolutely buggered. I wasn't surprised. Throughout the battle he had shown real nerve, real discipline.

'Well done, Jim, you fuckin' arse. You know, though, I will never be the same again after you dropped me off that bridge!'

'Sorry, Boss,' came the response in a thick Glaswegian accent.

Behind us, Al was starting to strip down the GPMG, looking for the round that had made it jam. The ANA soldiers were walking about, smiling, patting each other on the back, celebrating their heroics, pointing out the numerous bullet holes in the vehicles and the shredded tyres as if they were badges of honour to be worn with pride. Absent was the drone of the helicopter. After a last pass over the outpost it was on its way back to Bastion to rearm and refuel before being re-tasked to help some other poor sods out of the mire somewhere else in the province.

Someone put on a brew. I waited for my share. On the other side of the courtyard I saw an old friend, Lance-Corporal Malcolm 'Stewarty' Stewart. He had a mocking grin on his face as if to say, 'Welcome to Marjah, the shithole of Helmand'.

I waved back and turned to Brummie. 'We had better offload these stores pretty quick and then get the fuck out of here.'

'OK, but I think we should go back a different route.'

'That's a given. Which way do you suggest?'

'From Green 4, directly north until we hit the 604.'

I hated this route. With the irrigation channels hemming us in, forcing us to stay on the track, it allowed no flexibility. But it was also pretty obvious we couldn't go back the way we had just come.

'All right, Brummie, but this is the score. The ANA lead; the two WMIKs stay together as a pair; and then comes the Snatch. I don't want to be separated again.'

All the supplies we had painstakingly stowed back in Lash were removed from the vehicles in double-quick time. We were also leaving behind the two signallers, who, for their sins – which must have been great – were due to spend a week at the base.

The journey back was as quiet as I could have hoped for, the welcome bit of peace giving me time to think more about the balls-up I believed Marjah to be. As far as I could make out, the patrol base wasn't even in the right place. I thought the intention had been to set it up in the District Centre. Yet the DC was some three kilometres north of Green 4.

But, as we moved further away from the town, I started to think about other things. Whatever the problems here, they would be someone else's worry. I was scheduled to go home on R & R in only ten days and after that the men of OMLT 4 had been warned about a move to Garmsir. Anyway, the soldiers in Marjah now had supplies for the best part of a month so there would be no need to go back. I had time off due to me and I was looking forward to it.

EIGHT

THE GLORIOUS TWELFTH

LANCE-CORPORAL MALCOLM 'STEWARTY' STEWART, 1 R IRISH

12 JULY 2008

It had been another scorching hot day in paradise. But at last there was the chance of some escape from the blast furnace.

Walking into the shadow of the disused school building, I still couldn't quite believe where I was. Back in bloody Marjah. I let the relative cool (for everything in this country of extremes was relative) wash over me. I shrugged the daysack off my shoulders and gently put it down on the floor, careful not to damage the VHF radio tucked inside it together with the spare ammunition. These were my lifelines. I wasn't about to damage them.

Not so considerately I tipped the heavy Mk6A helmet off my head. It was used to punishment, designed to take it. With a thud it landed on the ground amidst the dust and debris, rolled a couple of times and then was still. I continued to unburden myself, unbuckling, untying and removing slings, pouches, buckles and straps. At last I could get to the Velcro fastener holding my body armour together. I gave it a tug and with a satisfying rip it parted. At last I could haul myself out of my protective shield. It too took its place at my feet. I was free. Finally the parts of my body that had been starved of oxygen for the past four hours whilst we were out on patrol had access to air. The effect was almost instantaneous. I felt a wave of relief as my super-heated torso began to cool down.

The patrol we had just finished had been a hard slog from start to end, through the increasing heat of the morning: a group of about fifty ANA soldiers and just five of us from the OMLT group – five of the meagre six that comprised the British presence in the town of Marjah. If I had been following the rules, then there wouldn't have been a patrol at all. Our orders were clear. At least six Brits had to accompany the ANA, but that would have meant there was no one back at the school to act as a link between our little party and the rest of the ANA contingent stationed there. I had already asked HQ for a couple more British soldiers to bolster our unit, but none had been forthcoming. Either my request had been ignored or things on the ground elsewhere were so tight that there wasn't the manpower to give me what I wanted. So I had a choice to make. Sit about all day and don't patrol, take all six men out with no middleman back at base, or break the rules. I chose to break the rules.

Out on the ground we tried to dominate it. Setting up vehicle checkpoints, interacting with the locals, carrying out stop-and-searches, house calls and overwatches. Overwatches were about observation. We would stop and look, absorbing the ordinary life of the town, people coming and going, minding their own business. It helped us build up a picture of normality, so the day that something was abnormal it would stick out like a sore thumb.

Everything we did was about showing our presence, making it at least look as if this was our territory and not the enemy's. It was as much a game of bluff as anything else, high-stakes brinkmanship, and we had to play. The locals needed to see we were in control. To a degree it was working. There weren't great displays of spontaneous adulation such as followed the Allied liberators' sweep across northern Europe after D–Day. The gestures were rather more subtle, inquisitive. Young boys following in our footsteps, wanting to know what each piece of equipment was for. Youths trying to practise their pidgin English. Old men keen for us to take part in their mini *shuras*, councils of elders, where they would explain in great detail how they hated the Taliban and were glad to see ISAF forces and the ANA. A shame then the ANA weren't glad to see them, or anyone else for that matter. If they could have spent all day at the school, then they would have. The Afghan soldiers were practised at complaining. They were always too hot, too tired, too ill–equipped to do anything. It drove me mad.

Anyway, for now it was over. The patrol and hence the moaning. I bent forward so gravity would peel my sodden shirt away from my chest and stomach and allow in a bit of that welcome air to try and stem the tide of sweat. Lifting my head I could see the others fighting the same battle to beat the heat. Jon was swigging greedily from a bottle, trying to stuff as much water as he could into his dehydrated body to re–establish some sort of liquid balance. The medics recommended we drink at least six litres of fluid per day. Only Lee Townson looked at ease with the world. Our signaller, he was the one who had stayed back with the other thirty Afghan soldiers. If we had hit trouble, then I could have reached him via my VHF set. In turn he would have used his TacSat to raise the alarm with command in Lash.

When he was sent to Afghanistan Lee never imagined he would be out in the thick of things. He had only been sec–onded to our OMLT unit for a few days. More than a month on he was still with us, lost in the system. He'd believed his tour would be spent in an air–conditioned ops tent, commu–nicating with some disembodied voice belonging to a poor sod getting shot at far away on the front line. Now he was that poor sod. Within twenty-four hours of arriving in Marjah he had been firing his weapon to help repel a Taliban attack aimed at driving us from our base. Any gaps in his military education were quickly filled.

Though at that particular moment I wanted to be in Marjah about as much as he did.

So much for taking it easy in the run-up to my R & R. The day after fighting our way into Marjah with supplies, and then getting out again, James took me to one side and said I was going back yet again – this time to take command of the base.

I was incredulous. 'What? Why?'

'Because Colonel Ed Freely wants you to.'

'But Ben Foster is there?'

There wasn't much James could say. Those were the orders. I could have said my R & R had nearly arrived. Could have said this would mean replacing me in just a few days' time. Could have said yet more movements in and out of the town by road were setting patterns (so much for no more journeys to Marjah for the next month). But I bit my tongue and tried to figure out how we were going to complete this latest trip without incident. In the end we again travelled in from the east but only after making a huge leap southwards first. With me were Matt, to act as medic, and Junior. On arrival, Ben took my seat and returned to Lash.

The situation in Marjah wasn't showing any signs of improving, in fact it seemed set to deteriorate. Not only was the local governor worried about the possible influx into Marjah of some of the 300 Taliban amongst the astonishing 900 prisoners who'd broken out of Kandahar Prison on 13 June. But with 2,500 US marines in and around the town of Garmsir to the south causing significant disruption to the Taliban's supply routes, he was also concerned the enemy's search for a new way to move men and weapons north would bring them to his district. And the intelligence we were getting suggested exactly that was happening. On top of all this the area was a big source of opium. Plenty of reasons then to have a force in the town, but not a force too small to make much of an impact and unable to defend itself properly. Ben had asked for more Brits and been refused. As had I. Hence just the six of us in Marjah.

Me.

Junior and Stewarty from 1 R IRISH.

Matt House from 4 PARA TA.

Lee from 216 Signal Squadron.

And Jon Mathews from 4 SCOTS.

Fantastic.

I stood up, stretched my back and let out a huge groan.

'I'm a fuckin' grandfather, Stewarty. I shouldn't be doing this shit at my age, you know!'

Malcolm 'Stewarty' Stewart grinned back at me. I had known him since my days in Kosovo in 1999. He was a likeable man with a quick wit and boundless energy. Slightly chubby, he was about 5´9˝ tall, with light brown hair. With a ruddy complexion, he looked the real outdoor type, a bit 'culchy' as they would say in Ireland.

A member of the regimental police, he normally worked for the RSM and his home was the battalion guardroom, where he was employed as a discipline tool by the CO. Which was slightly ironic, because in his early days with the regiment it was he who needed the discipline. As a young soldier, straight out of his mother's arms in Lisburn, he was a nightmare. He drank to excess, had an eye for the women, got into fights, missed parades and was generally a bloody nuisance. But he had a huge heart. Because he was so likeable, and never did anything maliciously, he was never quite busted out of the army. Certainly I had been happy to give him the benefit of the doubt and cover up for his slight indiscretions.

Now I wondered why I had bothered.

'I know you shouldn't be here, Boss, and I wish you weren't. My shoulders are aching from carrying you!'

'You should get that body armour off, mate,' I shouted back, knowing full well the bulge round his belly was from too much beer.

'You're just jealous of my muscles!' came the retort.

I pointed at the ragged weal that ran from his navel up to his chest, revealed as he had undone a couple of buttons on his shirt to improve circulation. 'Hey, fat boy, is that a scar from where they sucked all the fat from your gut, or was it where they did your chest augmentation?'

'Neither. It's where they finally removed my will to live, killed off by having to listen to you for eight years. And to think I could be at home enjoying myself on the Glorious Twelfth rather than spending it with you!'

With that last remark I remembered that even here in Afghanistan, 4,000 miles from home, it was 12 July, the so-called Glorious Twelfth. For many it was a day to celebrate, for many others in Ulster a day to forget, a day to get out of town. It just depended on your point of view.

Back in Portadown, in certain areas, like Union Street, where I grew up, the place would be awash with colour, mostly red, white and blue, but with a fair splattering of orange, commemorating the victory of King William of Orange over the deposed Catholic King James II of England at the Battle of the Boyne on the east coast of Ireland in 1690. People would line the streets, singing, as members of various Orange Order lodges, interspersed with bands, marched past on their way to The Field to hear speeches. It was time for a party. The Guinness would flow freely amongst the adults; amongst the children the race would be on to eat their ice creams before they melted. It was a day of general Protestant celebration and even those who had loved ones serving with 1 R IRISH probably weren't thinking about what their brothers, sons and fathers were doing at that moment. And even if they were, they couldn't possibly have imagined what six members of the regiment would be confronted with that very day as the clock struck twelve.

You rarely see it coming. The moment when calm is destroyed and lives are ruined. In the blink of an eye mayhem comes to reign. I had experienced such pivotal events time and again, yet almost without exception they had caught me by surprise, sucked my breath away.

The Glorious Twelfth was no different.

A number of shots signalled the start of our descent into madness. The shooting was coming from no more than a few metres away, out on the street. I could tell it was outgoing.

In the next second or so, a hell of a lot happened.

Soldiers of the ANA started sprinting for cover.

We six Brits started to scramble for the body armour and helmets we had discarded not five minutes before.

Lee began to send the usual holding message using the TacSat. 'Contact. Wait. Out.'

And then there was a huge eruption of noise.

A blast wave caused the windows of the school to shatter, covering the men who were crouched beneath them in glass.

'Fuck. RPG. That was close,' yelled Junior.

But it didn't sound like an RPG to me. Though I had heard a noise like it before. I tried to place it. The Afghans beat me to it. Several of them were now shouting, no screaming, at us.

'IED! IED!' came the cry, yet that didn't quite make sense either. How could an IED be so close to our camp? How had they managed to plant it without being spotted? Then the scream came again. It wasn't IED. It was SIED. Suicide Improvised Explosive Device. A shiver ran down my spine. No, not again. Not another suicide attack. Please no. My mind raced back a year and a half to Lashkar Gah and the carnage wrought by a suicide bomber in the compound of the provincial governor. It had been horrendous. A scene I never wanted to see repeated. And yet, here in Marjah, it seemed as if lightning had struck twice. Had struck me twice. I knew what to expect and that only made it worse. For a moment I wondered whether I could just leave the ANA to deal with it. After all, they were supposed to be in charge of the security of the camp, yet of course this was not an option. They would look to us for guidance, and even if they did get on with things themselves, who was to say they would do it right? I would have to lead rather than mentor. I was the one who had seen it all before.

'Matt, Junior, Lee, you stay in the school and secure the area. Jon, Stewarty, you come with me.' The calmness in my voice belied the trepidation I was feeling. The point of detonation was just thirty metres away, at a road junction. The ANA had positioned themselves there, checking the comings and goings of the civilian population as they passed directly in front of the school. There was still dust in the air, a fine mist trying, but failing, to veil the devastation around us. Slowly it settled on the grim scene. The first thing I really noticed was an Afghan soldier flat out on his back, legs together, arms at his side, as if still at attention even in his sleep. It quickly became clear it was an eternal sleep and there were plenty of indications of his violent end. His cheek, right-eye socket and ear had disappeared, ripped off by a hail of nuts, bolts and ball bearings, so-called shipyard confetti. All over his body there were small puncture marks where the metal had burrowed through his skin. In the moment of death, he had expelled a range of body fluids. The ground around him was not just covered with blood. There was a dark stain around his groin. The stench of shit was vile.

The three of us walked past him, without a second glance. His demise had made him irrelevant. There was nothing we could do, so on we went, to try and care for the living and the barely alive.

Just beyond the soldier was a leg, presumably that of the

bomber. It had been torn off at the calf – muscle and sinew hanging crazily from the stump, darkened by the heat of the blast. It was butchery. Without altering my eye-line I could also see half a head – again I assumed it was the bomber's – complete with an ear. From my unenviable earlier experience with a suicide attack I had been expecting to find an ear. It's strange but they always seem to survive intact, the shoulders protecting them from the upward force of the explosion.

'Stewarty, Jon, casualty check!' I yelled. And with that the two soldiers started searching for others caught up in the attack, ducking between the simple market stalls made of wood and topped off with either large leaves or the stalks of crops, all held together with rusty nails and bits of twine.

To my left, an old man sat on a step. He wasn't screaming or shouting, instead he was just looking down at the young man slumped over in his lap, clearly hurt.

Jon called out. 'I've got one here, Boss.'

Then Stewarty trumped him. 'Boss, I've got two and they're both in a bad way. One's just a boy.'

The noise was starting to build again. There were the cries of the injured, mixed with the pleading of some Afghan soldiers who had found a colleague by the canal, seriously wounded.

Other members of the ANA were at least trying to help manage the situation, blocking off all four approaches to the junction. From a mentoring point of view, if I was being objective, I could find plenty of faults in what I was doing. I should have been on the sidelines, now letting the Afghans take responsibility for the aftermath and all it entailed. But as a professional soldier, a father and a member of the human race I couldn't stand back and watch the ANA make a hash of things, knowing we could do things better, do them quicker and hence have more chance of saving some lives.

Stop and think, Doug. Stop and think.

Using the radio I called for help from Matt. As our medic, right then he was the most important member of the team.

'I need you out here. We have to get all the casualties into one location.'

A few moments later and he was with us. I told him the few details I had about what had happened and then he was straight into the thick of things, treating and organising.

As he set about his task, I returned to the school building to report to Lash. 'Topaz Zero, this is Amber 44 Alpha. Suicide attack at Green 4. Casualties over.'

I confirmed all six of the OMLT members were safe. The call came back for me to complete a nine-liner, a casualty assessment; but, as the injured were only just being brought in, I stalled them, waiting to get the full count.

I made for the makeshift medical centre, a classroom I had earlier earmarked for such a use should the worst ever happen – as it just had. On the wall there was a blackboard, a sprinkling of white dust hinting at the lessons that had once been written up on it. The rudimentary desks were pressed into service and covered with medical equipment and, as they arrived, the victims. The latest casualty was the wounded ANA soldier from by the canal, dragged in by my guys with little help from his colleagues. The Afghans have a very ambivalent attitude towards blood. Generally they are pretty useless in the face of it, tending to stand around wailing, waiting for instruction rather than getting on with things.

'What we got?' I asked Matt, who had followed the wounded back inside, not really expecting him to have yet got on top of the chaos.

As it was, Junior butted in before Matt had a chance to answer. 'Boss, this one is dead.'

'Are you sure?' Stupid question, I instantly thought.

'Yeah, massive head injury. No way he could have survived it.'

'Well, just keep working on him. Keep trying.' I grabbed Lee and pointed him in the direction of more casualties still, though these three didn't seem to be so seriously hurt.

Then Matt had his turn. 'Doug, I have two pretty bad ones in here.' It was an understatement. 'One has got his brain protruding from his skull. He can't be more than twelve or thirteen. The other must be in his twenties. The back of his head is missing. Can you give me someone to help?'

'All right, take Stewarty and Jon, but have a quick look at this one first,' I said, gesturing to the soldier Junior hadn't yet given up hope on.

It only took him a couple of seconds to give his diagnosis. 'Yep, he's dead.'

Amongst the confusion I tried to work out exactly what we were dealing with. There had been two wounded soldiers, but they were both now beyond help. There was also a pair of very seriously injured civilians. One was the young teenage boy, who, shockingly and seemingly unconsciously, was trying to push his brain back inside his head. It was truly horrific, yet we had to remain detached, mechanical in our actions. Pressure. Bandage. Tourniquet. Follow procedures, don't give these people personalities, avoid the temptation to superimpose the faces of your loved ones on to them. Stewarty and Jon were doing what they could for these two under Matt's direction.

Lee and Junior had taken charge of the other three casualties, who were all suffering from shrapnel injuries. One was just a boy. He looked no more than about nine or ten.

All of which left me to work on the security of the school, the nine-liner and the identification of a helicopter landing site (HLS) where the wounded could be picked up and taken away.

By now local people had started turning up and attempting to get into the school. Some were frantic to know if any of their loved ones were amongst those being treated. Others were just curious about the latest drama to unfold in their town. I tried to fight a sense of being crushed by events. So much was going on. So many sights, sounds, smells and tastes competing for attention. All of them so out of the ordinary. But what stood out, above and beyond every other horror, was a vision of Stewarty – drenched from head to foot in the blood of the young man he had carried in from the street and whom he was now desperately trying to keep alive. He appeared shattered by the feeling of helplessness brought on by the struggle to keep a dying person alive. It is to his utmost credit that he continued to fight for his patient in the most hideous of circumstances. Repeatedly he tried to breathe life into the victim despite his horrendous facial injuries. After each attempt at mouth-to-mouth he would turn and vomit. Then try again.

With every extra moment that passed, as Stewarty fought what seemed a losing battle, I became increasingly frustrated with the ANA. They continued to shrink back from the scene, happy to leave us to get on with it. There was little I could do to gain their co-operation. Pushing on a rope would have been easier.

I tried to concentrate on completing the nine-liner.

Just before I deployed to Marjah, I spoke to Major Chips Broughton, the man in charge of operational planning for Task Force Helmand (TFH), about calling in casevac helicopters with an Incident Response Team (IRT) on board. He had been blunt. He told me if we got into trouble it would be a one-shot deal. In. Pickup. Gone. There would be no repeat mission. The chances of the enemy recognising the landing zone and then laying an ambush were just too high. It was about percentages. When the possibility of losing both an invaluable helicopter and the men aboard it was weighed against a handful of other lives then there was no debate. Such were the hard choices of war. I had been left under no illusions. I thanked him for his honesty.

The place I now chose for the HLS couldn't have been closer: the school's dusty football pitch just metres away from the building.

I raised the HTF on the radio and started the nine-liner.

'Line 1. Grid of HLS 88674435.'

The location of the landing site.

'Line 2. Amber 44 VHF on hail.'

The frequency the pilots could speak to us on.

'Line 3. Three Bravo. Two Charlie. Two Echo. Roger so far, over.'

The type of casualties, categorised by the letters A to E, ranging from A, which is classed as a medical emergency (such as heat-stroke or a severe asthma attack) where treatment is needed within two hours, through B, which is a surgical emergency (such as trauma, gunshot wound or appendicitis), all the way to E, in which a patient can be treated at the doctor's convenience – or where they are beyond all help. Dead.

A positive acknowledgement came through.

'Line 4. Alpha.'

No special equipment needed.

'Line 5. Three Lima and two Alpha.'

Three stretcher cases and two walking wounded.

'Line 6. Papa. Roger so far, over.'

Possibility of enemy fighters in the vicinity.

Another positive response.

'Line 7. Charlie green.'

The HLS would be marked with green smoke.

'Line 8. All casualties are Delta, less the Echos, who are Charlie.'

All the casualties are civilians, except the dead who are non-ISAF military (the ANA).

'Line 9. Open area used as a football pitch. No obstacles. But heavy dust on the downwash. Roger, over.'

A description of the HLS.

'Topaz. Roger. Out.'

Then there was more paperwork to be done. This time a MIST report on each of the casualties.

M stood for mechanism of injury. That was easy enough. In

each and every case it was blast. I was for type of injury, lost limbs, puncture wounds, etc. S was for the vital signs of each casualty. What were their heart rates, blood-pressure readings and so on? T represented treatment given – perhaps morphine, the application of tourniquets, or maybe just the use of bare hands to apply direct pressure to wounds to prevent the red liquid of life oozing or squirting from the victims' bodies. As if all this wasn't enough I also made a note of the casualties' ages and consciousness levels. It turned into a long list. Finally, though, it was done and sent. At last the IRT would be on its way.

I lifted my head from the carnage and had a look around the room. Several ANA troops continued to look on with a mix of disgust, macabre fascination and bewilderment. One in particular seemed to be treating the scene as his own interactive TV show, as if he were on the set of a particularly realistic episode of *Casualty*.

I turned to our interpreter, nicknamed Bollywood, who had arrived in Marjah with me. He was good at his job but didn't let work get in the way of personal grooming. To him image was everything and he insisted on washing his hair every day.

'Bollywood, just tell him to fuck off, will you.'

'OK, Boss.'

Matt was still furiously trying to stabilise the casualties, in particular the young boy with his brain pushing out of his skull.

'How's it going?'

'I've never seen anything like it.' His voice was frantic, fatigued and high-pitched as he concentrated on what he was doing.

'That one's dead,' he said, pointing to the man Stewarty had been tirelessly trying to save, though now he looked on the verge of passing out. I could see in his eyes that he had given his all, yet he would still be wondering whether he could have done more. He looked deflated, as if he had physically shrunk, yet in my mind his stature had only grown. For anyone to be confronted with such a hideous situation – so far beyond normal experience – and yet find it in themselves to help and then help some more, well it was indescribable, and it made me immensely proud. There in southern Afghanistan, amidst the blood and the shit and the piss, the screaming and crying, the violence and its aftermath, I couldn't have been more proud of Stewarty and the others. They had been presented with a vision of hell and taken it in their stride. I used their example to give myself a kick up the backside.

Come on, keep moving, keep motivating, be inspired by the inspiring. 'Stewarty, who's the Afghan who's been helping you?'

'Don't know, Boss.'

'Well, get Bollywood to take him outside and see if they can locate any members of the dead man's family.'

It didn't take long for them to return, accompanied by a much older Afghan, with a long grey beard sprouting from his chin. He had the usual weathered face, stained dark by the remorseless sun and wind.

'So who's this?' I asked Bollywood.

'The dead man's father.'

'Does he know yet that his son is dead?'

There was a shake of the head.

'Well, tell him, and explain that he needs to get some sort of vehicle to take the body away.' I was shocked by the way my words came out. Emotionless, without a hint of compassion. What a dreadful place to learn of the death of your son, what a terrible way for him to be taken. I looked for a reaction in the father's face as he was told the news, just pleased that it was Bollywood who was doing it and not me. There was the briefest glimmer of acknowledgement, but the mask he wore betrayed no sense of what else he might be thinking. The anger, the pain, the shock. I believe there is a weary acceptance amongst Afghans that their lives are likely to be nasty, brutish and short. It is the way their existence has always been, the harsh environment conspiring with the ancient tribal system of feuds and vendettas to ensure they never become too comfortable with their lot. Add to that the civil wars and international aggression the country had been exposed to over the decades and it was perhaps easier for the population to steel themselves for the worst than dare hope for the best.

I stared as the father and the Afghan who had been helping Stewarty manhandled the corpse into a cart the ANA had brought up, struggling with the dead weight of the body and the slipperiness of the blood.

Something Bollywood said suddenly made the scene all the more tragic. 'The dead man, he wasn't twenty. He was only sixteen, just a boy really.'

It was heartbreaking.

I sent an update back to base. 'One of our Bravos is now an Echo.' It all sounded so two-dimensional.

Outside, Jon had been doing his best to herd the cats, struggling without an interpreter to get the ANA to secure the HLS and ensure it was clear of any IEDs or unexploded ordnance. There were still a few quizzical looks amongst the Afghan soldiers but – with a large dose of shoving, pointing and yelling – Jon had done a pretty good job.

Some sort of order was also being established in the medical room, though that might have been because of the dwindling number of survivors, now down to four. These included the thirteen-year-old with the cataclysmic head injuries and the nine-year-old with shrapnel wounds to his leg.

The ANA commander came up to me to explain what had happened. His men had been manning their checkpoint when a youth of no more than fifteen approached one of the soldiers. He was stopped and told to lift his loose-fitting top so he could be checked for IEDs. Obligingly he did so and as the gown was raised there to the soldier's horror was a suicide vest. Perhaps in a panic, the soldier shouted at the boy to go away and keep his arms outstretched as he went. The would-be bomber did as he was told, but kept turning to glance at a younger boy standing just a few metres away. As the human crucifix walked slowly backwards, his attention still taken up by the boy, the soldier lost his nerve and dived for cover, shouting a warning. The commotion brought one of his colleagues running from the canal, where he had been having a wash. Taking in the scene he grabbed the rifle of the soldier now flat on the floor and fired at the youth at least three times. As the rounds repeatedly struck home, the teenager exploded, sending out a deadly storm of metal. The man who shot him died, as did a second soldier. Amazingly the one spreadeagled on the ground survived.

I listened intently.

'So what do you make of that?' I asked the commander when he had finished recounting the story.

'Well, we think the bomber was detonated by a second person, the boy he was so fixated on as he withdrew.'

I wasn't sure I believed the story, but I had to act on it. 'Well, can you get a description of the boy and we will pass it on to the police and NDS to follow up.'

'No need, you have him in the medical room. It's the boy with the leg injury.'

I swung round to follow his gaze and saw the child, being tended to by Junior. I was stunned. 'Are you sure?'

'Absolutely. The sentry saw the pair of them talking together before the bomber approached the checkpoint.'

It was not unheard of. The enemy had used small boys to attack ISAF and Afghan forces in Helmand before. Indeed, some of those attacks had been in the form of suicide bombers. Women were used too, just as they were in Iraq and Palestine. Still, I was astonished. I really didn't want to believe what I was being told was true. Yet as I studied him I thought

I could see resentment and defiance in his face. I wanted to have some sympathy for this child, but I couldn't find any. He was the enemy and he had tried to kill us.

All I could do was pass the suspicions on up the line. At the hospital in Bastion he would be met by the Royal Military Police.

Lee shouted over. 'Ugly 52 is on station!' He was referring to an Army Air Corps Apache attack helicopter. Bristling with weaponry this would act as a minder for the lumbering, vulnerable Chinook. We needed to get the casualties out to the HLS and ready for evacuation. The pilot wouldn't want to wait for us. We formed a line of victims. First the injured, in order of priority, then the bodies of the two soldiers, the blankets covering them already sticky and wet with blood. We hadn't cuffed or bound the nine-year-old but we would let the IRT know our concerns.

'Throw smoke!' yelled Lee.

I lobbed a smoke canister into the centre of the pitch and it immediately burst into life, producing a cloud of deep green smoke to mark our position. A moment later the Chinook appeared low over the roofs and descended towards us. A huge brown cloud erupted from the ground and the helicopter disappeared into it. As the dust dissipated I could see the escort troops already down the ramp and securing the area. I recognised one or two faces. They were men of 2 R IRISH – the TA battalion. Not that we had time to chat. There was work to be done. Within a minute all injured had been carried into the bowels of the helicopter and, even as it lifted off, the onboard medics would be taking over from where Matt and the others had left off.

The Chinook had not got the bodies aboard though. That was down to another aircraft that had been waiting patiently in the wings and now made its grand entrance. The Sea King loomed into view and hit almost exactly the same spot as its twin-rotored brother. For the loadmaster there was an all-too-graphic view of what makes war hell. As the two stretchers were brought forward, the downdraught from the blades whipped the blankets off, exposing the corpses, flagellated by the ball bearings. Just as efficiently as those on board the first helicopter, the crew of the Sea King strapped down the new load and they were gone, disappearing after the Chinook, the Apache following behind.

As the aircraft disappeared and calm finally settled, all of us stood for a moment, lost in thought. We weren't there for many moments, but the solemnity seemed appropriate. Of course, too much time to think can be a bad thing, so luckily for us there were still plenty of other tasks we needed to apply our minds to, not least trying to recover bits of the bomb for forensic analysis. I followed Jon out into the street.

We were greeted with the most macabre sight.

There, strung across the street, was what at first looked like a washing line. But instead of wet linen being hung in the sunshine to dry, the ANA had put out body parts; the body parts of the bomber. I swallowed deeply, as I cast my eye along the line, moving from piece to piece. There was a leg, then an arm, then another arm, and so it continued. It was medieval. It was like the bodies of those killed at the gallows being put on public display as a warning to others not to repeat the deceased's misdemeanours. What disturbed me further was just how small and insignificant the hands and feet looked. How could they belong to someone grown-up enough to make the choice to kill themselves in pursuit of their cause? Then I remembered the nine-year-old. How on earth had he got involved?

I had become depressingly accustomed to seeing awful sights, had come to expect it even, but every time I thought I had experienced the worst, something else topped it. It was a sickening end to a dreadful day. The ANA had proved themselves to be unreliable when the chips were down and almost beyond contempt when it came to matters of life or death. Now this.

I shouted at one of the Afghan soldiers. 'What the fuck are you doing?'

'The people must know what happens to those who try and attack us.'

'No, no. Come on, you are better than this. This is not the Muslim way of doing things. Take them down. Now.'

I appealed to their better nature, but they didn't seem to have one. In the end it was only at the insistence of the Afghan commander that the jigsaw pieces of the cadaver were reluctantly removed. Though that didn't mean the scene was clear of clues to what had happened so recently. There was still so much bloody human tissue and debris lying about. At that moment I was convinced the casualty figures must have been much greater and somehow we had missed a whole group of the dead and the injured.

By now Jon had finished collecting and we made our way back to the school. In the coolness of the classroom, we tidied up; ourselves, our equipment, the medical room. We needed replacement kit, especially medical kit, though nothing would be forthcoming until a few days later, when a re-supply run had been scheduled. As well as bringing stuff in, the convoy would also take me out so I could finally get ready for my two weeks of R & R. I requested some of the men leave too, to be rotated back to Lashkar Gah for a rest. In particular Jon and Lee looked overwhelmed. I didn't ask for this because I thought they'd suffered any more from what they'd seen than the others (and even if they had, the advice is initially at least to keep together men who have been through a traumatic event). It was just because they had been there the longest. Why work men to a standstill if there is an alternative?

That evening, in the enveloping darkness, we talked through the incident. Sitting on plastic garden chairs on the platform running along the inside edge of the school complex we took it in turns to give our thoughts on the day's events. I made it my priority to reassure the men they were not to blame. For anything. What happened was caused by the suicide bomber. All we could do was react. We were not responsible, through our actions, or inactions, for the injuries or the deaths. The debrief was part of the Trauma Risk Management (TRIM) procedure. Using a defined set of questions I tried to gauge how people were coping. It was the first stage in identifying and dealing with combat stress and PTSD.

The last thing we did before turning in was to ask one of the ANA soldiers to take a photo of the seven of us (six OMLT members plus Bollywood). A reminder for the future that we had shared common adversity, that none of us had been through this on their own.

That night, as I lay on my cot, staring into the inky blackness, I wondered what would happen to the men in the photo. Would we get to the end of the tour unscathed? Years from now would we have reunions? Reminisce about battles we had fought and won, or at least survived? And even if we did get through the nightmare, what scars would be left on my mind, their minds? Despite my fine words of encouragement and support to the others, did I actually believe them myself? I wondered how I would cope. How would I deal with my imminent return to the UK and my daughter's wedding? The laughter, the brevity, the normality. Would it lift me up or drag me down? I shut my eyes . . .

I was getting ahead of myself. I hadn't even left Marjah yet.

NINE

BUNCH OF PIKEYS

RANGER JUNIOR STEWART, 1 R IRISH

13 JULY 2008

Throughout the night the grim thoughts continued, the horrors replaying themselves time and again in my mind.

Even when I woke there was no escape from my recent past. I kept coming back to the futility of it all. The waste of lives – on all sides. How had things got so bad a fifteen-year-old was prepared to die in such a hideous fashion? He hadn't even been the master of his own destiny. The younger boy had made the calls, flicked the switch, dispatched the bomber to the next life. Walking towards his fate, what had gone through his mind? Memories of friends and family? Parents? Brothers and sisters? Maybe in the very second he was obliterated he had realised the full implication of what he was doing and decided it wasn't for him, decided he didn't want to go through with the attack. Perhaps at the very instant he was ripped apart he had been about to turn back. Too late. The 'man' with the trigger had no such doubts. Boom, and the havoc was wrought.

I tried to apply cold logic to the emotional. What military

advantage had been gained by what took place? What was the purpose? Had it simply been an attempt to terrorise us, the military, or was the aim also to instil fear in the wider population by proving how impotent ISAF was when it came to protecting them? If it was the latter, then they had probably succeeded. We did our best, but there were nowhere near enough resources to dominate the town, keep the Taliban back and offer any real sort of security to civilians. Yes, we left the PB and patrolled, but little was achieved. We'd do our rounds and then scurry back to the school, leaving the enemy to act with impunity. If the operation in Marjah was to have any worth and not merely result in a steady stream of pointless casualties, then there had to be a change of emphasis across the whole of Helmand. The Task Force had concentrated men and equipment in places like Sangin, Musa Qala and Now Zad, yet the real centres of population and economic activity were Gereshk, Lashkar Gah, Nad-e-Ali – and here in Marjah. The weekly bazaar in Sangin would be doing well to pull in 600 people yet on hand to keep order were some 300 men of the British Army and a whole Afghan Army *kandak* together with their thirty or so mentors. Yet in Marjah, where attendance at the Saturday market was in the region of 4–5,000, there were no more than ninety ANA soldiers and six of us. I didn't understand the priorities.

That day, 13 July, we had to get out on the streets again – for what it was worth. We headed on foot towards Green 3. The locals were now intensely wary of our presence. They couldn't afford to be seen by the Taliban – or their informers – talking to us. It was literally more than their lives were worth. But they didn't need to say anything to us to make their point – it was obvious in their eyes. They were really coming to resent our presence in what had, until the arrival of ISAF and the events of the previous week, been a peaceful town. True, it had been controlled by drugs barons, but at least they ensured some degree of stability. Now we had upset the balance. There were enough of us to attract trouble, yet too few to guarantee security. We were turning Marjah into the front line. The inhabitants had little time for our vision of the future – reconstruction, development, education; none of it meant much to the majority of these people, who were engaged in a simple way of life, one now undermined by the arrival of foreign soldiers. Even the ANA were viewed with suspicion. From a different part of Afghanistan, they didn't speak the same language as the people of Marjah. They didn't even look the same. The antipathy only emphasised the lack of a cohesive Afghan state. When we look at maps we see blobs of colour defining countries, meandering lines tracing borders. Yet these features are all but meaningless to most Afghans. All they have regard for are tribal areas. That these might extend over some notional international boundary is of little significance. For example in Helmand – and Kandahar province – one of the dominant ethnic groups is the Balochi. Yet many of its members could also be found in Pakistan, and Iran for that matter. If they could choose which country to live in then it would be Balochistan. Of course such a nation doesn't exist (though there is a province of the same name in western Pakistan), but then when the map of the region had been drawn up no one asked the locals what they wanted.

The rest of the day was spent trying to shore up the school's defences as best we could. With one successful attack under their belts, there was every chance the enemy would be emboldened to try the same thing again unless we did something to prevent it. We spent a lot of time reminding the Afghan soldiers of the basics – stand-off searches, immediate actions, alarm drills.

In the afternoon I received my orders for the following morning. I was to carry out a meet with a team of men from the Special Forces Support Group (SFSG) who also had a mentoring job.

The meeting was to discuss the best way of co-ordinating our efforts in the district. The SFSG operated to the west, us to the east. However, if they fancied a little excursion to our side of the town to carry out a mission, then they had priority over whatever we were doing. An ops box would be placed around the area they wanted to enter and it would remain out of bounds to us until the SFSG had finished whatever it was they wanted to do. The theory was simple enough. Stop two groups of coalition forces carrying out separate and possibly conflicting operations in the same bit of ground and thus minimise the risk of fraticide – blue on blue. The rendezvous time was set for 07:00 hrs at an ANP checkpoint some four kilometres south-west of the patrol base, at a location known as Orange 7.

That evening the Afghan commander, a major, invited me to eat with him and one of his lieutenants, Tourjan. I had made it my duty to accept such invitations despite the potential damage that might be inflicted on my digestive system. Bollywood joined us for supper but when it came to talking with Tourjan he was redundant. The junior officer spoke remarkably good English. Tall, with thick black hair, unusually amongst Afghans, his face was shaven. He told me he originated from the Bamiyan Valley, one of the most scenic places in Afghanistan and the site where the Taliban had gleefully blown up two giant, 1,700-year-old statues of Buddha, carved into the rock, as part of their policy to eradicate the country of anything non-Islamic.

Tourjan possessed something rarely found in Afghans – an education. And in the brief time we spent together he changed many of my perceptions as to the value of teaching these people. If that morning I had been pessimistic about the scope for change and progress education could offer, then twelve hours later I was a convert, our conversation being my Damascene moment.

The four of us – me, Tourjan, the commander and

Bollywood – sat around a rickety wooden table in the senior officer's room. His own cot was pushed into one corner. In another were stacked boxes of ammunition. As we waited for the food to arrive we talked about things of universal interest. Hopes and fears for the future. Wives. Children. Home. It reminded me that for all the differences between us, there were common bonds, themes, which resonate with all human beings – whatever the cultural divides, whatever the bleakness of their circumstances – and bring people together more than they drive them apart.

Our chat was interrupted by the arrival of supper. A metal plate was set down in front of me, on it a bed of rice with beans and gravy, topped off with some sort of meat I didn't recognise. I poked at it with my fork.

'What's this?' I asked Bollywood.

'Goat,' he said.

Now, I had eaten goat on countless occasions before. Overcooked goat. Undercooked goat. Goat on the bone. Goat off the bone. Goat that an Afghan even tried to persuade me was fish. But never before had I seen goat like this.

I prodded it some more and took a very tentative taste. I wished I hadn't bothered. 'Bollywood, stop playing with your hair, my friend, and tell me exactly what this is.'

Despite my desire to retch I tried to keep a smile on my face for the sake of maintaining good relations with my hosts.

'It's goat. The inside of the goat. Heart. Intestines.'

Offal! Call me fussy but I wasn't going to be eating that. 'Bollywood, tell the major it is against my religion to eat the insides of an animal.'

My interpreter looked genuinely shocked. 'I am sorry, sir, I had no idea. I will tell him.'

I hated lying to these men who were offering me their hospitality, but I hated more the idea of eating what was on my plate.

The major apologised profusely and called in a soldier to

remove my plate. Shortly after, he returned with another dish. Again piled high with rice, thankfully this time there was something on it I did recognise as a lump of goat – with what looked like a bite taken out of it. It seemed as if some poor Afghan had just had his dinner snatched away from him for the benefit of the Irish infidel – and a plate of offal dumped in its place.

Despite resorting to religion to get me out of my predicament it was not a subject I wanted to discuss much further. From bitter experience I had discovered there would be no meeting of minds on it, no common ground, no chance even of agreeing to disagree. To them, as Muslims, the Koran is the exact and absolute word of God. It is not open to interpretation and revisionist views. And as an Irish Protestant I knew better than to get on to religion. Which made my subsequent attempts that evening to once again understand their faith appear all the more stupid – and I couldn't even blame it on having had too much to drink. As I sat and listened they told me more about the pillars that underpin the Islamic faith and provide a guide to how Muslims should live their lives.

I have never been religious. At least not in the sense of having much time for the Christian church. I regard it as a controlling organisation. A way of manipulating the masses through fear and dogma. To me the Bible might be a good read but not something to live my life by and certainly not something to evangelise about. Which is different from saying I don't believe in God. I think there is an omnipotent presence, an all-powerful being, but not one who can only be reached through a priest at Sunday service. I have no problem with blind faith, so long as those who possess it are content to accept that I don't. I am happy to recognise other people's beliefs but only if in return they understand my position. What I cannot abide are those who are holier than thou; those ready to condemn me to eternal damnation for what they regard as my ignorance of the one true path to salvation –

theirs. Given that my reservations extended beyond Christianity to Islam, it didn't bode well for much of a debate with the others sat at the table. After listening for a while I tried to explain my reservations through Bollywood.

'No, sir, I cannot translate that. I understand what you are saying because I work with you. But the others will not. They will be offended.'

With that the conversation petered out. Probably for the best.

I thanked my hosts and wandered off to find the other members of the OMLT. It was still pretty early but night had descended and I was looking forward to my bed. I took my boots off and stretched out in a chair. Which was when the telltale sounds of battle – RPGs and small-arms fire – suddenly echoed through the darkness.

'Sounds like the ANP checkpoints are being hit,' said Lee.

'Yep. Outside our box though, I think,' I replied, knowing full well they were very much inside our box. But I was fearful of what might happen with the Afghans on a night op and it was this that dictated my thinking – and my answer.

Jon came over with Bollywood. 'Sir, the ANA commander would like to see you again.'

'Do we know why?' I queried.

'The chief of police wants the ANA to go and help his men at one of the checkpoints being attacked.'

I headed over to the Afghan major. He was in animated negotiations with his police counterpart. After a few moments he turned to me and explained the ANA's help had been requested to stop Orange 7 being overrun.

'OK, Major, but this is the score,' I said, encouraging him to think through the various courses of action. 'If we go on foot in this darkness, then because your men do not have night-vision goggles, it will take three hours to safely cross the ground between here and the checkpoint, negotiating the ditches and streams as we go.

'If we go by road, and it will be your men leading, then we will be setting ourselves up for ambush. I am sure this is a "come on" situation, the enemy plan being not to take Orange 7 but to hit the relief patrol as it comes to the rescue.'

I stood back as the Afghan commander mulled over the options. Then he made his call. We were going. In vehicles. As the others formed up I got on the net to Lash to tell them what we were doing. I also requested air cover, but it was denied. Within twenty minutes we were on our way. Three ANA Rangers at the front, following an ANP vehicle, then the two WMIKs of the OMLT. Me in the front one with Matt driving, Bollywood in the back of it, but without any top cover. Stewarty in command of the second WMIK, Jon in the driver's seat and Junior acting as gunner. I left Lee behind as our linkman. I would speak to him on the VHF set and he would relay the messages back to Lash on the TacSat.

Heading west we passed through Green 5 and 6. At Green 7 we would turn south. Neither WMIK had its headlights on, but this gained us little tactical advantage because the Afghan vehicles had their lights blazing.

We had almost reached Green 7 when the shooting started ahead of us. Red specks of tracer flashed through the sky. Then the RPGs started to land.

'Amber 44, 44 Alpha. Contact. Wait. Out,' I passed word to Lee.

'Jon, go firm, keep the vehicle in the best cover you can,' I yelled, knowing as well as he did the only cover was the darkness.

With the ANA directly in front of us and the enemy directly in front of them, there was no way we could shoot back without risking hitting our allies. At the same time Taliban rounds not hitting targets at the head of the convoy were streaking towards us. Already an RPG had landed within a few metres of the other WMIK. By a miracle it failed to detonate. I ran forward to see what was going on.

ANA soldiers in the lead vehicle were furiously trading fire with the enemy. Behind them their colleagues had dismounted but seemed loath to do much more than crouch in the dust and watch the fireworks. I was worried we had bunched up too much. There were no more than 150 metres between the tail and the head of our little column and barely another 60 or 70 metres beyond that to the enemy positions, which seemed to be just short of the junction. Not for the first time I felt helpless. I wanted the Afghans to push on and use momentum to dislodge what was probably no more than a handful of enemy fighters. But instead of moving up, the Afghan vehicles started to carry out U-turns on a track hardly wide enough for a single vehicle. That done, one by one they somehow managed to squeeze past us and return the way we had just come, some ANA stragglers desperately sprinting after the trucks to avoid being left behind. From being at the rear of the convoy, we were suddenly at the front. In fact we *were* the bloody convoy. And now the enemy were starting to move down our left flank. As I turned my GPMG south to engage them, Jon pulled his wagon up alongside so his crew could get clear shots towards the junction where the initial ambush had begun.

'Jon, cover me while we turn!' I shouted into the PRR.

Nothing. He couldn't hear me over the clattering of weapons.

I tried again. 'Jon, keep firing towards G7 and get your top cover to fire south. We will turn round and then cover for you.'

This time he got the message and there was an instantaneous increase in the rate of fire from his WMIK.

Matt nudged our vehicle backwards and forwards, slowly rotating us through 180 degrees, giving it big handfuls with the wheel as he went from lock to lock. The trouble was I didn't have a gunner and Bollywood had already buggered off, joining the other Afghans in their fair impression of the retreat from Moscow. So now, having completed the manoeuvre, I had to jump out of the WMIK and swing my machine gun over the bonnet to shoot south. Which meant a steady stream of bullets flying less than a metre past the end of Matt's nose. To say he was rather unenthusiastic about this is an understatement, but it was a case of needs must. Finally Jon also managed to get his vehicle facing the right way for retreat and together we moved out, racing back through Green 6, past the Afghan pickups now parked at Green 5, and on to the school at Green 4.

In less than flattering terms I explained to the ANA commander how useless his men had been and that there would be no further patrols that night. I promised the police chief I'd try once more to secure air support for his men at Orange 7, though I still didn't believe it was in serious danger of being taken. As the hours ticked by and early evening turned into late evening, the exchanges of gunfire from the police checkpoint became increasingly sporadic before they died out completely. The ANP had held on to their ground though it was being reported one of the policemen had been seriously wounded. I was asked to go and retrieve him. And again I explained why I wouldn't be going out for a second time that night. The risk of taking casualties was just too high. Moreover I now had serious reservations about the following morning's meet with the SFSG. I was reluctant to repeat in daylight the journey we had just made in darkness. It seemed more trouble than it was worth. I passed on my thoughts to Dave in the ops room back at Lash.

'Understood,' he said. 'But the meet is operationally critical and is to go ahead.'

Operationally critical? I couldn't imagine why, but if the SFSG said it was important then it must be.

The bright sunshine made Green 7 appear almost benign. No enemy forces, no noise, just some pockmarked buildings hinting at the goings-on of the previous evening. We turned left and headed south towards Orange 7. Arriving at the police checkpoint, I could see it too bore some battle scars. Ducking down through the low door, I went inside. There were eight Afghan policemen. Other than looking tired and hungry, seven of them were not really any worse for wear. Even the wounded soldier we had heard so much about over the radio was in pretty good form. He had been shot in the back – but was still managing to walk about. I told Matt to clean the wound. As he went about his duties, I took a closer look at the checkpoint. A simple compound, the mud walls topped off with sandbags, it was easy to see how it had become a target. All around were other, smaller dwellings, almost abutting the police's so-called stronghold. Between the buildings, along the narrow passages, it would have been child's play for the Taliban to get up close and hammer the occupants. I tried to explain to the police commander how he might try and improve his beleaguered situation. More barriers, some wire, but all beyond the checkpoint walls. Stop the enemy getting so close to their main target. He didn't seem very interested, happy instead to ride out any storm within the compound, finding solace – as so many Afghan soldiers and policemen did – behind bricks and mortar. It was precisely the wrong tactic. To avoid being besieged he needed to get men out and about, start to dominate the ground around their HQ, use offensive tactics, seize the initiative. I could see it wasn't going to happen. There wasn't much more I could do. I'd said my piece.

I checked my watch. 06:50 hrs. We had ten minutes to travel half a kilometre west away from habitation and away from prying eyes to a location that soothed the SFSG's phobia about being seen.

In two WMIKs we five Brits travelled to the rendezvous, leaving the ANA soldiers who had come thus far with us back at the checkpoint.

07:00 hrs came and went. Nobody arrived.

I gave it another few minutes, then got on the radio to Lee back at the patrol base to find out where they had got to. The answer came back quickly. The SFSG guys were running late. They wouldn't be there for another thirty minutes. Military planning or what? Well, I wasn't going to sit waiting for them. I relayed the message that we'd return to Orange 7 and they could come and find us there if they wanted.

(It was staggering that although we were in the same army as the SFSG, in the same theatre of operation as them, prob-ably not more than a couple of kilometres apart, I could not actually speak to them directly. Not because it was technically impossible, but rather because they and we had chosen to use different kit configurations to suit our varying missions. Essentially our radios were fitted with different 'fills' to theirs.)

Back at Orange 7 we sat and twiddled our thumbs. Thirty minutes turned into forty. Forty turned into fifty. Finally, nearly an hour late, they showed up. And as they did, the true, two-tier nature of the British Army became all too evident. The SFSG, funded by the Director of Special Forces, who had clearly got his chequebook out, looked like they were taking part in a photo-shoot for a fancy-equipment catalogue.

They were riding about in new Jackal vehicles. On their heads were the latest lightweight helmets, and around their torsos they wore the most recent, equally light, body armour. And they had the firepower to match – GPMGs, GMGs, .50-cals on their vehicles; Demarco M4 rifles as personal weapons. To add insult to injury they were also kitted out with TacSats fitted with omnidirectional aerials. Not for them the indignity of stopping every time they wanted to use the radio, grabbing hold of the antenna and thrusting it aloft. And to top it off, whilst there were just six Brits from the OMLT, mentoring ninety Afghans, the SFSG was a much larger formation than us, but actually had a far smaller group of Afghans to look after. The ratio was a mere 1:2.

'Fuck me,' said Junior. 'They make us look like a bunch of pikeys!'

I glanced back at my motley crew. Four of them, sitting in a pair of rusty, beat-up Land Rovers. Dusty, dirty and blood-stained, we looked like the poor relations come for the party and confined to the kitchen. Yet not for the first time I mar-velled at what was being asked of the men of 1 R IRISH and how well they were responding to the challenge. As for this other lot – well, I wasn't feeling charitable. Special? My arse, they were. They hadn't even turned up on time. They could keep their flash kit. I'd take my chances with the men and equipment I'd already got.

The young, fresh-faced officer in charge stepped forward and said hello.

'I just wanted to introduce myself and put a name to a face.'

'What?' I was incredulous.

'I knew the OMLT were operating in the area and I just wanted to say hi to you.'

Was he fucking joking?

'You had better come up with something better than that for dragging us out here, fella.'

I could see the look of uncertainty in his eyes. He realised I was angry and that he had misjudged the mood. For the next thirty minutes he attempted to make it up to us, passing on details of his ops, and intelligence he had gained about enemy movements on his side of the town. He also promised to do what he could to stop Taliban fighters moving through from the west and attacking us. To his credit, when I returned the compliment and told him what knowledge I had of enemy activity in our area of operations, he took copi-ous notes. Perhaps he was writing out 100 times 'Irish bastard', but at least he went through the motions of being interested.

Meeting over, the SFSG mounted up and disappeared whence they'd came. As for us, we trundled self-consciously back to town, our pikey presence knocking thousands off house prices as we passed through the neighbourhood.

I had been in Marjah for nine days, but at last it was time to go on R & R. With Lash having finally agreed to my request, Jon and Lee, plus Stewarty, would also leave with me. Matt was coming too, his time with the OMLT over. The only one remaining was Junior. My replacement was the man I'd taken over from, Ben Foster. Amongst those with him was Rab McEwen.

Thank God, the journey by road back to Lash was uneventful. From there it was a short helicopter hop to Tombstone, where I handed in anything directly linked to theatre – weapons, body armour, ammo – then had a chance to do a bit of very welcome 'admin'.

For the first time in sixteen days I was clean – showered and shaved, my uniform went through the wash too. I was ready to go home. Except the RAF wasn't ready to take me. I got from Bastion to Kandahar easily enough on a Herc, but then problems. The flight was delayed for twenty-three very long, very frustrating hours, and that was twenty-three hours I wouldn't be getting back. One day of my fortnight of leave already gone and I had not even left the sodding country.

When we did eventually get away, progress was still frustratingly slow because of stop-offs we made in Muscat and Cyprus. At last back at Brize there was at least a bus waiting to take me and the other men of the Royal Irish who had been on the same plane back to Tern Hill. There I picked up my car and drove for three hours to get back to Catterick. After four months away, at last I was home. It was what I had been looking forward to more than anything, and yet, at that moment, I hesitated before going in. I stepped off the path to the front door, on to the grass, and looked through the window. I could see Margaret and Luke sitting, watching TV, all relaxed. Peering through the glass, it was as if I was an outsider looking in on someone else's regular, happy life. I really didn't want to break the peace of the house by going in. I wasn't sure what to do. I almost turned and headed for the pub to get some Dutch courage. But I didn't. I went in and walked into the living room.

It was clear from Margaret's expression she was shocked. I might have been spick and span, but this wasn't the Doug Beattie she'd seen off back in March. My face was weather-beaten, my hair thin, unkempt and bleached by the sun. The dark rings around my bloodshot eyes betrayed the lack of sleep, the pressures I'd been under. But it was my emaciated frame that must have rendered me almost unrecognisable from the husband she'd watched go to war. I had lost at least two stone. I couldn't fill my uniform, my beer belly long gone, hollows in my cheeks. I was a shadow of my former self.

In the days before you go on R & R you think about the million and one things you are going to do when you get back. The beer you are going to drink, the curry you are going to eat, the football you are going to watch. You look forward to walking down the High Street in jeans and T-shirt, unburdened by a helmet or body armour, a radio or a rifle, or any of the other things you are forced to carry in theatre. But even before you get home you realise things might not go quite as you hope. There is a briefing at the airhead that warns of the dangers of over-expectation, of the gap between dreams and reality.

I had been determined not to reveal the horrors of what I had been through, determined to smile and laugh and enjoy being with my family. Yet in the very first seconds of being there, I was convinced I'd blown it. It was clear Margaret could sense a distance between us. I feared I would hug my daughter Leigh but have my mind on other things. Was terrified I'd shake the hand of my son and think of men his age whom I'd left behind in Afghanistan to continue fighting and, Heaven forbid, dying. Most of all I dreaded cradling my grandson whilst thinking of Shabia.

In fact picking up Tristan for the first time was spellbinding. So fragile and pure, he was untouched by anything bad, blissfully ignorant of the evils of the world. If only I could have shared his innocence. I was in love with him and so proud of my daughter. Yet over the next few days increasingly I shrank back into my shell, sitting silently on the couch, watching whatever was on the box, remembering Afghanistan, unable to forget Shabia. Around me frantic last-minute plans were being made for Leigh's wedding due to take place in just a few days. I wanted to share in the excitement, have it sweep me up, yet instead it just swirled around me. I was like an interloper. I was the head of the family and yet I didn't belong. I was marking time, waiting to return to the world I knew best. One of war. Fighting. Death.

The wedding took place on 26 July. Two weeks after coping with the aftermath of a suicide bomb attack I was walking Leigh down the aisle. She looked absolutely stunning and for that day, for her sake, I fought off thoughts of what had gone so recently before. We couldn't have wished for a better day. The weather was great, warm summer sunshine bathing the church in Richmond, North Yorkshire. I could not believe where the time had gone. All parents say their children grow up in the blink of an eye, yet for me it seemed quicker still because I had been away for so much of Leigh's childhood. I had missed her being born and then so many birthdays after that. I was in Kenya training for Afghanistan when she discovered she was pregnant, and in Helmand when my grandson appeared. It was all the more important then that I had actually made it home for her wedding to Mark, who served with the RAF. I had always warned Leigh never to bring home a soldier. She hadn't and yet she'd still managed to get her man in uniform.

After the ceremony we all decamped to a hotel in the town for the reception. My turn came to make a speech. I couldn't help but wonder what people would make of me. Should I tell them why my clothes were too big for me? Explain how I had such a good tan when there had been nothing but rain for the past couple of months? In the end I just thanked everyone for coming.

As I spoke, the emotion welled up. It must have been a combination of everything. The joy of seeing my daughter getting married, the full realisation of being a grandfather, the experiences of Afghanistan and the fear of going back, the memories of a lifetime being married to Margaret.

I looked at the newly-weds. 'There will be many happy times over the years to come. And many sad times, too. Mark, just try and make sure there are more of the former than the latter, that you make her laugh more than you make her cry, and that you always treat her like the princess she is.'

How well had I managed to do what I preached? Was I anyone to lecture on being a good husband? If nothing else I hoped Mark would learn from my mistakes. It was time to have another drink. All too soon I would be in Helmand again, away from my wife once more. But this would be for the last time. I had broken so many promises before. But not on this occasion. Margaret was still with me. She hadn't carried out her threat to turn her back on our marriage. And soon it would be my turn to deliver on what I had vowed to my wife. I'd run out of chances. This was it. All I had to do was go back, do my duty for a couple of months and then come home. Alive.

As the clock counted down to my return I scanned the papers, listened to the radio, watched the TV, looking out for any information about how the boys had been doing since I'd left.

On 28 July came the news I had dreaded. It was reported that a soldier from 4 SCOTS had been killed close to Lashkar Gah. And because the only troops from 4 SCOTS were serving with OMLT 4, that meant Marjah. And if it was Marjah, then the dead man must be Rab McEwen.

Only it wasn't.

Twenty-four hours after the announcement of the death of the soldier, he was named and a few more scant details released: 'Sergeant Jon Mathews of 4th Battalion the Royal Regiment of Scotland (the Highlanders) was killed while conducting operations with the Afghan National Army close to the provincial capital of Helmand province. He left behind a wife and young daughter.'

Perfunctory, clinical, two-dimensional – that was that, all that was said about a man I had liked and admired. A man I'd first worked with in Catterick and had just been serving alongside in Helmand; someone who had shown great courage and leadership in Marjah when the suicide bomber struck. And now he was gone. And with him, his humour, bravery and friendship.

PART THREE

THE END: ATTAL

TEN

POINT OF THE SPEAR

WO2 BILLY ROY, 1 R IRISH

1 AUGUST 2008

'In . . . Out . . .'

Jon was going home.

'In . . . Out . . .'

Leaving Afghanistan for the final time.

'In . . . Out . . .'

The words whispered by the NCO marching behind the coffin.

'In . . . Out . . .'

His orders slowly, respectfully, propelling forward the six men bearing Jon, their arms linked at the shoulder to take the weight of the vessel and the body it contained, heads not bowed, but raised high, proud they had the honour of carrying a brave soldier on the first leg of his final journey.

'In . . . Out . . .'

The only other sounds; the occasional crunch of boots on sand and grit as the party crossed the apron towards the rear of the C130; and the low melodic notes of the piper leading the way. The tune, 'Flowers of the Forest', a lament to the

Scottish defeat at the Battle of Flodden in 1513, rolling out through the darkness of a Helmand night.

Otherwise there was nothing, just 150 men standing in silence, some illuminated by the clusters of arc lights throwing out thousands of watts of light, others hidden in the shadows, surrounded by colleagues but alone with their thoughts.

In the splashes of brightness I could see a variety of head-dresses – the green caubeens of the Royal Irish, the maroon berets of the Paras, the tam-o'-shanters of the Royal Regiment of Scotland, the men wearing them formed into two lines between which Jon passed.

And not just Jon. For as if to emphasise the peril British troops faced there was a second bearer party, this one for a soldier of 2 PARA killed in Sangin, led by the battalion's colours.

I followed my friend's coffin with my eyes as it slipped by. Just as those carrying him were honoured to do so, so too was I to say I had known him. I couldn't help but wonder why Jon had died? Yes, I knew that after a few days' rest he had gone back to Marjah to replace Rab McEwen, who was pulled out to Lashkar Gah for some medical treatment. Yes, I knew he had been shot, a single Taliban bullet entering the side of his body where there was no armoured plate. Yes, I knew bad things happen in war. People die. But what I still couldn't reconcile was the fundamental question of why we were in Marjah in the first place. Two weeks after I left the town, the OMLT was removed altogether; plans to extend our reach into the desert shelved. So what had been the point of ever setting up the PB? Of allowing ourselves to get bogged down in yet another fucking DC, with limited man-power, poor equipment, inadequate command and control, and no simple way of being re-supplied? In my mind it had been a waste of time, waste of resources and a waste of Jon's life.

To my left the coffin disappeared up the ramp and into the cathedral-like belly of the aircraft. Disappearing too was Rab.

Jon's wife had asked if he be allowed to accompany his best friend home.

I had been with Rab earlier in the day at the memorial service to those who had recently died, including Jon and the Para. Rab looked as if he hadn't slept for days. The pain was evident in his eyes. Not only had he lost his mate, but Jon had been killed after replacing him in Marjah. The guilt hung heavily around his neck. You couldn't see it but you could sense it.

We had crowded around the brass cross in the centre of the HQ compound at Bastion that is the tribute to those who have died in Helmand. When I had first served in Afghanistan in 2006, the plaque below the cross bore no more than 20 names. Now there were over 100. Several I had known. Several I had known of.

The padre gave the eulogy. 'At the time of his death Jonathan 'Jon' Mathews was attached to the 1st Battalion the Royal Irish Regiment Battlegroup in southern Afghanistan, serving as a mentor and a trainer to the developing Afghan National Army. On Monday 28 July 2008 Jon was on a joint foot patrol with the ANA, which was helping to protect Afghan Police in a town near the provincial capital Lashkar Gah. As the patrol moved forward a single shot struck Jon. He was evacuated to Camp Bastion but despite the best efforts of all the medics Jon's life could not be saved. Jon Mathews was born in Edinburgh on 6 September 1972. He was a family man who was passionate about his city, his wife and his daughter.'

The words spoken, the prayers said, I had shaken Rab's hand as we dispersed. I didn't dare say he shouldn't blame himself. It was his right to come to terms with his loss in whatever way he wanted, but at that moment he was as much a casualty of war as Jon. He had been wounded; something had changed in him for ever. You don't get over a loss like that; you just have to learn to live with it. Everyone has a cross of some sort or other to bear. It's just a question of whether you have the strength to carry it.

'Take care, mate, I'll see you when you get back.' I never saw him again.

The gaping hole under the tail of the Hercules tightened and closed as the ramp settled back into place. The moan of the pipes replaced by the thunder of the four turboprop engines. The stillness of the night disturbed by the backdraught and the storm of dust whipped up by it. I turned and walked away.

The front wheel of the American Humvee dropped into yet another pothole on the road and, not for the first time, sitting in the rear seat, I whacked my shins on the metal bar running across the vehicle interior, against which my legs were jammed. It was literally pinning me to my seat. I didn't dare contemplate what would happen if we struck an IED. Even if I didn't die I could see me leaving both my feet behind as I got blown out.

Instead I tried to concentrate more on where I was going and why. Given that the journey to Patrol Base Attal was scheduled to take some six hours, there was plenty of time to do so. The route would take us from Camp Tombstone up to FOB Price, where we'd collect some stores, on to the town of Gereshk for a briefing with the local ANA commander, before we finally headed north through the desert of the Upper Gereshk Valley to the base.

All well and good, except until about twenty-four hours earlier I had been getting ready to head in the opposite direction, south to Garmsir. I had been looking forward to returning to a town I hadn't revisited since we had first wrested it from Taliban control in September 2006 and then held on to it with a contingent, on occasion, of only three British troops. I was eager to find out what had been happening since the 2,500 American marines had moved in.

But it wasn't to be. The ever-shifting sands of operational requirements were to take me to Attal instead.

The PB was established in May 2008, with an initial strength of 120 Afghans mentored by twenty-five Brits under the command of Jon Huxley. In the heart of bandit country, on the western side of the Helmand River, it was in contact daily. However, the resident force repeatedly beat off the Taliban onslaughts and also managed to get beyond the four walls of the camp to take the fight to the enemy on their own turf. More recently Jon had been replaced by Sergeant-Major Billy Roy. Now he was on his way out, too. Hence the call to me.

It was strange, I had only been back in Afghanistan six days and yet it was as if I had never been away, my mind quickly re-tuning to the realities of life in a war zone. Just as back home I couldn't easily imagine being back in the heat, dirt and danger of Helmand, now I couldn't envisage walking down the High Street on my way to the shops.

By now we had made our stops and were on the last bit of the route to Attal, traversing the so-called 'Desert of Death', an inhospitable wasteland where nothing seemed to grow and nobody seemed to live. Even the road we were following eventually melted away, swallowed up by the desolate landscape.

I mulled over the command structure I'd be faced with in Attal. We would be working alongside some American National Guards who had initially been assigned to a training detail with an Afghan counter-narcotics *kandak* up in Kabul. Unfortunately it was a company – ninety-five strong – from this *kandak* that was now in Attal, having been deployed south to make up the numbers as their previously resident ANA colleagues were moved on elsewhere. This created another problem. There weren't enough of the Americans – members of the Embedded Training Team or ETT, the US equivalent of our OMLT – to do the mentoring role in an operational environment. Which was why we Brits needed to be involved. Including me, there would only be nine OMLT soldiers helping out (plus three guys from the fire support team). We'd be answerable to the ETT, which would number just two. To add to the confusion, the area Attal sat in was controlled by the Danes, who had command over Battlegroup Centre. If you had wanted to create a set of circumstances from which chaos would ensue you couldn't have done better than come up with the scenario I was just about to be thrown into the middle of.

I looked around at the other men in the Humvee with me. In the front were the US driver and one Colonel Hamilton, the ETT commander, who was coming along for the ride. A third American provided top cover. Alongside me, in the other backseat, was Acting Sergeant Malone, known universally as Bugsy. From the Shankhill Road in Belfast – the big smoke, as he referred to it – Bugsy must have been about thirty, married with a child. He was a member of the Bugles, Pipes and Drums, a platoon in 1 R IRISH unique to the British Army. Whilst other regiments might have had bugles and drums, or pipes and drums, we were the only one to have all three. Which is not to say Bugsy and his colleagues were musicians first and soldiers second. No, their main job was to man heavy weapons. They only got to play their instruments – in Bugsy's case, a bugle – in their spare time, but they were damn good and highly thought of by the rest of the battalion.

We made our final approach to Attal. Peering through the thickened glass of the narrow windscreen I could see the large watchtower that dominated the western approaches. There was also no missing the burned-out shell of an ANA Ranger vehicle that had probably fallen victim to an IED.

We passed the tower and entered the base. With blessed relief, I hauled myself out of the Humvee and stretched my back, and my battered and bruised legs. I looked around at the place I would be calling home for at least the next month. Attal was essentially a large compound split into two: the northern part occupied by the OMLT; the southern part, by the ANA. Out to the east an extension had been built using HESCO cubes. Plenty large enough to accommodate a helicopter, in fact it was used as little more than a vehicle park. With the extension, the compound measured perhaps 200 metres by 100 metres. Around the perimeter there were man-made stand-to positions, essentially scaffolding poles and angular metal pickets lashed together with wire. Along the top of this metal frame ran wooden planks we could stand on. At each firing point an ammunition box had been fixed to the compound wall to hold extra grenades, illumination flares and range cards. Our makeshift defences afforded us a clear view over the high wall, as did a series of sentry posts dotted around the compound.

The OMLT area was dominated by a long low building, split into rooms, each with its own arched door. Along the length of one side ran a veranda. Jutting out over this was an overhanging roof made of mud and wood, against which a lean-to of corrugated iron and HESCO had been constructed to provide a bit more shelter. Off to one side of the building was the toilet. It happened to be the most heavily fortified part of the camp, given that a sangar to house a .50-cal had been built on top.

Away to my left was a pen made of sandbags within which all our ammunition was stored, other than what the men needed for the current day. Beyond this was another small building with a corrugated roof. It contained jerrycans full of petrol. Unlike diesel, petrol expands in the heat and so had to be kept out of direct sunlight. As for the diesel jerrycans, they were stacked against a hut occupied by the interpreters. I had seen as much as I was going to from where we had stopped. I had a last stretch, rescued my kit from the rear of the Humvee and set off to find Billy Roy.

'Want a brew, sir?' Billy asked in his mid–Ulster accent.

'Just some cold water if you've got it, please, Billy.'

'Crocky, get the boss some water!' Billy shouted past me before taking hold of half my kit and leading me to the living quarters. The accommodation room was ten metres long and five wide. There were three cot beds along one wall. It was oppressively hot, there was no electric light and other than the door the only opening was a small window. Billy pointed me to a bed with a mosquito net already hung around it. Kit dumped, I headed back outside into the harsh light to seek the rest of the OMLT, the Americans having already taken themselves off to their own corner of the camp.

'Hi there, I'm Sven.' Robert John Hay of Laxfirth introduced himself.

A captain in the Royal Horse Artillery, he had a Scottish father and a Norwegian mother. Hence the name Sven. Standing about 5′9″ tall, he was follicly challenged, his hair receding from the front. But there was no missing the shock he still had. It was wild, sticking out at crazy angles. Crazy too was his long beard.

'Hi, Sven, Doug Beattie. How long have you been here, then?'

'From the start I suppose, back in May?'

'Fuck that! Four months?' (Hence the beard.)

'Yep. Enjoyed it as well. Have done more than most here.'

Sven commanded the fire support team comprising himself, Bombardier Morgan 'Morgs' Armstrong from Bolton and Gunner Karl Shields from Larne on the Antrim coast in Northern Ireland. The fourth member of the team, Bombardier Kevin Penny from Mansfield, was on R & R.

'Here you go, Boss, water.'

I turned as Crocky tossed me a bottle.

'How was Kajaki?' he asked.

Crocky was one of the men I had taken over from up at the dam, way back in April. Jesus, that seemed a long time ago.

'Yeah, all right, mate. Got a bit hairy at times but the guys from 2 PARA were a good bunch. What about you?'

'Well, we were manning a PB at Witch's Hat close to FOB Gibraltar. Had a bit to do with 2 PARA, too.'

'Fuck, you were there with Basim, then? What happened?' I queried, already half-knowing the answer. Crocky filled in the detail. He explained how men from 2 PARA had inadvertently killed a child and wounded its mother in an incident close to Gibraltar when they fired two bursts of warning shots to deter a pair of Taliban lookouts who had the base under surveillance. Both casualties were brought by locals to Witch's Hat, from where the woman was evacuated for treatment. But this did little to placate the angry locals or indeed the ANA, many of whom vented their anger on the OMLT. A large group of civilians gathered outside the base and demanded the ANA soldiers leave and let them deal with the OMLT. The ANA were split. Some left the camp, others washed their hands of the matter and refused to intervene on behalf of either side. Some remained loyal. There then followed an attack on Witch's Hat. Under fire and with little support from the ANA, whom he decided he could no longer trust, Basim decided to abandon camp.

The incident had many repercussions. Had Basim bailed out too quickly? Had he failed to anticipate events? In particular, could the ANA ever be completely relied on not to turn on their allies?

As Crocky finished the story I drained the last drop of water and looked around the lean-to. When I wasn't on patrol or asleep this was where I would be spending most of my time, eating, briefing, giving orders, sorting equipment, even socialising — if that is the right word. And yet what I saw reminded me of a shit-heap. It was dirty and disorganised; frankly, it was disgusting. This wasn't about being tidy for tidy's sake — it was about looking after the gear that was going to keep us alive. In a corner there was a pile of radio batteries gathering dust.

There was ammunition strewn about on the sandy floor. In another corner was what looked like bits of demolition kit, including volatile detonators. Then there were 81mm illumination rounds just lying there covered in grime. Yet who was I to criticise? Billy had been doing a fantastic job in and around Attal and he had also developed good relations with the Americans. I would be doing well to emulate what he had achieved. The clean-up would have to wait.

It was about then he came over to give me the ground brief.

He began by explaining that the Attal area of operation was basically cut in half down a north–south line.

Just thirty metres to the east the Green Zone started – the lush fringes of vegetation that straddled both sides of the Helmand River. It was in the Green Zone that most enemy activity took place. Some 1,500 metres into it you reached the river. This was where our sphere of influence ended. Between us and the river lay a patchwork quilt of green and blue. Man-high fields of corn (also known as maize), tree-lines, tracks, streams, irrigation ditches. Our PB was on elevated ground above all this but, given the density of the plant life, it was impossible to see more than a few hundred metres into the zone.

Out to the west there was little more than desert and a few isolated settlements. Just north of us was a dry watercourse known as Star Wars Wadi (so called because the village in it looked like part of the set from the film. Soldiers give odd names to things. They don't have to be accurate; they just have to stick). To the south was another wadi. Both offered good routes into enemy territory.

Once Billy had explained the ground, he explained the situation. His first sentences were the most telling.

'Doug, if you imagine the Upper Gereshk Valley as a spear, then the Danes are sitting at the middle of it, at the grip. We, at Attal, are the point of the spear. To the north there is nothing but enemy until you reach Sangin. To the south there's only more enemy until you get to FOB Armadillo. Across the river and down a bit you come to FOB Gibraltar and 2 PARA. But they're not in the Danes' area of operations. Don't be in any doubt. We are on our own.'

Billy continued the briefing, but to be honest it was difficult taking it all in. The best way to understand what he was talking about would be to get out and about and see things for myself. What was abundantly clear, however, was that we were surrounded. To all intents and purposes we were beyond easy help. The only thing that had previously even half-levelled the playing field was the sheer numbers of ANA and OMLT in Attal. With 120 of the former and 25 of the latter it at least meant that through heavy patrolling they had managed to hold the ground around the base. But that looked set to change.

The mentoring force would now be just 14 ISAF troops with the ANA numbers down to 95. And as I was about to learn from the Americans who nominally had the job of mentoring them, the Afghans were woefully ill-equipped for the job. Billy's handover complete I next spoke to Oliver, one of the American National Guards. He explained that the *kandak* from which the Afghans now in Attal were drawn had been formed to work with the poppy-eradication programme. In effect they were force protection for those whose job it was to destroy the opium crop. But barely were they established than this group was sent to Helmand with no relevant training, little cohesion because of ethnic divisions within the group, and next to no respect for their own leaders (not surprising given the company commander had only a bit more experience than his men and had been given his position primarily because of his standing in the community. It was real jobs-for-the-boys stuff).

There were also concerns about collusion between the ANA and the Taliban. Unlike most of the ANA in Helmand, some of these men were Pashtuns and came from the same tribe – the Alozai – who effectively controlled the Upper

Gereshk Valley. This nervousness about our movements being leaked to the Taliban had resulted in the ETT being increasingly reluctant to go out and patrol. Just the previous month a number of French troops had been killed in a large-scale insurgent attack and the word was that Attal was next.

To round off the day I took a stroll to the Afghan part of the camp. It was clear they had little sense of personal hygiene, no willingness to tidy up after themselves. The cooking area was squalid, as was the site where they dumped all their rubbish, supposedly for burning.

Day Two in Attal started much like Day One had finished. More briefings, more chats with those who had been at the sharp end for a while. And, just as the previous day, no patrolling had been scheduled. This was an ETT decision so I went off to find Oliver and his colleague Samuel to ask why. The pair's explanation was that the ANA had issues and didn't want to go out – they were tired, had problems with supplies of food and ammunition, needed more specialist equipment. It was a list of excuses I had heard before, yet the ETT took them at face value. What nobody seemed to grasp was that staying in camp was no safer than going out. It simply encouraged the enemy to be bolder in their actions and get closer to our position. Something that was underlined the next day.

It began with the telltale sound of firecrackers going off – bullets zipping over our heads, coming from the north. A few seconds later there was a large explosion to the west, perhaps sixty metres away – probably a mortar.

'Incoming!' The warning went out.

Then came a second explosion and the sound of firecrackers intensified.

Just a bit earlier I had been eating a late breakfast/early lunch – swordfish casserole. Not normal fare in the British Army, but then this wasn't British rations, it was Norwegian and had come via the Danes. It made a welcome change from

Lancashire Hotpot, sausage and beans, and the dreaded corn-beef hash. Around me the others had been equally relaxed, most dressed in nothing more than military-issue desert shorts and sandals. Not any more. Everyone, myself included, was scampering back to the lean-to and the accommodation block to grab helmets, body armour and weapons.

As I ducked into the building I shouted to Ranger Jon Kerr, who was manning the radio in the ops room. 'Contact north, SAF and indirect fire.'

'Roger, Boss.'

Running back out with my kit, I tried to shrug the straps of the radio pack over my shoulders. As I emerged from the building, I saw most of the men, American, Afghan and British, crouched down against the HESCO, taking cover.

'What the fuck are you doing?' I yelled as I darted past them, over the open ground of the compound and up a ladder to the firing position on the north wall. I shouldered my SA80 and began shooting back.

Others were now clambering on to the firing steps. Samuel, the ETT sergeant, was there, as was Corporal Alwyn 'Stevo' Stevens, one of my commanders, plus Bugsy. Our targets lay in a tree-line some 400 metres north. The ANA were now venturing forth too. Along with their normal assortment of PKMs and Kalashnikovs (as this ANA counter-narcotics *kandak* was merely attached to the Afghan brigade in Helmand and not an intrinsic part of it, there was no plan in place to switch the men from their AK47s to M16s) they also had an SPG-9 recoilless rifle.* The sound of it being fired was about as loud as an incoming mortar shell detonating.

---

* A recoilless rifle is a weapon, usually mounted on a tripod, that fires much larger-calibre rounds than small arms. The Russian-made SPG-9 fires fin-stabilised projectiles. It has been widely copied around the world. It is recoilless because rather than the blast being contained in the breech, some of the gases are let out through the back of the weapon, reducing the kick.

A minute or two later Sven arrived, having already established contact with the gun line some eight kilometres south of us in FOB Armadillo.

'Doug, I have the guns,' he shouted, referring to the 105mm artillery pieces now at our beck and call.

'Roger, Sven, just wait.'

I dipped behind the parapet and studied the map, the sweat already running down into my eyes. I had seen three enemy positions to the north and north-east. One was in the desert in a deep wadi. The others were just inside the Green Zone, closer to the compound but hopefully still far enough away to safely bring the artillery shells in. Sven wanted the main target first.

'I have at least four of the enemy in a wood-line at Grid 654346.' I didn't bother telling him the area indicator as he would already be well aware of it. There was a pause whilst Sven found my reference on his own map.

After getting on the radio again, he yelled up to me. 'Doug, I'm going to drop in the open ground to the north-east of the grid and from there we will adjust on to the target.'

Whilst theoretically we might have been outside the 150-metre danger area of a detonating 105mm shell, we'd be in big trouble if it fell short. This way the first rounds should land well beyond the target and, when that was confirmed, Sven would talk the gunners back in from there.

'There will be two guns on task, so you should see two detonations.'

I grabbed my rifle again, checked the magazine, and stood back up, my head above the parapet.

We had now got the enemy's range. Tracer from a .50-cal and a brace of GPMGs was slamming into the Taliban positions. There was also steady fire from an American GMG on top of one of the vehicles. The ANA fire wasn't so accurate – in fact it was like a mad dog's shite, spread all over the fucking place – yet at least they were having a go.

Through the noise I heard Sven shout out.

'Shot!'

He meant the first shells were on their way. Even he couldn't resist taking a look and hauled himself up to peer over the wall. He had plenty of time. Fired from such a distance, they would take about thirteen seconds to reach their target. You could hear them coming. It was strangely comforting. Not a whoosh, but a low rumbling noise coming from behind us, which increased in volume until the rounds were directly overhead, and then tailed off as they continued inexorably towards the target. It was like having surround sound on your TV or hi-fi system, only rather more dangerous.

Then they exploded. Landing in the Green Zone, much of the blast absorbed by the soft earth, the effect from where we watched didn't look tremendous. Yet I still wouldn't have wanted to have been anywhere near the impact site with the red-hot, razor-sharp fragments of casing spinning out in all directions for more than 100 metres.

In a moment Sven had made his adjustments. 'Opal 82, this is Opal 70. Drop 200. Four rounds. Fire for effect.'

The reply came back in the same precise gunnery language. 'Opal 70, this is Opal 82, shot over.'

'Doug, we should see eight impacts, keep an eye open for me.'

It is at times like these that you quickly get the measure of the men you are serving with, men who – like Sven – you might have only just met. I didn't know him, or his team, from Adam. Didn't know their backgrounds, their experience, their capabilities, their judgement. And now my life was in their hands. There wouldn't be much of us left if Sven fucked it up and dropped a shell on the PB by mistake. But from the look of confidence in his eyes, that didn't seem about to happen. He gave off an air of assurance. And it rubbed off on me.

Way to the south I heard the reports as the guns fired in

rapid succession. Then came the rumble overhead, followed by a string of explosions – all on the nail.

I gave Sven the co-ordinates for the next targets.

As our small battle continued, I at last had a chance to send a more detailed contact report – known as a SALTA report – to Gereshk via Jon, who was still sitting patiently in the ops room.

'Sierra – 6–8.'

The strength of the enemy.

'Alpha – enemy engaging with SAF, RPGs and mortars from three locations to the north and north-east.'

What the enemy was up to. Jon acknowledged the details so far and I continued.

'Lima – firing-points grids . . .'

I passed on the map references for the enemy positions but didn't bother with our own – Attal had already been registered as our location.

'Tango – 11:45 hrs.'

The time the contact had started.

'Alpha – engaging the enemy with SAF, RPG, SPG9, HMG and 105mm.'

What we were throwing back at the Taliban.

It was now down to Jon to put this into something more formal and send it up the chain to the ops room in Gereshk known as Sierra 60. From there it would go to the brigade HQ in Lashkar Gah. In Attal, as in Lash, we didn't have our own JTAC to call in air-strikes. We would be relying on a Danish JTAC back in Armadillo to do the job for us, call-sign Norseman. Almost immediately he was on the net, asking what we needed. I declined his offer of help. The enemy weren't great in numbers and anyway, Sven and the guns had got them bang to rights.

The situation coming under some sort of control, I looked around at the men from the OMLT. It was clear they understood what was required. Some were in a direct fight with the

Talibs, trading bullets. Others were below the battlements – for in effect that is what the walls and the firing steps were – running around the compound, gathering and delivering ammo to those who needed it. Whatever else I would have to do in Attal, teaching them my methods of getting the job done wouldn't be part of it.

There was one thing that didn't seem quite right, though. During breaks in the shooting I could just make out another sound. I could distinguish SAF from the .50-cal. The 40mm underslung grenade launcher, from the American GMG. The SPG-9, from the PKMs. But there was something else. I strained to listen. It was singing. Bob Marley. 'One Love'. Now I might not have been well up on my music but even I was aware the reggae legend was dead. So patently the great man himself wasn't in Attal. Which meant one of the guys had found time, in the heat of the battle, to turn on his iPod. The song was completely out of place, and yet at the same moment completely apt. The music belonged to our medic, another of our resident Fijians, Ranger Qalitakivuna – or, as everyone referred to him, Q.

Around me the noise of battle – if not Bob Marley – was dying away. The fire mission from Armadillo had had the desired effect, enemy activity initially subsiding to a trickle and then drying up completely. Our return fire eased up too.

'Watch and shoot,' I shouted, wanting the men to keep a keen lookout for the enemy and fire at will if the situation presented itself.

As we stood at the wall I received a call from Norseman. A French Mirage was *en route* even though we had not requested it. It was decided the aircraft should over-fly the enemy positions and look for any activity.

A few minutes later and Norseman relayed a message from the pilot saying he could see movement at one of the three locations from which the enemy had engaged us. He said if we could positively identify enemy fighters, then the aircraft would engage. But I couldn't. I passed the buck back to Norseman.

'If you can identify the enemy, then the call is yours.'

Many of the coalition planes had real-time cameras mounted in the nose, pictures from which were downlinked back to the JTAC. It was now up to him. I wasn't going to be the one responsible for bombing innocent civilians who might just have walked back into the target areas as the Taliban fled.

In the end the decision was taken not to drop any ordnance. For thirty minutes the Mirage circled overhead but there was nothing to report. For another half an hour after that we remained on the ramparts, but with little going on I closed the TiC and stood the men down to resume life within the PB.

As everyone dispersed, I grabbed hold of Oliver. 'When was the last time we went out on patrol from Attal?'

'About two days before you arrived, I think.'

'So there has been no attempt at ground domination for four days, perhaps longer?'

'Yeah, but we are able to monitor the ground from here.'

Samuel, the other ETT guy, came over to join in the conversation. 'It's all about observation. If we can see into the Green Zone from here, then we can dominate it without venturing out.'

'Guys, I think that is complete folly. I have been in enough situations where we didn't dominate the ground and the enemy had complete freedom of movement, meaning they hit us at will. We need to be out and about. Patrolling, searching, ambushing, taking the fight to them, not waiting for them to come to us.'

Samuel seemed to be against the idea, whilst Oliver had at least come some way round to recognising the need to get out of the gates. He wanted to set up a permanent checkpoint at a crossroads in the Green Zone, but in my eyes this was a mistake too. Not only would it be in another static position but, surrounded by the lush vegetation of the Helmand River hinterland, the soldiers manning it wouldn't have any chance of seeing the enemy until they were all but on top of them. I wasn't the only person who thought this way – the plan was rejected by Brigade HQ.

Against my wishes, the next couple of days were spent in camp. Billy had now left and at least it gave me the opportunity to get things the way I wanted them. First on the list was to build a medical centre. There was always the danger of having to deal with mass casualties and it would be sod's law that the day a bus full of injured arrived we would have nowhere to look after them. We toiled to get the facility finished – well, mainly Q toiled. It was his baby, his design, and mostly his sweat that got it built. Made of HESCO, wood and corrugated iron, it was rudimentary but, equipped with an operating table and a fridge to keep drugs in, plus stretchers for the lesser wounded, it was as good as it was ever going to be in such circumstances.

I also devoted time to getting a shelter built to house the lubricants and fuels for the pair of WMIKs the camp had call on. We also enhanced the ammo-storage area and refurbished the mortar pits. Although to call them mortar pits was a bit misleading. Yes, they had once contained a pair of 81mm weapons. No, they weren't there any longer. Someone higher up the food chain had decided the weapons and their operators would be better located elsewhere. So instead we were the proud owners of two holes in the ground lined with sandbags. The best use for them now was as trenches to dive into when enemy fire got a bit close for comfort.

I had got to the point where I had done as many makeovers as one camp and one captain could endure. What I was increasingly desperate to do was get beyond the four walls.

The next morning my wish came true.

Entering the Green Zone was like leaving behind a drab world of unimaginative browns and greys and stepping on to a set of a movie filmed in the most vivid Technicolor. It was as if, hand in hand with Dorothy, we had left Kansas behind and entered the Land of Oz. In normal times the natural point of entry to Oz would have been via a narrow bridge over a small stream. But these were not normal times and the chances of the crossing being booby-trapped were high. Instead we waded through the water. For 500 metres we pushed eastwards through the verdant landscape, the foliage doing its best to smother us, visibility through the suffocating crops no more than five to ten metres. Periodically we would emerge into a patch of open ground and see a ploughed field ready to receive the next poppy crop. These were usually close to a single compound from which the cultivator could guard and tend his livelihood. Then, all too soon, we'd plunge back into the clawing jungle of corn. Eventually we reached what was known as the enemy's main supply route (MSR). Stretching away both north and south it was regarded as the Taliban's principal route for shifting men and equipment – not to mention drugs – through the region. Only just wide enough to take a small car, the route – in reality little more than a rough track – was more frequently used by motorbikes. It was on the MSR that the primary team of ANA, led by Stevo, one of five soldiers from St Helena serving with the Royal Irish, set up a vehicle checkpoint (VCP). The secondary team – the one I was with – was responsible for providing cover and protection.

Stevo's group would bring to a halt any approaching bikes several yards short of them and order the rider to get off and prove, by lifting his clothing, that he had neither weapons nor explosives on his person. Once he was declared safe the ANA would check any mobile phone the driver might have for numbers we recognised as being linked to the Taliban. Then they'd expertly search his transportation. They always seemed excited when they discovered any drugs and were quick to confiscate them. Not to be handed in, but rather to keep for their recreational use back at the camp.

Even once the search was complete the disruption for the unfortunate Afghan wasn't quite over. To make sure he didn't ride off and simply call all his mates to warn them what was going on, he would be directed to a holding pen and held under armed guard until the VCP was dismantled.

In little more than twenty minutes Stevo had collected a motley assortment of nine riders plus a gaggle of children who had come to watch the strange goings-on. Whilst Stevo was doing his thing, Bugsy and his group of ANA had pushed on through to a village we regarded as friendly. After chatting to the locals and carrying out a couple of low-key searches they moved to the periphery of the settlement and took up a position on the edge of a field covered with the biggest, healthiest cannabis plants you were ever likely to see. Well over six feet tall, they obviously thrived in the warm, damp environment found on the fringes of the Helmand River. Bugsy came through on the radio.

'Just picked up some Taliban chatter. The enemy can see a patrol near the shop and are preparing to attack.'

The Taliban used simple, insecure press-to-talk radios to convey messages. Our interpreters carried similar devices to intercept what was being said. It was one of these 'terps' who had first overheard the information Bugsy had just relayed. The difficulty was that, because the Taliban were aware we monitored their radios, a lot of what they said was either an attempt to deceive us, or mere bravado. But as Stevo's VCP was right by a shop, we had to take the chatter seriously, though as it happened we were about to move on anyway, wary about overstaying our welcome in one location. We headed north along the MSR, staying with it as it swung north-west and then exited the Green Zone into Star Wars Wadi.

The final part of the patrol took us up the seemingly sheer side of the plateau on top of which Attal stood. Struggling to put one foot in front of another and sweating like a bastard, I realised just how exhausted I was. The patrol had lasted little more than two hours but I was totally fucked, not least because of the oppressive humidity and scorching heat in the Green Zone. I reckoned the temperature was at least five degrees hotter down by the river. It certainly felt that way. And obviously not just to me. Most of the men shrugged off their equipment and headed for the fridge – not the one in the medical centre with the drugs, but another in the lean-to – to retrieve the water they had stashed in it before leaving 120 minutes earlier. Others sat down to clean their weapons. And those unlucky enough to have contracted the shits made a beeline for the single toilet to unburden their bowels.

But we wouldn't be allowed too much time to relax. Just half an hour after we got back, the enemy struck again from almost the same positions as three days before, the incoming fire consisting of mortars, AK47 rounds and RPGs. Hurriedly I donned the kit I had just taken off and made my way to the wall.

I shouted out my instructions to the others, giving each a specific target area to hit. I glanced round just in time to see Morgs Armstrong clambering up on to the roof of the accommodation block to man the 51mm mortar. Coming up the ladder behind him with some ammunition was Q. It was then the rocket-propelled grenade struck, impacting somewhere behind Morgs and sending up a huge billowing cloud of dust that enveloped him completely. The debris started to descend on Q who dipped his head to try and stop the sand and grit getting into his mouth, nose and eyes.

'Fuck it!' I thought to myself, the words escaping my lips at the same time.

'Q, get up there and check on Morgs!'

He didn't really need telling. Like a rat up a drainpipe he pulled himself from rung to rung and disappeared into the dust still hanging in the air. I turned my attention back to the enemy. A minute or two later there was the most welcome of sounds – the 51mm firing.

'Morgs, you OK?' I screamed.

The reply came in the form of a thumbs-up. From Q there was a pair of open palms and a shrug of the shoulders, as if he was asking, 'What's all the fuss about?'

The firefight turned out to be short and sharp. We had been hit with at least six RPGs, but the enemy was once again quelled by the booming presence of the 105mm guns. When the action had died down, Sven came to find me. It seemed I had been wrong about mortars being part of the enemy's arsenal.

'Doug, that wasn't indirect fire. You reported it as such, but it wasn't. It was just RPGs.'

'Sorry, mate, I didn't realise.'

This wasn't Sven being petty. It was about knowing the exact strength of the enemy and whether they had a mortar team in the vicinity. Sven explained that, before my arrival, a Taliban mortar unit had been wiped out. Since then there hadn't been any more mortars fired into the PB, hence why what I said had given him kittens.

(It also meant I had been wrong about coming under mortar attack previously. That time Sven had bitten his tongue, but now I'd got it wrong twice, he let me know.)

Once we stood down from the attack we made for the accommodation block to find the RPG that had struck so close to Morgs had actually penetrated the roof of the building and detonated, of all places, on his cot. Shrapnel had gnawed big chunks out of the wall. Moving closer, I saw the fin of the grenade was still on Morgs's bed, having burned through his mosquito net and sleeping bag. There was no doubt about it, if anyone had been in the room at the time we would now be dealing with casualties. It had been a lucky escape and proved once again just how vulnerable we were.

For a second time I spoke to the ETT guys Oliver and Samuel and expressed my concerns that we had become too static. They trotted out the same lines about failings amongst the ANA leadership and the threat of collusion. What they said wasn't wrong. These problems existed when I first arrived in Helmand in 2006 and they existed now. You had to assume a degree of corruption and complicity amongst the Afghans, allow for tribal factionalism, take into account poor leadership and training. And then you had to put it all behind you and get on with the job. The only way to make a success of things was by demonstrating good mentoring. Lead from the front. Demand action. Demand the Afghans went out on patrol. Demand they did what they were supposed to do.

As I walked away I remembered what Billy had said to me: 'The ETT are front of house, but the hard work is down to us.'

And if we didn't give the ANA a kick up the arse then there would be serious consequences. Not just for us, but also for the rest of the valley. If the ANA didn't start dominating the ground, then how could we prevent the Taliban from moving downstream towards Gereshk, the commercial capital of the province? The more time that passed, the more I was worried I was going to have a serious falling-out with the Americans.

The next day, however, it seemed there might be a thaw in our relationship. We were going out. With the ANA, we set off to clear and search a group of buildings on a piece of high ground to the south-west of Attal where it was thought the enemy had an observation post which gave them a commanding view straight into the PB little more than a kilometre away. The Afghans were split into two groups. The first, commanded by Stevo, initially moved out to the west before turning south. The other group was Bugsy's. American Samuel was with him. Sven, Morgs and me, we were at the back. Things moved along pretty smoothly. There was good depth, good ground coverage and good mutual support. What there wasn't, were any bloody locals to interact with. We were dominating an open desert – one that had no people. At least it allowed the OMLT to give the ANA some more on-the-job training. We arrived at the forming-up point (FUP) short of the buildings. At an FUP, in the British Army, we would stop, shake out into whatever formation was in the orders and then fix bayonets. The fixing of bayonets had a huge psychological effect on the men. It marked the point where things were about to get serious and readied them for battle, any illusions they might have been under about what they were doing evaporating as the blades slotted home. I wanted to take the ANA through the same motions.

I gave the order over the PRR to start moving and then stood up. Slowly I started walking towards the target. It sent out the clearest signal to the Afghans. They were left in no doubt that they should come too. Bugsy moved from the low ground of the wadi he was in up towards the small compound, the men with him now eager to get on with the task. Within a few minutes they were swarming all over the tiny settlement, rummaging through the main building, turning over some outhouses, inspecting a corral used for animals. They didn't find anything out of the ordinary. It seemed as if the 'Taliban' who had been spotted from Attal were probably just kids coming and going to tend the animals.

I turned my attention to Stevo's section. They had continued patrolling in the direction of another set of compounds, south of the first target, that also needed to be cleared.

'Stevo, I'm coming to join you,' I said over the radio before setting off along a ridgeline with Sven.

Then the inevitable happened: small-arms fire and RPGs from the direction we were heading in, mostly aimed at Stevo's team. I had only been at the PB for four full days and this was already my third contact. I was going to enjoy myself at Attal. Not. Bloody place.

'Stevo, what have you got?'

'Enemy position some 350 metres south-east of my location. I would say six Taliban.' His voice was calm despite the difficulty he found himself in.

'Roger, mate, suppress and I'll join you in a minute.'

Heaving myself up from the prone position I'd instinctively adopted when the shooting started, I began to work my way to where he was. A quick glance over my shoulder revealed Bugsy and his men were in heavy contact too.

'Bugsy, what can you see?'

'Boss, the ANA have spotted some enemy moving along the main supply route.' He went on to describe their exact location close to a group of compounds.

I reached Stevo just as two RPGs whizzed over our heads, seemingly fired from a location much nearer than the one Stevo had initially reported. Soon I'd seen enough. I was off and crawling again, this time to Sven.

'Got enemy here.' I jabbed my finger at the map, making sure he understood exactly what I was talking about. Message received loud and clear, and it was time to complete another leg of my battlefield relay. But by this stage I'd had enough of dragging myself around on my hands and knees. I picked myself up and started running back to Stevo. I arrived amidst a hail of bullets. As I wriggled into position to help return fire at the fleeting enemy, Sven came through on the radio.

'I am hearing fire from the north. Not sure where exactly, but it could be Attal under attack.'

Fucking hell. Immediately I got on the VHF to speak to the ops room at the PB.

'Amber 92, this is Alpha, send sitrep over.'

The reply came in a flash, confirming they were in contact from the north.

'Roger 92, I will see what support I can get for you. In the meantime ensure Sierra 60 knows your situation.'

The problem was I didn't have much in the way of support to offer. To mentor out on the ground I needed at least six men with me, plus Sven and his fire support team. That left just three men back at Attal with another contingent of the ANA. Tommy (a lance-corporal with a flair for cooking) wouldn't leave his post in the ops room, which meant there was only Crocky and the American Oliver out on the walls.

Thanks to Sven and the 105s, our situation out on the ground was improving, though. Two of the three enemy positions had gone quiet. I asked him to turn his attention to helping relieve the pressure on Attal. Now I wanted to drop the ANA with us down into the Green Zone and then work them up through cover towards the enemy attacking the PB. I told Samuel my plan.

'No,' came the reply. 'The Afghan commander wants to go back.'

I didn't mince my words. 'Well, fuckin' tell him otherwise. Get him to agree. Make him understand. Do your fuckin' job.'

'Hey. It's not my job. I only mentor the ANA, I don't command them. If they want to go back, then we go back.'

I was livid. We had the advantage of the 105mm guns. We had requested air support. And I didn't really believe the attack on the PB was anything more than a diversion, merely a way of making us abandon our ground activities and scurry back to camp. Which is exactly what we did. Under cover of smoke we withdrew, tails firmly between our legs. ISAF nil, Taliban one. The foreign aggressors defeated by the fearless defenders. At least that's what the headline would be.

At the risk of labouring the point I talked through the matter yet again with the Americans, hopeful at least Oliver might now see the virtue in striking out. His view was that the defence of Attal was the important thing, yet we were still diametrically opposed over how this would best be achieved. He still couldn't see any value in creating a buffer around the camp to stop the Taliban getting close enough to attack. On top of this he trotted out the same old excuses about the inadequacies of the ANA. If he was bored by me, then I was equally bored by him.

And as for patrolling, there wasn't going to be any of that for at least another few days. The Afghans were needed by the Americans to construct some new watchtowers within the camp. So that meant there was little for the OMLT to do other than sit and wait. Wait to be attacked. Like fish in a barrel.

Maybe I was wrong. Maybe I had badly misjudged the situation. Perhaps the ETT and the ANA were more on the money in their views than I was. But I doubted it. The recent history of my own regiment showed how bloody things could turn if you remained holed up in one location. In Musa Qala in 2006, troops from 1 R IRISH were effectively under siege as they repeatedly tried to fend off enemy attacks on the platoon house they occupied, prevented by the chain of command from carrying out any offensive operations. The result? Two of my friends were killed and several more wounded. Now here in Attal, I feared we too would start taking serious casualties. I regarded the American plan as utter bollocks.

I endured another two days of inactivity. Inactivity, that was, except for repelling the attacks launched by the enemy as the bloody watchtowers got higher. It got to the point where I could take no more. I was at boiling point. I had been in Attal for a week and only been out of the camp twice, both times on short patrols. To cap it all, some twenty of the Afghan soldiers were withdrawn from the base after discussions between Colonel Hamilton and the ANA *kandak* commander. We were down to just seventy-five ANA troops.

I sent an email to my direct superior Dave Harrison. A large, likeable soldier, Dave was a major in the Royal Horse Artillery. Based at FOB Price, he was the man in charge of OMLT operations in the Upper Gereshk Valley.

I'm not sure if you are fully aware of the situation up here, but it is clear the ANA are not being properly mentored. The ETT lack understanding of the role at Attal and will not take the ANA out on patrol to dominate the area. My OMLT are now sitting around doing little as the enemy surges forward and attacks the PB at will.

In order for me to achieve the mission in Attal, the ETT need to get the ANA out of the gate and allow us to tactically mentor them on operations. If they are not prepared to do this then it is clear to me the ETT should be withdrawn from forward bases such as Attal and allow the OMLT to conduct all patrolling.

I believe it is only a matter of time before the enemy have a success in their many attacks on the base and without a doubt if we do not dominate the GZ then soon Armadillo and even the DC will be under a far greater threat.

I pressed send.

Unfortunately the sympathetic reply I got back from Major Dave came complete with my initial message still attached. Which somehow the Americans got to see. They were furious.

I tried to explain to them I didn't doubt their courage in the face of the enemy, and I understood they had to some extent been thrown in at the deep end. After all, they had taken on a job mentoring a bunch of Afghans who were supposed to have an anti-narcotics role but suddenly found themselves defending an isolated FOB. Even so, I was frustrated by their failure to have any meaningful influence over the ANA. My attempt at justification fell on deaf ears, and Oliver and Samuel reported my remarks to Hamilton, who in turn demanded that Colonel Ed Freely – my battalion CO – remove me. The demand was studiously ignored.

My dealings with the ETT were now at breaking point. So much for the Anglo-American special relationship.

The whole situation annoyed me. But I tried to put it in perspective. What was my minor spat compared to the sacrifices being made by coalition forces up and down Helmand?

ELEVEN

KILLED IN ACTION

TELEVISION NEWSREADER

Just another day.

You turn on the TV news and there, somewhere after a report on the credit crunch and before the footie, you get the other stuff, events in brief, the stories they haven't got pictures for or don't think are important enough to warrant two minutes all to themselves. Amongst these fillers you hear the presenter say, 'A British soldier has been killed in action in Afghanistan after being hit by a roadside bomb.' Killed in action. KIA. It all sounds so unsentimental, so impersonal, so clinical. But it's not. It is usually brutal and bloody and painful. So here it comes, the wretched truth about KIA, a truth you'll never hear, let alone see, on *News at Ten*. This is what KIA is all about.

11:46 hrs
This was the time a British soldier stood on an IED, an improvised explosive device, a roadside bomb. It wasn't clear whether it was the heel of his desert boot that made contact with it first, or the sole, or perhaps he was already springing off his toes and well into his next stride when the weapon that he

trod on killed him. It doesn't really matter, for any of these scenarios would have set off the same catastrophic chain of events.

As the weight – several stone of the soldier, and a few more of his equipment – came to bear on the track, it also fell on the part of the bomb that would trigger the explosion. Just below the surface, encased in a motorcycle inner tube to keep them free of dirt and moisture, were a pair of old saw blades: one connected by a wire to an electrical power source, a pack of six or so domestic batteries; the other attached by a different wire to a Russian mortar shell. The blades were wedged apart at each end by pieces of wood. In this configuration the blocks acted as a circuit-breaker, preventing the flow of electricity, keeping the system inert. With the soldier's full weight now coming down inexorably on the top blade, it buckled and bowed in the middle, then made contact with its twin beneath. And that was that. The circuit was complete and a current started to flow, at the speed of light, from the battery, via the saw blades to a detonator. In turn the detonator was connected to a booster charge, which in itself was hooked up to the mortar shell.

The weapon could have lain there for a day, a week, a month. It might have been there for a year or more. Of course, it wouldn't have mattered to the bomb how long it had gone undiscovered. It had no feelings, no sense of time, no memory, only an endless patience it wasn't aware of. But now its moment had come. It was about to do the one and only thing it had been created for. Wreak death on the enemy of those who had first dug a hole for the weapon to sit in and then carefully buried it, hiding all signs of the earth having ever been disturbed.

In that most routine and instinctive of movements, walking, the British soldier had sealed his fate, self-selected himself as the victim. And life for his family was about to be irrevocably altered. Shattered beyond recognition. Not that they knew it yet. Though, it seems, he possibly did.

Because even as he was completing his step, as events were about to unfold beneath him out of sight, he suddenly stopped as if he suspected something. Had he already seen something, felt something not quite right through the rubber sole of his boot? It was as if he already had an inkling of what he'd just done.

But by now it was way too late to alter the course of history.

The chemical reaction going on inside the mortar shell was rapidly generating an extreme amount of pressure and heat – as much as several hundred tonnes per square inch of the former and anything between 1,500 and 2,500 degrees Celsius of the latter. It was all happening so fast – unimaginably fast – and it had become impossible to turn the clock back; things had already gone far beyond the point of no return. Yet for a few more milliseconds there was still no outward sign of the impending disaster. Because at that precise moment the destructive power was still, just about, being contained within the shell. The original makers of the shell had been ruthlessly exact in their calculations. They hadn't wanted all the heat and the pressure to burst out too soon. No, they'd designed the casing to be strong enough to resist its own demise for as long as possible – long enough for the force of the imminent explosion to have reached its absolute zenith. And only then did it break free.

The mortar disintegrated into a million pieces of metal that hurtled away from the seat of the blast. There would be no dodging them. Not at the immense speed they were travelling – as much as several thousand metres per second. The fragments were followed by the blast wave. It radiated from the epicentre of the explosion even faster than the splinters of the bomb casing, at a velocity many times the speed of sound. For good measure there was a heat wave too. And a hell of a lot of noise.

Because the mortar had been buried only just below the

surface of the track the soldier had been walking on, most of the energy was funnelled skywards, following the path of least resistance, up through the thin veneer of the Afghan desert. It took with it bucketloads of dirt and grit.

In the moment the explosion mushroomed clear of the ground, both of the soldier's legs were shredded. It was as if someone had furiously rubbed them up and down a giant cheese grater, not stopping until the white of the bone was clearly visible through the bloody, ragged remains of human tissue. If the soldier had had the chance to take in what was happening to him, then he might have been tempted to count his blessings, pleased at least that both of his lower limbs remained anchored to the rest of his body. But he would have been wrong to do so. Already they were useless to him; indeed they were hardly recognisable as legs. There was little or no skin left to speak of, and much of the mass and most of the definition of the muscle had gone too, hacked off by supersonic, super-sharp pieces of twisted metal. That which remained had become blackened in places – charred, seared by the extreme temperature that accompanied the blast. The torn remnants of skin and uniform had been similarly singed.

As the cuts of human meat, some minuscule, others the size of a hand, were hacked off the bone, other fragments of the bomb now buried themselves deep inside the ragged flesh that remained. They also tunnelled into the man's thighs and groin, peppering the muscle. For good measure the billowing cloud of dust then further contaminated the wounds.

The blast wave continued running up the length of the victim's torso, forcing its way under his body armour, eventually tearing it off. The two removable, protective ceramic plates worn to the front and back of the armour had already been blown from their pouches, and now, as projectiles, they had become part of the problem rather than the cure.

By this stage the soldier's weapon had been ripped from his

right hand, then the hand and the arm were flayed as the legs had been.

As the blast reached his head, it got beneath the rim of his helmet, and forced it off, the chinstrap of the MK6A offering only limited resistance before giving way. There was also massive damage inflicted on the man's throat and jaw. A large piece of shrapnel – or maybe it was the plate from the body armour – had torn out his voice box and smashed his chin. A fold of skin now hung limply from his cheek. Even if he had wanted to call out for help, to scream in pain, he wouldn't have been able to do so.

There was also the damage done that you'd struggle to see. The force of the explosion had caused serious internal injuries. The soldier's eardrums burst. So too did the blood vessels in his eyes. His lungs probably collapsed as the blast wave rippled through his body. By now he was no longer in contact with the ground. Instead, he and his barely attached limbs were sailing through the air, tumbling and turning, before crashing back to earth. He was flung a good ten metres from the point of detonation.

The very worst thing of all was that – despite everything – he was still alive.

Eyes rolling; trickles of blood seeping from his ears, nose and mouth; torrents of thick red blood pumping from at least three severed arteries; he was still alive.

And conscious.

In the immediate aftermath of the attack, the medic did a heroic job of trying to treat the soldier, applying tourniquets, inserting a drip, giving morphine. And then it was a case of clock-watching, waiting for the IRT helicopter to arrive. Knelt down alongside the casualty, the medic held on to the soldier's remaining good hand, offering what comfort he could, reassuring him everything would be all right. Except it wouldn't.

Because twenty minutes after he had detonated the bomb,

the soldier succumbed to his horrendous injuries, the lifeblood finally drained out of him, away into the dust.

The brutally dispassionate message went out over the radio: 'UK Bravo now KIA.'

That is the reality of killed in action. For some, death comes mercifully quickly. They are the lucky ones. But for others dying is an agonising, lingering, terrifying experience. Their last on earth.

Now, where were we? Ah yes. How did Chelsea get on against Man U?

TWELVE

FUCKIN' AFGHANS

SIGNALLER DAN ANDREWS, 216 SIGNAL SQUADRON

27 AUGUST 2008

There's war.

And then there's murder.

And in between I suppose there are the grey areas, occasional events in the fog of conflict when a split-second decision can later be picked apart and concluded to be fractionally to one side or the other of legality. There are likely to be mitigating circumstances; explanations for doing what one did, which justify actions or at least make them understandable.

But this wasn't one of those cases. There was no ambiguity here. This was crystal-clear. This was a cold-blooded killing. Murder, through and through.

I looked down at the body again. The man wasn't a casualty of war. He was a victim of crime. Death is an occupational hazard for soldiers, they know about it, fear it, expect it; the majority escape it. Occasionally some succumb to it. Their loved ones grieve; their colleagues mourn and move on. For those left behind, there is a crumb of comfort to be clung on to; the knowledge that the dead have been taken in the heat of battle, doing what they were trained to do, aware of the possible consequences. Whatever the squalid, nasty reality of fighting and dying, there is awareness that being killed in the face of the enemy is just part of the job description.

But this . . . this was a million miles from that.

This was an execution.

An execution of a prisoner, of someone who – even amidst the violence and chaos of southern Afghanistan – would have expected to survive, not least when he saw that amongst his Afghan National Army captors were British soldiers. He might have been prepared for some abuse from the ANA. A bit of roughing-up perhaps; a hands-on interrogation maybe. But to be shot dead? Jesus fucking Christ. What a mess.

A rage surged through my veins. I wanted to scream and shout. At that moment I wanted to raise my own gun and shoot those who had just cut down a man in my charge without a second thought.

I couldn't take my eyes off the corpse. His hair and beard were matted with blood and dirt. His tunic had been ripped apart by the bullets, the material around the holes stained crimson. The left arm was contorted at a wild angle, completely unnatural. In life it would have been unbearably painful – now it was just another sign of his violent death.

But it was his face that most vividly portrayed the brutality of his departure. Or what was left of his face.

It was as if the prisoner's head had been cleaved with an axe, the blow first splitting his skull down the middle, from the crown to the bridge of the nose, before veering diagonally to the left; the blade passing just above the eye, skimming his cheekbone and then exiting halfway through his ear, leaving his brain exposed to the elements. Already the fleshy mass – that which hadn't been scythed away – was darkening, drying and shrivelling in the heat, the healthy pink hue giving way to a ghastly grey. Folds of skin hung limply around the cavernous wound, their skeletal support blasted away.

I was totally stunned, desperately trying to work out what to do next. This had come out of nowhere, out of the clear blue Afghan sky. Everything had been going so well.

The plan for that day involved moving into the Green Zone and pushing south to make ourselves known to the locals in an area where we believed the enemy to have a number of outposts. There would be two platoons – each one consisting of twenty men from the ANA, three British soldiers from the OMLT and one member of the American ETT. (The transatlantic relationship had warmed significantly, as by this stage Oliver and Samuel had been replaced during a normal rotation of troops. I was glad to see the back of them and no doubt they were glad to see the back of me.) And then it got more complicated still. A pair of Danish Leopard 2 tanks – sent up in support from FOB Armadillo – would be positioned on the high ground running above the Green Zone to offer support if necessary. With them would be two Danish command vehicles – armoured Piranhas – and for good measure a British fire support team (FST A), made up of Sven and Karl; their job, as usual, to call in indirect fire when we needed it.

As for me, well, I stuck close to the Afghan company commander and a second FST – comprising the other half of Sven's four-man gang.

Although I would be making the decisions on the ground, technically the responsibility for mentoring the ANA troops still fell to the Americans. We Brits were only there to back up our Yank colleagues because they still didn't have enough men to support the Afghans.

The ANA commander had been briefed about the mission the night before. Without much enthusiasm he noted down the start time, how many men he needed to bring and how this multinational force was going to be divided up.

He was told we'd leave the camp gates at 14:00 hrs.

As H hour approached we all made our final preparations.

I loaded myself up with kit, variously clipping, hanging and packing gear into and on to the pouches and slings attached to my Osprey body armour and belt:

1 × Personal Role Radio
2 × red phosphorous smoke grenades
2 × L109 HE grenades
1 × pack of mini flares
1 × green signal smoke
1 × Sig Sauer 9mm pistol in the drop holster on my thigh
4 × spare magazines, two on my belt and two on the left
    side of the body armour
1 × medical kit containing two field dressings, two
    tourniquets and a couple of morphine syrettes. The kit
    was on the right side of my body armour, carried in
    the same place as every other soldier in the battlegroup,
    so it could be found immediately by others if the worst
    happened
1 × bayonet on my back
1 × daysack with another radio – the Bowman 353 VHF
    set – water and yet more ammunition in it.

Weighed down like a packhorse, I still had a few minutes until it was time to leave. Every soldier has a different routine, a different ritual, they follow before going to war. Some write letters. Others have a cup of tea and a cigarette. A few check their weapons for the umpteenth time. For Ranger Q it involved putting on some of his bloody music. As I'd already discovered, Bob Marley was a favourite. So too was Kenny Rogers. Rather than pump you up, though, it mellowed you out – and perhaps that was no bad thing.

As for me, I took a few minutes to slump on my cot and think about what might lie ahead. To do so brought me to the verge of being physically sick, the responsibility of taking these men – most of them young, all of them looking to me for guidance – only adding to the physical weight already on my shoulders.

The patrol moved off, Stevo taking the lead as he always did, even though I repeatedly urged him to let the ANA go first. With him and the Afghans went nineteen-year-old Dan Andrews, a signaller, and Q. I followed with my two-man fire support team, Bombardiers Kev Penny and Morgs Armstrong. Last came Bugsy with his ANA group. The Danes and their Leopard 2 tanks had been in position for about an hour now, above us and to the west. Sven was there too.

Within five minutes we were at that stark transition point where the desert abruptly gave way to life. One by one men disappeared through the green curtain and into another world. Bayonets fixed, the advance continued through eight-, nine-, ten-foot-high stems of corn, so dense you could see no more than a couple of metres ahead. Hemmed in and without reference points, disorientation could have been a big problem, but technology ensured otherwise. I looked down at my watch, except it wasn't a watch – it was a small GPS device strapped to my wrist; the ultimate backup to my trusty map and compass.

Navigation-wise, our journey could have been made easier still if we had stuck to the small tracks which dissected the fields; however, the threat of pressure-point IEDs was so great we were all happy to take our chances amongst the corn. The same went for the watercourses we encountered. Whilst they could be crossed by the numerous bridges and dykes, we preferred getting wet rather than risking being blown to pieces by a booby trap or mine.

Patrolling the Green Zone, there was never any question of staying dry. If you weren't soaked through from sweat, then you would be from water.

By now we had fanned out.

With Bugsy 400 metres out to the west, Stevo was making his way south, staying parallel with the Taliban's MSR, clearing the ubiquitous compounds as he went. Along the way he chatted to the locals, occasionally using his pidgin Pashtu, more often speaking through his interpreter. Asked when the Taliban had last been around, most Afghans lied.

Haven't seen any.

Not for weeks.

They never come round here.

It was all taken with a bucketload of salt and then Stevo would push the men on again. On towards trouble. Somewhere ahead of me a handful of shots rang out, accompanied by frenzied shouting from the ANA.

Stevo came over the PRR, talking back to base. 'Amber 92, this is Amber 92 Charlie. Warning shots. Wait. Out.'

I called him on the radio. 'What's happening, Stevo?'

'The ANA have taken a prisoner. They just walked up on two dickers* who tried to do a runner. They've caught one of them. He had a rifle and a radio.'

'Good. Make sure they search him and put the cuffs on. Then take him back to the company commander.'

Then I heard from Sven up on the high ground.

'Doug, I can see large numbers of civilians heading east. Mostly women and children, plus a few old men.'

There was only one reason why they would be clearing the area – the Taliban were about to attack. I started to feel nervous again, the sick feeling returned. I hated these moments. It was all but inevitable someone was about to shoot at us but it was impossible to know who they had in their sights. Was it my head they were aiming at? That of the man next to me? The one behind? There was no way of knowing until it happened. And by then it might be too late.

---

* The term dicker is a throwback to British operations in Northern Ireland. Patrols would be constantly watching for republican lookouts; men, women and children who just dicked around on street corners ready to pass information about the movements of troops back to their IRA masters.

Without warning, my questions were answered. An RPG snaked through the undergrowth, fired from a compound no more than eighty metres ahead of us. It flew past us. I was still alive. Then the enemy opened up with small-arms fire. Everyone dived for cover.

I fumbled for the switch on my PRR that allowed me to send a message over the VHF radio system. 'Amber 92, this is Amber 92 Alpha. Contact. Wait. Out.'

Reporting an engagement had become a well-worn procedure for me. And it set off a tried-and-tested train of events, involving a veritable army of acronyms. Amber 92 would send the initial contact report to the Danish HQ, who in turn would pass it on to the Task Force Helmand HQ in Lashkar Gah. The JTAC in FOB Armadillo would be requesting air support, as Sven scanned for targets to relay back to the fire-planning cell, also at the FOB, so we could get indirect fire support from the 105mm artillery pieces.

As for me, I was face down in the dirt, working out how we were going to get out of the shit. Cautiously I raised my head to try and see exactly where the enemy positions were, but all too soon a torrent of lead came my way and I was back, flat on the ground. 'Stevo, get the ANA into a line along this stream and have them clear the cornfield with fire.'

I started crawling to try to find a better position to direct operations from. As I got an improved view of proceedings, I turned to Morgs. 'I need indirect fire on that tree-line to the south-east. Grid 644325. If the enemy thinks we are going to hit their line of withdrawal, it might focus their minds and encourage them to get out sooner rather than later.'

I thrust my map under Morgs's face. 'Once you've got the initial fire down I want you to adjust it to this compound here.' I gestured to a point on the paper marked GF2-2.

As for Bugsy, he was still out to the west and that's where I wanted him to stay.

'Cover our flank and be prepared to move on my command.'

Fire continued to whip towards us from the south and south-east. I didn't find it easy to identify where the enemy was firing from, but somehow the ANA troops had a knack for doing so.

We were starting to make some impression on the enemy but our rate of fire still wasn't as heavy as the incoming. Amidst the noise of our SA80s and the Afghan Kalashnikovs, the heavier bursts of a GPMG broke through. It was Q. He might have been our medic but he was never one to miss out on the action and the machine gun was his weapon of choice. He would wave the eleven-kilogram piece of kit around as if it were a twig.

'Boss, shot, heads down!' It was Morgs warning me the first shell was on its way from one of the two 105mm guns back at Armadillo.

'Get down!' I shouted.

The round landed some 600 metres away, but gave me a real sense of destructive power and was as comforting to me as it must have been hellish to the enemy.

'Morgs, bring the gun in and hit that tree-line. And stand by for a second target. It's all yours now. Just get the fuckers.'

Stevo was making his way along the course of the stream, stopping by each Afghan soldier to make sure they knew what they were doing. Just a few metres away from me lay the Afghan officer. I shouted to him. In return he gave a big smile and held up the arms of the bound prisoner, who was trying to take cover next to him.

'Alpha 15, can you see any targets?' I said to the tank commander over the VHF.

'Can't identify any enemy, you are just too deep in the Green Zone for us to be certain who is who. Can you mark your position?'

I pulled at a pack of mini flares and fired a couple directly above my head, the green light arcing high into the sky, a white tail snaking away behind it.

Fighting from the walls of Attal. Map in hand, with Sven close by, I'm calling in indirect fire whilst the others engage the enemy at close range.

Morgs and Sven look down at the IED they unwittingly lay on top of. If it had detonated this would have been their final resting place.

Patrolling from Kansas to Oz – the Green Zone.

The guys pose on a Danish tank. Q is on the left with Jon Kerr, Robbo and Crocky in the middle.

Down time in Attal.

A Russian-built Hip helicopter piloted by civilians. At Attal this became our lifeline to the outside world.

A Danish Leopard 2 tank in the Upper Gereshk Valley.

Morgs and Q.

Stevo in the Green Zone. Note the customised badge on his arm.

The claustrophobia and fear of the Green Zone. Karl Shields patrols with bayonet fixed, the strain evident on his face.

Morgs.

Sven completing a radio check before another excursion to Oz.

Target indication at its most basic. If lost for words, just point.

The capture of a suspected Taliban fighter.

British soldiers stand around the body of the prisoner after he has been
murdered by ANA troops.

My last patrol in the Green Zone, just moments before my final contact in Helmand, close to Attal.

After Attal. My team just prior to departing Afghanistan. Bugsy is top right.

Civilian life. Twenty-seven years fighting done, it's now time for my family and new grandson.

'Got you. We will continue to scan for targets.'

Now Morgs was screaming at me again, asking for details of the second target. I had to decide what our objective was.

We seemed to be holding our own and I decided this was an opportunity to push the ANA forward. What normally happened at Attal and across the rest of Helmand was that we would pound enemy positions with air-strikes, indirect fire and anything else we had to hand. Then when the enemy had stopped shooting we would withdraw. But not this time. We were going to assault the Taliban's defences. My decision was in part made by the information we had got from the prisoner, who was now singing like a canary, telling us what the enemy's strength was and where they were holed up. I was sceptical about everything he said, but it was worth taking a chance on.

A second 105mm fire mission was now under way and this time the rounds were landing a lot closer.

'Stevo, when the artillery stops we are going to advance through the cornfield.'

'Roger, Boss,' came the slightly hesitant reply.

'Morgs, as we advance I want another fire mission on that tree-line.'

Two more shells landed on the compound at the end of the trees. The sound died down to almost nothing.

'OK, let's go.'

Immediately Stevo, Q and Dan were on their feet, but amongst the Afghans not much was happening. They seemed happy to stay where they were, their way of judging the success of a mission being based pretty much solely on returning to base safely. I had an element of sympathy with their point of view, but at the end of the day we were soldiers, there to fight, not to flee, and more than anybody it is a commander's job to set an example.

'Come on, let's fuckin' move!' With that I too scrambled to my feet and waded through the stream.

Slowly the ANA troops started to do the same. They would have to get a move on – as would I. Already the younger members of 1 R IRISH were putting some distance between themselves and us. The skirmish didn't last long. With increasing zeal the Afghans moved through the field and towards the compound. Faced with a trapped enemy they used their RPGs to clear buildings and rooms without compunction. The result was devastating, at least for the six Taliban who were killed. And our success wasn't just confirmed by the body count. We also recovered several weapons, including a prized RPG and two PKMs, and a pair of radios.

Now the prisoner was giving us more information, about an arms cache he said was hidden in another, apparently unmanned, compound another fifty metres south of where we now were.

'Stevo, I want Q and a couple of the ANA guys to go and investigate.'

A moment later they were off. As well as being fearless and compassionate, Q was also pretty switched-on. As he reached the front of the compound and carried out his checks, he found an unwanted surprise. The Taliban had placed a mine in the frame of the door; a pair of wires connecting it to a pressure pad hastily hidden under some loose soil and old stalks of corn. One step on the pad and – boom – we would have been scraping up bits of our medic and putting them in a bag.

'Boss, I've got an IED,' Q said quietly in his unique Fijian-Ulster accent.

He asked whether I wanted to come and see his discovery.

'Do I, fuck,' I replied with a genuine lack of appetite for his offer, quite happy enough to send a report – a so-called ten-liner – about the device back to HQ without setting eyes on the offending item.

It was time for us to call it a day. We had ridden our luck and I wasn't going to push it further; anyway, we had been successful. We'd killed a number of the enemy and recovered some of their equipment. Crucially the ANA had – eventually – stepped up to the mark and done the job. We'd even taken a prisoner, though, as I looked round at him, I could see he was taking a bit of punishment from one of his captors.

'Oi! Don't be doing that,' I shouted.

The soldier meting out the blows gave me a quizzical look and wandered off.

We started to pull out, covered by Bugsy and more thundering shells from Armadillo.

As we covered the ground and entered another field of corn, the dull crumps faded from my ears, to be replaced by the sound of men crashing through the crops, heading west, out of the Green Zone towards the openness and relative safety of the desert.

We were heading for a small, dry wadi that cut into the high ground flanking the western side of the valley floor. From there we would be able to see back towards the tangle of crops we were now trying to escape from.

The exertion of the fighting had left me drenched with sweat; rivulets of perspiration followed the paths of least resistance down my head, back, chest.

As I barged between the stalks, pieces of foliage clung to my face, like pollen sticking to the legs of a bumblebee. Close by were Morgs and Kev. Somewhere ahead was Stevo and his group.

'Stevo,' I said over the PRR. 'Slow down a bit. Every time you go off at speed, the Afghans are running and bunching up after you and we're getting left behind.'

'OK, Boss,' came the reply. I could hear the exhaustion in the voice, the culmination of two hours of mental and physical effort. 'I'll slow down and then stop when I get to the mouth of the wadi, then call you in from there.'

It wasn't that I was scared of getting lost, just that I didn't want the Afghan soldiers with Stevo – high on adrenalin, and trigger-happy at the best of times – taking a decision to shoot us as we emerged from the undergrowth in a possibly different place to them.

My own high, brought on by the contact with the Taliban, was fading fast and I was getting nervous again – I always was with the Afghans around me. No matter we were there to lead and teach them – and that they had done well that day – the chance of them acting unpredictably, on a whim, was a constant danger.

The ANA soldiers with Stevo also had our prisoner. They were leading him back to Attal and due process. Once there we would question him ourselves for more local intelligence, then pass him back to a holding facility at Camp Bastion. Finally he would be handed over to the Afghan National Directorate of Security.

From what I had seen a few minutes earlier, I was worried the ANA would be more hands-on with our captive than I might like, but I was close by and anyway it wasn't far back to Attal.

'For fuck's sake, which way did Stevo go?'

'No idea, Boss,' came Morgs's reply. I looked back at him. He was bent forward, head down, his hands resting on his knees, trying to take some of the weight of the TacSat radio off of his back.

'Right, then, we're heading straight for the wadi.' I warned Stevo we had lost contact with him and were making a bee-line for the dry watercourse. 'Whatever you do, don't let those Afghan soldiers fire due east.'

Then I passed on our movements back to the signaller working at the Danish battlegroup HQ at Gereshk. 'Sierra 60, this is Amber 92 Alpha. We have broken contact and are heading west out of the Green Zone. Roger so far.'

'Roger, over.'

I started to tell him the locations of the other two groups of British soldiers.

A burst of gunfire cut me short.

All three of us instinctively ducked as three, four, five shots – probably from a Kalashnikov – rang out from the direction of the wadi.

A moment later and there was more firing. This time at least twenty-five rounds from heavier weapons.

'Wait. Out.' I cut the signaller off.

'Stevo, what the hell is going on?' There was panic in my voice.

Instead it was Sven who answered. 'They've shot the prisoner. The Afghans, they've bloody shot him.'

'What, say again?' I couldn't quite believe what I was hearing.

The story didn't change at the second time of telling. 'They've just killed him.'

I waded through the field for a few more metres before emerging out of the shadows into the harsh glare of the desert. We weren't far from the mouth of the wadi – and the body now lying in it. Dan was crouched beside it.

'How did it happen?'

Without turning he told me, his voice full of emotion. 'Fuckin' Afghans, they used a knife to cut off the plastic ties around his wrists and then shot him.'

'Where were you at the time?' Instantly I regretted the question.

It sounded accusatory.

'I told them to stop, but what could I do? One of them pointed a gun at me, while the others killed the prisoner. Then they ran off.'

Stevo had come to join us. He filled in a little more of the detail. Not that there was much to say. It had all happened so quickly. The ANA soldiers had dragged the prisoner behind a rock and one had stepped forward to execute him, the volley of shots spinning him round and leaving him lying face down in the dust. There was no hesitation, no discussion, no qualms. And who had pulled the trigger? Only their fucking medic. Using his AK47 the one Afghan supposed to actually save life had happily taken one. At this point Dan was still struggling to intervene but was held back at gunpoint. And the criminal activity wasn't over. Four more ANA members had moved in and from a range of no more than a few metres simultaneously opened fire with their heavier PKMs. The young man had twitched violently as the fusillade ripped into him, peppering his back and demolishing his skull, churning up the ground around and beneath him. Then they disappeared, smiling as they went, shouting 'Allah Akbar' – God is great.

Too late, Dan was free to try and help. With one hand on the victim's shoulder he had turned him over, before recoiling from the sight that greeted him.

'Fuckin' Afghans,' Stevo said as he finished his story. Fucking Afghans indeed.

None of us standing there was sparing a thought for the Taliban or the contact we had just been involved in. It was as if it had never happened; it had been erased from our memory. How can you think about the enemy when your allies have just done this? We were supposed to be on the same bloody side. Even Bugsy and his team, still stuck in the Green Zone – aware of the shooting, but unaware of what had caused it and why – were briefly banished from my mind.

I was completely shocked. In twenty-seven years of soldiering I had never come across anything like it. I had never considered something like this could happen. It was so far beyond my comprehension. Murdering a prisoner. For God's sake.

All right, I realised this particular group of Afghans could be a handful. Based in Kabul, supporting counter-narcotics operations was their thing. Here in Helmand, being used to take and hold ground, they were out of their depth, short on leadership, training and discipline, and the ETT had been struggling to keep them in line. But even so, how had these Afghans gone from being a group of disobedient and hot-headed soldiers to a bunch of murderers? For that is what they'd become.

What the fuck was I going to do?

The killers were goodness knows where, certainly out of sight. I couldn't pull myself away from the mangled remains.

'Stevo, secure the area while I get on the radio to Price.'

I called FOB Price to tell them the grim news. 'Sierra 60, I need you to speak to Amber 95 and find out exactly where we stand in relation to what's happened, given that we've just witnessed a murder.'

It was a surreal moment.

Here I was in the middle of a battlefield asking for legal advice. 'Do we go after those who did it and what should we do with the body? And I need to know quickly.'

'Roger, wait. Out.'

The radio went silent and I slumped to the ground, my back sliding down the rock behind which the atrocity had been committed. I looked down at my fatigues, darker below the waist than above, still soaking wet and heavy, despite the temperature, from the numerous irrigation ditches and streams we had waded through during the day. I let my head sink into my hands, trying to rub the frustration and anger out of my eyes. How had it come to this? For five months we had trained and tutored and mentored and advised, trying to equip the ANA with the skills and standards necessary for them to provide security for their country and its population. At that moment, the prospect of such a thing happening was about a million light years away. These people were never going to preside over a just system. Look at what they were capable of. What a waste of time. I glanced up and saw the blokes around me were thinking exactly the same thing.

We sat there and waited to hear back from Amber 95 – Major Dave Harrison. Dave had a wonderful ability not to pester his men whilst they were out on the ground, but to let them get on with the job in hand, safe in the knowledge they could call on his help and advice when necessary. Quite what his advice would be now I couldn't wait to hear.

Dave came back on to the radio network. 'Legally this is not your problem. It is an Afghan issue. You are to return to base immediately. Do not talk to the ANA. I don't want to take the risk they'll turn on you. As for the body, it stays where it is, but take as many photos as you can.'

This last request was easier to carry out than might have been thought. Part of our group comprised an American free-lance journalist who had been with us for the last six days. What a story he had.

Despite the major's reassurance that no blame was attached to me or my men, I couldn't shake the thought that I was in some way responsible. Should I have seen it coming after the rough treatment I'd witnessed just half an hour earlier? It didn't matter that he was the enemy and had sent Q to a com-pound he probably knew to be booby-trapped. He was murdered by the Afghans and I was mentoring them.

I dragged my mind back to those around me. We needed to get moving. As we headed up the slope away from the Green Zone, the enemy opened up with some sporadic small-arms fire. Given their distance from us, it was speculative shooting, but no matter, a poorly aimed bullet can kill just as easily as a well-aimed one. At last there was something for the Danish Leopards to do and they opened up with their BFGs; Big Fucking Guns. As they engaged the enemy Bugsy and his team finally made it to the open ground of the desert.

As we progressed back to Attal we were attacked twice more, and twice more the tanks went into action.

But even these skirmishes I couldn't really take seriously. My mind dwelled on what had happened. We had achieved a victory of sorts but I was feeling like a beaten man. The Afghans had spent three hours putting their lives on the line, trying to make a difference to their country, carrying out actions they should have been proud of, and then this. In a few seconds any respect I might have had for them had gone. And through my role as their mentor I was part of what went on. For five months I had been in Afghanistan, fighting and surviving. Through all the blood and bullets, the dead and the wounded, the sickening sights, I wanted to believe I had done some good and changed things for the better. Now I seriously wondered whether I could ever make any difference, whether anyone could? What was the fucking point of being here? What was the point of risking my life, of risking anything, for a country that at that moment didn't seem worth saving – perhaps couldn't be saved?*

---

* The Afghan medic who carried out the killing was actually back out on patrol with us the next morning. It was only several days later that he was finally withdrawn from Attal. Dan Andrews was also withdrawn from Attal for his own safety in case of any retaliation by the ANA.

THIRTEEN

SMELLING OF LAVENDER

RANGER MARK 'ROBBO' ROBINSON, 1 R IRISH

29 AUGUST 2008

It was the strangest thing. There I was – there we were, British soldiers – in Attal, trying to stay alive, and yet half of my bloody time was spent not worrying about the enemy's bombs and bullets, but rather what my allies were up to. I wouldn't have believed the military equivalent of office politics would play itself out on the battlefield, but there it was. Every time I thought my disillusionment with the Americans couldn't get any greater, it did, despite the change in personnel.

We were all out on a patrol. Us. Them. And the Afghans. And from the start it was clear to me the US ETT had lost it. They stood back as the ANA soldiers acted with impunity, doing what they wanted, when they wanted. If the Afghans had displayed a bit of initiative fighting the enemy, then everything would have been fine, but no, that day they were working to their own agenda, and it had little to do with taking on the Taliban. At this particular moment they happened to be looting a shop. And the ETT clearly had next-to-no idea how to halt it.

'Stop or we will dock your pay!'

Not much of a threat given most of the Afghans hadn't been paid for several months anyway.

'We will tell your commanders.'

It was the commanders who were leading the free-for-all.

'We will have you removed from Attal.'

This was the most meaningless threat of all, because that's what the Afghans wanted – to get the fuck out of Attal.

Though, as it turned out, it was the Americans who were about to leave in pretty short order. This was how their CO explained their departure.

'With the loss of a couple of men, I need to consolidate my guys back at FOB Sandford. We simply don't have enough resources to support Attal.'

And that was that – off they went, taking a few more Afghan soldiers with them. Despite the depleted manpower I actually saw this as an opportunity. Ramadan – the ninth month of the Islamic calendar, revered as the time the Koran was first revealed to the prophet Mohammed, and during which Muslims are expected to fast between sunrise and sunset – was just about to start and would limit the number of hours the enemy were likely to be out on the ground. Which meant we had a chance to fill the vacuum they'd leave behind.

But I soon discovered my plan had a rather large flaw. The ANA would also be observing Ramadan. They had been ordered not to patrol in the Green Zone until it was over. This meant they looked set not to leave the base for at least another four weeks, which was about the time we were due to hand over Attal to the incoming unit. It was ludicrous.

I sent my observations up the chain of command. Dave Harrison burned the midnight oil trying to get the senior Afghan officers to review their decision. But they wouldn't budge.

I had my own decisions to make. Attal was not just a sand-bag wall behind which to hide as we were attacked. It was a patrol base and that title gave a pretty big clue as to what we were supposed to be doing there. We also had a responsibility to soak up, and then respond to, Taliban pressure. If we didn't, then Sandford, Armadillo and Gereshk itself would get targeted more frequently as the enemy became emboldened. Our duty was not just to stand our ground, but to try and extend it.

But now, contributing to making this even harder still, was the fact that our lines of supply were looking increasingly vulnerable.

Because of the threat of IEDs, the Danes essentially viewed Attal as a no-go area unless they were travelling in armoured vehicles. On every occasion they had come to the PB over the past three weeks there had been an IED strike. The worst incident was on 25 August when a re-supply column leaving Attal hit a mine. The damage appeared relatively minor. A badly broken femur for the commander of the vehicle involved but at least he'd live. Or so it was thought. He was brought back to Attal to be put on an IRT helicopter to take him to Bastion for treatment. But during the flight he died. Unknown to the medics who first treated him, he had struck his skull on the cab roof and this caused severe internal injuries. The death of Sergeant First Class Henrik Christian Christiansen affected us deeply. It also curtailed many logistical patrols and general movement to and from the base by road in anything much less than Leopard 2 tanks.

We came to rely on a civilian helicopter to provide us with the most basic supplies – food, water, etc. An ancient and weathered Russian-made Hip, it was piloted by Romanian and Bulgarian civilian crews contracted in for the job. It was not employment for the faint-hearted.

I gathered my men together so they would be under no illusions about what I intended to do over the coming days and weeks. I had already primed Sven and got his support. 'OK, this is where we are. The American ETT has fucked off. We only have fifty-five ANA left, and even they aren't going to be going out for a while. But I still intend that we – Brits – keep patrolling. That means two four-man teams out in the Green Zone but close enough to the PB to get some support if needed.'

I looked at the faces of the men surrounding me. I could see they understood exactly what I was saying – outnumbered and outgunned we would still be taking the fight to the enemy.

'What we need to do is stay flexible,' I continued. 'Stay off the tracks, use the corn to our benefit, never let the enemy know just how small we are in number. We will go as far as the MSR, and dominate it and the neighbouring compounds. Treat the ground as if it were ours; display no hesitation to the Taliban. I'll also speak to Gereshk about more men. Any questions?'

I was sure there would be none.

'Happy?' I gave them another chance to raise objections.

Still silence.

'OK, then, first patrol out is tomorrow morning at 08:00 hrs, to the MSR. More details to follow.'

And that was it.

The next day, a few minutes after eight, two small units of British soldiers dropped off the high ground down through Star Wars Wadi and melted into the Green Zone – the heart of enemy territory. One team was led by Bugsy. With him went Crocky, Jon Kerr and Ranger Mark 'Robbo' Robinson from Lisburn. The other team was under Stevo's command and comprised Q, Morgs and Kev Penny. Me, I floated between the two. Sven and Karl were back on the high ground at Attal with a grandstand view of the valley.

Surrounded by dense, lush foliage, it was all we could do to stay in contact with each other. Continually, using the PRR, we reported our relative positions. Progress was slow. It was gut-wrenching, nerve-racking stuff. Each time I parted more stalks of corn I expected to be confronted by the enemy. And there was plenty of time to conclude that my actions were stupid, reckless, downright dangerous even. Had my exuberance got the better of me? The sweat was flowing freely now, the fear of being killed and the fear of having fucked up competing for dominance.

We went firm in the middle of a huge field full of maize. As I breathed deeply to try and catch my breath, I also inhaled a particularly sickly scent, one I was sure I recognised.

I turned round to confront Robbo. 'What the hell is that smell?'

'Lavender,' Robbo retorted.

'What?'

'Lavender, Boss. We are a patrol smelling of lavender.'

Now that I had noticed the smell it seemed to intensify. There's often a great deal of debate over just how much the Great British public cares about what its soldiers are doing in their name, or indeed whether it has any interest in their welfare. Well, I can't vouch for everyone but there is certainly one group who has our best interests at heart – ladies of a certain age with time on their hands. Now I might be stereotyping slightly, however I imagine they mostly live in the shires and are steeped in the finest traditions of this country. They are women who recognise and appreciate a sense of duty and responsibility amongst others in society, women who perhaps care less about the politics of the situation in Afghanistan and more about the hardships endured by those sent there to do their country's bidding. And to show their appreciation they send endless supplies of goodies: predominantly tissues, toothpaste, mints . . . and shower gel, mostly Tesco and ASDA own-brand, and almost without fail lavender-scented. And as our supplies of army-issue kit became depleted, these modern-day equivalents of the food parcel that had remained relatively untouched were being dug into with increasing relish.

'Fuck me. The stony-faced dealers in death reeking of lavender! The enemy will fuckin' die laughing.'

We carried on deeper into the Green Zone. Keeping well in amongst the crops I was hopeful we hadn't been seen – or smelled. But we were almost at the MSR and would have to reveal ourselves to do the next bit of our job, establishing a vehicle checkpoint. In fact we positively wanted to be seen, at least by the locals. There was no point in getting this far from the base if none of the civilians were aware of it. We were actively trying to create a presence and appear to be a bigger force than we truly were. But it was a balancing act. Stand out too much in one place and for too long and we were going to attract the interest not just of the locals but also of the Taliban. And, as we had seen in Marjah, the enemy was able to organise an ambush very quickly. So I decided to follow the rule of thumb we had been taught in Northern Ireland way back when. No more than twenty minutes static in any one place and then out of there. I told the others.

There was another point to the VCP, other than just showing we weren't hiding behind the walls of Attal, and that was to gather intelligence for so-called key-leader engagements. We wanted to get information from those we stopped about the local big swinging dicks, the leaders and elders who decided to whom whole communities gave their allegiance – us or the enemy. They were the ones who were respected by the locals, the ones who were approached for guidance and advice. And they were the ones ISAF needed to talk to if there was to be any hope of winning over the resident population. What you hope to find out about these people are their tribal backgrounds and their position in the local political and social hierarchy. What contact do they have with the imams? Have they held meetings with the Taliban? What work do they do and where does their income come from? The knowledge gained, it would then be used by others to interact with these people and, if possible, to win them over. Sometimes, buy them over. But if there was no real expectation of co-operation, if they had already committed themselves to the enemy, if in fact they were the enemy and orchestrated attacks on ISAF forces, then they'd be arrested . . . or killed. At the end of the day there were really only two options for dealing with these leaders – targeted talks or targeted strikes.

Not that our little operation was going to yield much intelligence – certainly not in a mere twenty minutes – but you were never sure, it might just fill in a few blanks in the bigger picture. And what didn't seem relevant to us could be key for those whose job it was to fit the pieces of the jigsaw together.

Time was up, and after that only a fool would push his luck (I was one to talk).

Now I wanted to get back to base, before the Taliban could get their act together. The route was straightforward – north up the MSR until we hit the junction by the shop at compound 10 and then due west, out of Oz and back to Kansas.

But it wasn't easy to maintain speed, pushing through vegetation and crossing waterways. At each obstacle we would stop and then inch forward, team by team, one covering the other. There would only ever be a single man in the water at a time. Despite continually breaking our journey, I almost welcomed fording these barriers to our progress. Wading waist-deep through the cool, fast-flowing water offered some relief from the oppressive heat, even if there was always a real danger you'd get swept off your feet by the strong undercurrent. And whilst I didn't mind being half-wet, I was not in the mood to be completely soaked.

We were back in the desert, the confines of the Green Zone giving way to the expansiveness and far-reaching views of this wholly different landscape. Just 300 metres north of us lay Attal – we were on the last leg and I felt myself starting to relax, coming off the nervous high that had sustained me over the past couple of hours. We had got away with it. If my high-risk strategy had gone wrong, then it would have been my neck on the chopping block and rightly so. But nothing had gone wrong. We were as good as home and dry (figuratively speaking anyway).

I could see the ANA manning the walls of the PB, covering our final approach. Bugsy's team was in the lead and had just passed through the main gates, where they stopped and took up position to help see us in.

Now there were only 100 metres between me and a bottle of cold water from the overworked fridge.

The sound of firecrackers filled the air.

'Contact. Contact. Contact!' screamed Bugsy as the rounds whizzed over our heads and thumped and thudded into the HESCO just ahead of me.

The ANA were quick to respond. There was now heavy two-way traffic of lead with me, Stevo, Q, Morgs and Kev in the middle, trying to get out of the way. We half-ran, half-scrambled towards the gates. But with just thirty metres to go, the increasing volume of fire had us dropping for cover. I slithered around, desperately looking for a deep rut or dip in the sand in which to conceal myself. The others were doing the same. Off to my right, from the corner of my eye, I could see a handful of Afghan soldiers who had been manning the observation post just in front of the main base now standing in the open excitedly firing their AK47s and PKMs from the hip. Rather them than me. I attempted to squirm my way further into the landscape. I couldn't clearly see all the enemy firing points but this was the closest they had yet come to attacking the PB.

'Sven,' I shouted over the radio.

'Yeah, Doug, I have the enemy. They're in the wadi you have just come out of.'

'OK, mate, can you get fire into it?'

'I can but it is going to be danger close and I would rather you were in the compound before I called it in.'

That did it, then.

'OK, moving now,' I replied before yelling at Stevo. 'Mate, we'll have to make a run for the PB. We have fire coming in from the 105s.'

And with that we were all up and away in a mad dash to get into Attal.

Almost immediately someone said the word I had come to dread more than any other. 'Casualty!'

In the confusion, the sound of my heart pounding in my ear, I couldn't tell whether the call had come over the PRR or I'd heard one of the guys shout it out loud. A few seconds later and I was through the entrance to the PB. Diving to my right I collapsed behind the HESCO, gasping for air. Thank God, the other three guys were there, doing the same.

As I gathered my senses Sven rushed over. 'I need those Afghans out there back behind their sandbags before I call this in.'

'OK.'

Still trying to catch my breath I cried out to Bugsy, who by now was also up on the walls. 'Mate, get those fuckers to get down, will you.'

'Boss, one of them is wounded. They're trying to bring him in.'

'All right, but they had better get a move on because we're firing now. Sven, call it in.'

There were two low crumps as the guns in Armadillo fired, followed by two more – much louder this time – as the shells exploded just where we wanted them down in the wadi. Another pair of shells arrived from Armadillo. The Taliban shooting dried up, but Sven kept the pressure on. For good measure another four 105mm rounds whistled in and slammed into the dry watercourse.

As things calmed down I managed to take a look at the casualty. He was walking-wounded. Q led him away to the

OMLT section of the camp where we had built the medical shelter. A single high-velocity round had hit the Afghan in the upper arm. Incredibly painful for sure, but the good news was that it had missed the bone. Q bound the wound and gave the man a jab of morphine. I hoped it would stop him screaming.

'Fuck sake, Q, tell him to get a grip,' I said in my best bed-side manner.

As Q continued to work on his patient, I prepared the nine-liner. I would send it straight away but I would put in some delay timing. We were still in combat and I didn't want the IRT arriving under fire just for a gunshot wound to the arm. The Afghan could wait.

After another half an hour though, I closed the TiC. Having taken a pasting in the wadi the Taliban had disappeared back to whence they came. I sent an update to Sierra 60 and asked them to now dispatch the IRT as soon as possible, requesting the Chinook land at the HLS on the western edge of the camp.

Twenty-five minutes later and the evacuation team arrived.

As an Apache kept a watchful eye over the landscape from on high, the CH-47 came scudding in low over the horizon, crossed the perimeter and aimed for the green smoke I had thrown to mark the exact location for touchdown. As the air-craft came in and flared ready to land, it threw up the familiar storm of grit. I turned my back and shut my eyes. As the hail subsided we hauled the casualty – who was now on a stretcher – towards the gaping hole at the rear of the helicop-ter and then up the ramp. Q gave a handover to the staff on board and that was it. The Afghan had become someone else's problem.

We scurried back to the sandbag wall to wait for the Chinook to depart.

Which was when the Taliban decided to have another pop.

'Contact. Wait. Out,' came the call from Bugsy, who was in a covering position to the south of the HLS. The clattering of the aircraft's twin engines had drowned out the noise of the small-arms fire, but as I looked up I saw a tracer round scribing a gentle arc through the air over the top of the helicopter. Bugsy returned fire. As did Robbo.

'Two enemy have moved into the compound just below me. Am engaging.'

The Talibs had clearly turned their sights on bigger prizes, yet thankfully, with an agility and speed that belied its lumbering bulk, the Chinook was already away, keeping low, heading west at a breakneck rate of knots.

Loping along behind it, easily keeping pace, was the Apache.

The aircraft disappeared into the distance. And the further they got, the clearer I could hear the exchange of bullets between us and the enemy. But already it was becoming increasingly sporadic. With their main target now long gone, the Talibs had had enough.

Back in the ops room I closed the TiC – the second in just a couple of hours – and thought more about our obviously precarious position. It was a depressing business. The Taliban had got seriously close to the PB and been brazen enough to target the helicopter even though there was an Apache in the air. I had to face facts: despite my best efforts we didn't possess the manpower to really influence the locals or have a real effect on the enemy. For all the good I was trying to do, it was clear we were not winning the battle. All I could do was try and stop us losing it.

I needed help and I asked for it.

The response was that another OMLT would be sent to us from Gereshk. They would come in as part of an armoured patrol, but wouldn't arrive for at least another two days. Which left me with the same dilemma. Sit tight and risk getting picked off one by one, or do like we'd done that day – make our (albeit limited) presence felt. I chose the latter.

Which from a personal level was exactly what I didn't want to do.

In an ideal world I would have been quite happy to spend my days in the khazi. Not just because it was the most heavily fortified part of the PB, but because I had an extreme case of the shits. It had started off as diarrhoea and vomiting, but now it was only coming out of one end. Not that that made me feel a great deal better. It was almost completely debilitating and sapped what little energy I had. Yet there was no way I could sit out the patrols. I was the bloke in charge. I needed to set an example. Even if, more than once, that meant squatting in a cornfield, my trousers round my ankles, shit pouring from my arse as enemy rounds were flying all about. When you've got to go, you've got to go, and no way was I going to crap in my trousers. Funny how your priorities change. If there's little dignity in war, then there's absolutely no dignity in war whilst you've got the runs.

Our reinforcements arrived at last, the British OMLT led by one Captain Meddlines of the Royal Anglian Regiment. Amongst those in the convoy was the CO of the Danish battlegroup in Gereshk. I gave the Dane the full tour of the camp and told him exactly what we were facing on a daily basis.

He listened intently and at the end of my brief said something that went a long way to boost morale. 'Doug, you know you and your men are achieving more for me here than anyone else in the whole area of operation.'

Because we were bearing the brunt of the onslaught in the Upper Gereshk Valley, Armadillo had not been attacked and nor had Sandford. And life in the Gereshk DC was also improving. Obviously some people were feeling the benefit of us putting our lives on the line on a daily basis by continuing to patrol the Green Zone. All for the greater good, I suppose.

And the CO had more than just warm words. There was welcome news, too. He was deploying a troop of tanks to support us for a few days – it would be the same men who had been with us the previous month. For good measure an

ANA colonel was also about to visit us to try and work out how we could get the Afghans patrolling again. It looked like there was genuine interest in the work we were doing at Attal.

The only downside to the visit came on the convoy's return journey. Once again there was a mine strike and it was the CO's vehicle that was hit. Fortunately no one was seriously hurt. But it finally put paid to any movement by road. Our only way of getting stores into Attal was by the Hip helicopter (the unarmed, civilian-owned and -operated aerial packhorse) or the tanks when they arrived. Not that even the Leopards were immune to IEDs and mines. When one ran over a mine, the explosion killed the driver and badly damaged the vehicle, which careered on down the side of a hill. With no way of stopping it, the other two crew members were forced to bail out whilst it was still on the move, and both were injured doing so. I had also had my own close encounter with an IED. Out on patrol very early one morning, I took up position in a dip in the ground. It was still dark as I did my five-metre check – that is, a search of the ground immediately around me for signs of booby traps. In the murk I found a piece of flex protruding from the dust. To my mind it was a bit of discarded old wire. But as the sky lightened I examined it again and gently lifted it up out of the dust. It was the best decision I ever made. This was no offcut bit of cable. After a lifetime of searching for command wires, I realised I had actually found one. Fuck. One end ran off towards the Green Zone. The other seemed to head into a hollow where Morgs and Sven were lying, oblivious to my discovery. Fuck, fuck.

'Sven, move now, mate. I've got a command wire. Move!'

The pair must have been as surprised as I was because their reaction was slower than I would have liked. I was worried that right then, somewhere out of sight, a Talib was about to put his finger on the button. And boom. That would be that. I grabbed hold of the wire in both hands and pulled. The metal core and plastic sheath came apart. Then. Nothing. I stared at the two ends. Still nothing. We had got away with it. I could have screamed out loud, the tension lifting as quickly as it had descended.

'Hey, big man, I've just saved your life!' I shouted to Sven as he started to burrow down into the dirt to uncover the device and get a couple of snaps for the EODD.

'Guess I owe you a pint!' came the retort.

'Why don't we call it something eighteen years old and Scottish. And I don't mean a hooker.'*

But despite the threat from IEDs and my own close shave – despite supply problems – overall I was feeling more content with our situation than I had for a while. We now had extra Brits on hand and we were shot of the Americans. We were going to take the fight to the Taliban, get them to show themselves and have a good crack at them. Happy days. If only I could get rid of the shits too, then I really would be laughing.

9 SEPTEMBER 2008

I walked up to the wooden door in the high wall surrounding the village. It was already half-open. I crossed the threshold and stepped inside. Instantaneously I was in another world; a frantic, dangerous world of bombs and bullets, of men fighting for their lives against an enemy who in at least two places were no more than fifteen metres away. Grenade-throwing range. As if to prove the point, there were two large explosions as grenades hurled at the Taliban by Gordon 'Gordy' Mair (a sergeant from 4 SCOTS attached to 1 R IRISH and one of those recently arrived) and his team detonated. I

---

* When I did at last return home from Afghanistan, I found the eighteen-year-old was already there – a bottle of malt whisky sat on the table. The note attached to it read, 'Thank you for saving my brother's life'.

flinched as a cloud of dust and debris blossomed out from the seats of the blasts. To my right the wall that enclosed three sides of the village (I haven't a clue what the local name for it was, but we referred to it as GF1) ran away from me, only to end abruptly where cornfields began. Before the cornfields, there came several more compounds. Somewhere out there were several Talibs, firing furiously at our position. Their rounds were churning up the ground and smacking into the buildings behind us. We literally had our backs to the wall. Captain Meddlines and two of his men were returning fire, using everything at their disposal. SA80 rounds, 40mm grenades, L109 HE grenades. They were all being offloaded on to the enemy, with a vengeance. Some of the ordnance ripped through the crops in the field, and hopefully took out some of the enemy in their invisible positions, hidden amongst the foliage. But most of it was concentrated on the mud walls of the compounds much closer – no more than twenty metres away – that the Talibs were using to attack us from.

Risking a glance to my left I could see the alley where the initial contact had taken place and where 'Engineer Robbo' (not Ranger Mark 'Robbo' Robinson of 1 R IRISH, but a Royal Engineer also recently arrived with Captain Meddlines) and a couple of others were still involved in a fierce exchange.

The fighting had begun in the most bizarre fashion. Pushing through the same door I had just used to gain entry to the village, Engineer Robbo had warily started out down the track, hemmed in by big mud walls on either side. As he went he saw five, possibly six, men squatting down against the wattle and daub, all in a row. For some reason he thought they were locals. It was only when he was almost level with them he realised that what they had in their hands were not shovels and hoes but AKs and RPGs. The Talibs must have been as surprised as Engineer Robbo was – though, dressed in combats, with a light machine gun in his hands, and wearing the face of a foreigner, quite who they thought he was other than a British soldier, we'll never know. Astonishment got the better of them.

For another second or two not much happened as everyone tried to compute what the next step was going to be. It seems as if they all came up with the same answer. Suddenly it became a race to the death, the enemy raising their weapons. Outgunned and outnumbered, Engineer Robbo nevertheless had two advantages. He was already on his feet and he already had his finger on the trigger. Shouting out a warning to the rest of the patrol and stumbling back to try and put some distance between himself and the enemy, he pulled the crescent-shaped piece of metal at the bottom of his Minimi and a storm of 5.56mm rounds flew down the alley at a range of less than ten metres. Contained by the compounds forming the passageway, the deafening noise of gunfire reverberated from side to side. Some of the Taliban managed to get a few inaccurate shots away but the ferocity of Engineer Robbo's onslaught was devastating – and, that close, a lot of the bullets were going to find their target. Two of the enemy were already motionless down in the dirt and another had stopped firing, seemingly hit. The injured man and his unscathed colleagues desperately scrambled away. Engineer Robbo did the same thing, but in the opposite direction.

By the time I arrived there was a stand-off, the Taliban holding one end of the alley – darting in and out of cover to spray rounds along it – Engineer Robbo, Gordy and a couple more guys at the other.

Over the roar of the battle I shouted into the PRR. 'Stevo, hurry up with your men.'

Then I turned to Gordy, shouting again. 'What we got, mate?'

He was just about to answer when we were both inter-rupted – by an RPG snaking towards us. Fired from twenty metres away, there wasn't much time for us to get out of the way. Flying past it slammed into a compound wall, cratering it badly.

'About six to eight enemy shooting at the captain, and there must be another four down here,' he said, pointing towards the scene of Engineer Robbo's earlier good work.

'OK, just hold your ground until Stevo gets here and we can get some more guns into play.'

The radio was full of chatter and the sound of men crashing through the undergrowth surrounding the village to join the fight. There was also the disembodied voice of Sven up on the roof of a building, saying he could see more enemy fighters converging on GF1 from the south-east. Shouts and screams split the sky, fighting their own battle to be heard against the rattle of gunfire and the slapping and cracking noises of rounds fizzing overhead before smacking into something solid.

'Grenade!'

'Magazine!'

'Cover!'

'Get down!'

'Fuck me!'

'Watch the corn!'

'Stoppage!'

It was the vocabulary of war, being deployed by men frantically trying to maintain the toe-hold they had in the village. Come on, Stevo, where are you?

At last, after what seemed like an age, he appeared at the door and stepped through into hell, leaving behind the rich, vibrant, multicoloured landscape of the Green Zone and entering a stark black-and-white world of life and death.

Under orders from me, he replaced Engineer Robbo and Gordy, who moved over to support Captain Meddlines on the right flank.

I now had another decision to make. Consolidate, or advance and push the bastards back further.

'Stevo, Gordy, we are going to assault the enemy. Stevo, I

want you to get down the alley. Gordy, move along the open flank. Stevo will go first after the initial 105mm fire mission.'

I turned to Sven, who was now at my side, map in hand, calmly talking into the radio as enemy fire continued to rattle past.

I waited for a break in transmissions. 'All right, Sven, where did you see the enemy?'

He explained where he'd spotted them, towards a tree-line directly east of us. He'd already sent the co-ordinates to Armadillo. All he needed was the OK from me. Which I promptly gave.

'Shot!'

Rounds were incoming, aimed at a position some 200 metres away.

'Stevo, when they land, you clear the alley. Gordy, stand by.'

There were two muffled, rumbling explosions in quick succession. Corn, mud, clay, soil, grass, dust, dirt, sand: it was all sent billowing skywards. The trees were shredded as branches and leaves were ripped away.

Seconds later and there were another pair of explosions as two more shells detonated. Then there was another pair, and another.

'Sven, hold the mission. Stevo, go. Go. Go!'

What followed was an awesome display of firepower, skill and bravery. In the narrowest of confines the men pressed forwards, firing their underslung grenade launchers, and throwing HE L109s and red phos. The narrowness of the passageway – seven or eight metres – contained the blasts, making them all the more devastating. There was nowhere to run and hide. The only way was ahead. The men pressed on, covering each other as they went, manoeuvring around the dead bodies of those Talibs who had decided to stay and fight. All the endless hours of training in Lydd and in Kenya and on Salisbury Plain, this was what it had been for – thirty seconds in a dirty, smelly Afghan village. Together the patrol had assaulted two enemy positions and had gained more than 100 metres of ground. It had been pure FIBUA – fighting in built-up areas. Clearing the buildings and compounds had meant expending vast amounts of ammunition. But it was like having an expensive camera and not taking any pictures. What was the point of having a weapon, if you didn't use it when you had to? If some bean counter had an issue over the cost of the war, well, good luck to him – there was no way we'd be counting bullets. Not knowing what lurked in the shadows of a room, or round a corner, no one was taking any chances. First a grenade lobbed in, then two men following it up, firing high and low into every corner. Most rooms were empty, but not all. Each time a Talib was discovered, he was the one who came off worse.

Captain Meddlines, Gordy, Engineer Robbo, Stevo and the others – they had all behaved in exemplary fashion. The fight to take GF1 was never likely to feature on any list of battle honours, but that didn't mean what the men did that afternoon wasn't bloody magnificent.

We had secured the northern section of the village, leaving men behind us to cover our rear as we cleared, but with only twelve soldiers in total we were about to become too thinly spread and the danger of getting cut off was rising. If it wasn't for Sven and his 105mm fire missions – six in all – that moment could already have been upon us. Some had been danger close, 150 metres away and less; the compounds we'd been fighting for actually helping protect us from the supersonic, super-hot, super-sharp fragments of shell casing thrown out on detonation.

'Sven, I think that's us, mate.'

'Right. I can call in one more mission to cover our withdrawal if you want.'

I passed on the good news to the others and at the same time warned them some of the enemy might already have got behind us.

It also appeared Attal was getting hit – a favourite tactic for the Taliban when an ISAF patrol was being effective against them elsewhere. But back in the ops room, Bugsy seemed pretty calm about everything. There had been a number of RPG strikes but the ANA were doing a good job in reply.

Cautiously, we retraced our steps out of GF1. By my assessment the enemy had been of platoon strength, maybe some 28 to 30 men, not including those who had been attacking Attal. And by that same assessment we had killed eight of them and wounded at least three more.*

Back at base we talked through how things had gone and what we thought we had achieved. I was proud of my men and told them so. I was also realistic about what we remained up against. And as a reminder of our precarious existence the enemy hit us again from both the north and the south. It came to nothing, but was yet another demonstration that we were camping in their territory, not the other way round.

There were just two weeks left before I was going home. But as I knew from events in Marjah before my R & R, a lot of things can happen in a fortnight.

---

* The bodies would normally disappear from the battlefield once we had gone, local people collecting them and either returning them to the Taliban or, if the dead were from the area, taking them for burial.

FOURTEEN

TASK FORCE BEATTIE

CAPTAIN JON HUXLEY, 1 R IRISH

10 SEPTEMBER 2008

I tried to put our position in perspective.

Our CO was now describing Attal as a place where the likelihood of troops being contacted when they went out on patrol was 100 per cent.

On a map of the region where red was used to signify enemy-held territory, and green was for areas of ISAF influence, Attal was a pea bobbing about in an ocean of crimson.

As if to underline our isolation and vulnerability one of the Danish officers who'd visited us a few days previously had explained how the northern limit of coalition activity was the 32 northing. Being way beyond this we were effectively operating behind enemy lines.

And we had just lost one of our last lifelines to the outside world. The Hip helicopter had made its last visit after nearly becoming a prized scalp for the Taliban. Whilst the chopper was on the ground and the men were feverishly trying to offload much-needed food and water, the insurgents opened up with RPGs. In the chaos, as the ANA manned the walls, returning fire, Stevo had to grab hold of the aircraft's loadie and tell him to get out of there. Either that or watch his helicopter be hit and then have an enforced stay at holiday camp Attal. As enemy fire continued to whiz around the aircraft, it lurched into the sky and, skimming the perimeter wall, headed away never to be seen again. Also never to be seen again were most of the supplies on board that there hadn't been the chance to remove.

After the shooting died down we did an inventory of the kit we had.

'What's the situation?' I asked Stevo.

'OK, we have got 250 litres of bottled water.'

Not much when you think that needed to be shared between seventeen men. There were two wells in Attal, but we had already tested them for purity. Both were found to have salmonella at dangerously high levels. Certainly their water could not be drunk, and several men were wary even of washing or shaving in it. We were told not even to bother trying to boil it to make it palatable. In fact the medical advice was: Don't touch it with a barge pole.

'And food?'

'Yeah, we're OK there – got about twenty-four days of supply.'

Whilst Stevo was responsible for rations, it was Bugsy's job to count the ammunition.

'Ammo state, mate?'

'I have got the most recent numbers on the wall,' he said, referring to the scribble board he kept updated in the ops room. 'But, to hit you with the headlines, we don't have any 40mm bombs for the UGLs except what the men are already carrying. We are also very low on all forms of illumination and signal smoke. On the plus side we could invade a small country with the amount of 7.62mm and .50-cal we have.'

'And 5.56mm?' I asked about rounds for the SA80 and light machine gun.

'Short on 5.56mm belted for the Minimi, and we could use some more 5.56mm ball, but otherwise should be OK for a while.'

As well as all the other problems we were up against I was still fighting my own (losing) battle against the shits.

The previous day we had again been deep in the Green Zone, under constant threat from the enemy, and yet my constant priority was not staying alive but keeping my pants clean.

Repeatedly I had to worm my way into the undergrowth, drop my trousers and squat down as the shit poured from my arse like liquid chocolate. There wasn't a solid thing in it, yet it still felt like I was passing house bricks. And, just when I thought I had expelled everything from my bowels, out would come another wave of filth, gushing to the ground and splashing over my boots. For good measure there'd be an accompanying surge of pain in my abdomen, caused by cramps.

In the military, going for a shit out in the field is called a shovel recce. You're supposed to dig your hole, do your business, cover it up and move on – leaving no trace of your activities. Not much chance of me managing to do that. When the feeling came, that was it, I had to go. Afterwards I would clean myself up as best I could, and try and brush some soil over my own dirt, before getting back to little matters like life and death.

The diarrhoea had been with me for three weeks by this stage and showed no signs of abating. Yet I was committed to leading our operations and, given that we were well into Ramadan and the ANA were still refusing to do anything other than guard the camp, my presence was required. Shits or not.

'Bugsy, take your team forward and clear the mosque,' I ordered as we stood at the main crossroads in the village of GF8, though to call it a crossroads was perhaps overstating its scale and importance. It was little more than a spot where two rough tracks intersected, each bordered by imposing compound walls. Gordy – Amber 93 – and his team were out on my left flank, to the north.

Only a minute earlier we had been chatting to some locals. They were adamant. At least six Talibs were holed up in the religious building no more than eighty metres ahead of us and just round the corner out of sight. The locals described how the Talibs were from the Qal-e-Gaz area further up the valley. They had been taking food from the residents of the village and effectively forcing them to support their operations against ISAF. They had turned one room of the mosque into a makeshift training camp, where they'd make the villagers undergo rudimentary weapons training in exchange for the normal, nominal fee – $10.

'OK, Bugsy. Go for the mosque,' I repeated.

Bugsy looked hesitant, but I wasn't about to burden him with any more instruction. The order was simple and the choice of how to carry it out was his. He knew what he was doing, he knew where the rest of his forces were located, and he knew what fire support was available through me. What else was there to say?

His team moved off, crossing over a trickle of a stream. They hadn't got very much further on, only to a point where the track bulged, opening out into a large patch of ground bordered by walls, cornfields and ditches, when the enemy started shooting.

And it wasn't just a few haphazard rounds of unco-ordinated fire. This was a murderous wall of bullets. Lead churned up the ground, tore and bore its way into the compound walls. Fizzed and snapped overhead. Cracked around us. There was no slow build-up to a crescendo; it was an instant cacophony. It was an ambush and a well-planned one at that.

Tracer streaked before my eyes. It would have been mesmerising if it hadn't been so dangerous. Still slightly trailing Bugsy's team, I dived for cover, joined by Q, Morgs and Kev.

At least we had some cover to hide behind. Bugsy and his guys were pretty much out in the open, a shallow trench the only sort of shelter they had.

Fumbling for the switch on my PRR, I yelled more orders.

'Morgs, cover south. Kev, talk to Sven and get the guns on line. Use the ground to the east of the village as your starting point.'

I also managed to get a first contact report back to the ops room in Attal. But my priority was Bugsy. Each time one of his men half-raised himself out of the dirt to try and put some fire down on one of at least three enemy positions, he would become the target for a vicious torrent of return fire and be forced back on to his belt buckle.

'Bugsy, what's the situation?'

'We're pinned down and ain't going anywhere.'

Which was rather an understatement.

'OK, mate, I am going to get Amber 93 to push up on your flank and try and clear the enemy from there.'

'Roger, but be quick.'

'Amber 93, this is 92 Alpha. Give me a call on the other means.'

I spoke to Gordy on the VHF because I wasn't getting any reply from the PRR. Now I wanted him to try using it again, so we didn't clog up the VHF net.

'Boss, Gordy, send.'

That was better; perhaps he had moved position and got a better signal.

'OK, I want you to push east and clear any of the enemy in the fields and compounds north of the ambush site. Understand?'

'Roger, moving.'

'NO. NO. Wait!' There was real urgency in my voice. 'I'm going to try and get some fire down to the east and see if that helps the move. Don't go anywhere until you hear the rounds land.'

'Kev?' I shouted.

'Two minutes, Boss.'

One hundred and twenty seconds before the first fire mission.

Kev had a no-nonsense attitude. He was confident in what he did, understood his job inside out and had already proved himself on numerous occasions. Now, as link man to Sven up on the high ground overlooking the Green Zone, I needed him to get it right again.

The first two 105mm rounds landed. Too far east. Kev brought the guns in a couple of hundred metres.

'Gordy, move now. Kev, Morgs, come with me.'

My aim was to get forward to try and offer Bugsy and his team some support. But the enemy had other ideas. We had moved no more than ten metres when the enemy firestorm centred itself on us. We were deluged with lead. Looking down, everywhere there were puffs of dust as the bullets tunnelled into the earth around my feet. More flashed past my head, which was throbbing with pain from the ceaseless noise. I crouched down, just in time to glimpse an RPG flash out of a neighbouring field and smack squarely into the corner of the building in which we had just been sheltering. Another RPG was fired from the same location. It airburst just above Bugsy's position. Then a third came arcing out of the crops, only to land slightly short.

'Fuckin' hell,' was the most appropriate thing I could find to say and with that I led Kev and Morgs back to our starting point.

We were in a pretty major engagement and it was clear we weren't going to make much progress with just thirteen of us.

It was a view echoed by Gordy: 'We are unable to move forward, we are now taking fire from another position to the north at close range.'

'Roger. Go firm. Send grid.'

Things were grim. To the east, Bugsy and his men were

pinned down by heavy fire in open ground. To the north, beyond a large compound I couldn't see past, Gordy's team was also pinned down. My four-man band was stuck at the crossroads but at least we had something to hide behind. There was no way any of us were going forward on this one. I needed to get the men out of there and consolidate our position before all or some of us were completely surrounded.

To that end I needed help. 'Kev, get Sven to key up the GMLRS. And we need an AH on task now!'

'Roger, Boss.'

'And, listen, I need the guns to keep firing to fill the void before the GMLRS does its stuff. Bring the guns in as close as you can. Hit the eastern edge of the village at grid 64033468, where the tree-line is.'

I wanted to get everyone back to the crossroads. And from there, once regrouped, have another go at the enemy.

I spoke to Bugsy. 'I want you to pull back to where we are.'

This time his reply was packed with emotion: 'Not a chance at the moment. If we try and run, we are going to get fuckin' shredded.'

I tried to keep my voice calm as I responded. 'OK, understood. We will give you covering fire and there will be a fire mission about 150 metres east of you. Move when I call.'

I turned to Q and told the Fijian to give some support with his GPMG.

What happened next was astonishing.

From his crouched position behind the corner of the compound with me, he stood to his full height of 6´2˝. Grabbing the machine gun as if it were a toy, he wrapped a spare belt of 7.62mm link around his strong, bulldog neck. The long end of the belt already fed into the weapon lay loosely over the top cover.

And with that Q waded out into the torrent of fire and began to run towards the enemy, one size-eleven boot after the other. Metre by metre he covered the ground in long loping steps. It didn't take long for the enemy to decide he posed more of a threat than his colleagues pinned down in the dirt ahead of him. All the enemy fire seemed to converge on the big man. I couldn't understand how they missed him.

'Morgs, give Q covering fire!' I yelled, raising my rifle and opening up with short bursts into the Taliban position closest to me.

And still he moved forward. Some of the rounds concentrated on him dug into the earth at his feet, others ricocheted off the rock-hard surface and disappeared into the cornfield to his left, the tracer rounds amongst them having travelled just far enough to ignite before they disappeared into the wall of vegetation. It was only when Q got level with his colleagues, but some fifty metres north of them, that the massive Fijian dropped to the floor, pushing the GPMG ahead of him and immediately engaging with it. It seemed as if a duel was going on between Q and the numerous enemy – an unfair duel at that. Because in the state of mind he was in, I wouldn't have bet against the South-Sea Islander. He would use sustained fire to suppress one Taliban position before twisting round to take on another, hauling his weapon with him through the dust, then settling it down on the bipod fixed under the barrel, pulling the stock back tightly into his shoulder, and opening fire again, a steady stream of spent cartridge cases spewing from his weapon as he did so. With the first 100-round belt of ammo now a thing of the past, he ripped the spare from his neck, reloaded and continued where he had left off.

It was as if the Taliban had forgotten about everyone else. Q had become the target. For Bugsy and his team this was good news. It was time to get them out of there. I started screaming at them.

At the same time Kev screamed at me: 'Shot!'

The 105mm rounds were on their way.

With Q still drawing an incredible amount of fire, Bugsy was up and moving, followed by the others. I had never seen them run so fast. Then the artillery shells arrived, exploding with a vengeful ferocity. Bits of tree, mud and bodies were all sent flying. So too was a fountain of water. As the debris started crashing back to earth, at last Q was on his feet too and sprinting back the way he had just come.

'Fire for effect,' I yelled back to Kev, telling him to let the gunners do their own thing.

Then came news about the air support. What I had been hoping for was an Apache that could self-designate its own targets. What I was being offered was a fast jet, to which I couldn't talk. Fuck it. It would be like Chinese whispers. Me passing on enemy details to Sven. Him passing them on to Norseman, and finally Norseman telling the pilot. The chances of something going wrong were fucking enormous. There was now no chance we'd be pushing forward again. Without the AH there would not be the real support I needed. Added to this we were being hit from three sides – leaving us all but cut off.

I spoke to Gordy. 'Right, here's the situation. We are now holding the crossroads at 665347. I have CAS on its way and GMLRS being set up by Sven as well as the 105mm you can hear going in now. I don't think we are going to be able to push forward and I am going to have to get the CAS to drop danger close to our location. I need you to move to compound 10 and secure it. That's going to be our rally point. Let me know when you are there and I will join you with Bugsy's team.'

If garbled all at once it would have been more of a diatribe than a sitrep, but I had broken it up into easy chunks for Gordy to digest, waiting for his acknowledgement after each line.

'Moving now!' was his final reply.

Then for the first time that day I heard over the radio the voice of Karl Shields – the man from Larne was with Sven on the desert high ground overlooking the Green Zone.

'CAS on task. Require target grid.'

To the north Gordy was making his fighting withdrawal, there was still incoming fire from the east towards the cross-roads, and south of us another bunch of Talibs were continuing to fire their RPGs and AKs.

'Opal 70, this is Amber 92 Alpha. I need enemy at compound 5 hit now. Do you require grid, over?' I knew he'd have the compound clearly marked on his map.

'No. Send your location.'

Not a fucking chance! In the heat of the battle, over a busy and confused network, I wasn't about to send my grid to the pilot via the FST and the JTAC in Armadillo and risk it being confused with the enemy position.

'We are at compound 3, withdrawing to compound 10, in figures five, over.'

'Roger, CAS will not engage until you have withdrawn a safe distance.'

Jesus, it must be a French Mirage. They had caused me problems before. Coming to our aid, they seemed less than willing to engage whilst we were still in contact, which begged the question, Why the hell were they there at all?

I asked how long the GMLRS was going to be.

'Good to fire once CAS out of airspace.'

It was a hell of a job for Sven and the others to keep all the balls in the air. Artillery pieces, air support, GMLRS, even the Danish tanks – there were plenty of assets to play with and plenty of scope for things to go horribly wrong.

'OK, clear the CAS and engage now with the GMLRS on compound 5.'

A few seconds later Karl confirmed the seventy-kilometre sniper had been fired. Which gave me about forty seconds to think of the worst-case scenario. Maybe the grid was wrong. Perhaps they'd hit the wrong compound. What if we were too close? The damage the ballistic material would do to us was hideous to contemplate. I felt physically sick.

'Cover! Cover!' I shouted, watching men frantically search for any sort of shelter – behind walls, in hollows in the ground, down in the stream.

I shouted the warning again. 'GMLRS danger close!'

Then I did what the others had just done and hit the deck, face flat to the floor, my hands tucked under my body in case of blast or flash damage. I prayed, hoped, the strike would have a horrifying effect on the enemy. It would be carnage. And yet I had absolutely no reservations about it. I didn't care what I had to do to preserve the safety of my men. No qualms about what might happen to these fellow members of mankind. At that moment I had no understanding for their cause or their points of view, no sympathy for their families. They were the enemy and, just as I was trying to kill them, they were trying equally hard to annihilate us. How my out-look had changed since Garmsir in 2006. Back then I had thought deeply about it. What had changed? What did my attitude say about me now? Had I become a harder, heartless person? Had the seemingly endless cycle of violence torn from me any last vestiges of humanity? Suddenly my thoughts were interrupted.

By what sounded like a nuclear bomb going off.

If some of the other explosions I had witnessed in Helmand during 2008 had failed to live up to the billing, then this impact made up for them many times over. The rocket arrived with the momentum of a runaway freight train. It was the irresistible force colliding with the immovable object. The ground shook beneath me. But I didn't feel any great shock wave wash over me because the target compound had some-how managed to contain much of the blast, a ferocious mix of heat and shrapnel and other debris careering around the enemy's position. The insurgents would have been cut and sliced, choked by the smoke and dust, their internal organs left traumatised by the enormous build-up of pressure. And I was pleased. Pleased because it was them and not us.

I pushed myself to my feet and punched the air, overcome with relief.

Which was when the second rocket hit and I was sent tumbling back to the ground, this time more of the blast wave escaping the confines of the mud structure, and increasing in intensity as it was funnelled down the alley towards our position.

'Bugsy! Move now towards 10.'

Then, to Gordy: 'Where are you, mate?'

'At 10 but taking fire from the north-west.'

This wasn't great news as our escape route was due west and from their position the enemy would have a prime view of our pull-out across open ground.

'How bad is it?' I asked.

Before Gordy could respond, an RPG fired from the north-west flew over the heads of Gordy's team and smashed into the wall next to Bugsy and his men, sending them all slithering for cover again.

'Just keep going, Bugsy!'

We seemed to be missing someone. I looked behind me, only to see Q fighting his own rearguard action, apparently oblivious to what everyone else was doing and intent on staying where he was.

'Come on, Q, for fuck's sake.'

The retreat to 10 was like something from the film *Black Hawk Down*. We were running the gauntlet of enemy fighters who were crowding in on us from all sides. Either they had regained their confidence after the GMLRS strike or else they sensed that they might actually be safer by being close to us as it limited our ability to bring in indirect fire for fear of a blue-on-blue. We showed them the errors of their ways.

It was frenetic. We were engaging the Taliban in every direction. Nobody was bothering to send enemy locations. They were too numerous and too obvious for that. In a stop-start fashion we staggered towards 10, covering colleagues who had tripped and fallen or whose guns had devoured their ammo and were hungry for more. All around me people were exchanging mags on the move. Belts of 7.62mm and 5.56mm were being flung from man to man in a relentless battle to keep the weapons fed. Eventually one of the Minimi's just gave up: bone dry after all the firing, it seized. The soldier released his grip on it, so it hung around his neck from its sling, and pulled his pistol.

We were making an impact. I didn't stop to count those we had killed but there must have been many. I watched as Talib after Talib appeared. Watched as they were engaged. And watched as they fell out of sight – some dead, some wounded, some just hiding from the murderous fire we were putting down. It didn't really matter to me as long as they were out of the game. As one soldier stopped, so did the others. If not joined at the hip it was as if we were held together by a length of rope. No one was going to be left behind, no one was going to have to fight alone.

And still we moved on – until exhaustedly we reached 10 and, covered by Gordy, collapsed through the door. All thirteen of us were now in the same place. Gasping for breath, I immediately questioned whether we hadn't just gone from the frying pan into the fire. My surroundings gave me little reason to be relieved. Some seventy metres by fifty, the whole thing was in a ruinous state of repair, with gaping holes in the crumbling walls. With a long perimeter and more ways into it than I had men to cover, we were in the shit. I tried to allocate each soldier an area to defend, giving them arcs of fire that in some cases saw them engaging targets no more than fifteen metres in front of them. If the enemy were minded to storm the compound now, that would be it. I turned to Sven for help. It was time for him to really earn his pay.

'I need CAS on task now. I need a second GMLRS strike. And I need the 105s to take care of the enemy to the northwest, over.'

It would need masterful conducting from Sven to get his extensive orchestra playing in harmony. A difficult job given he couldn't even look the operators of his assets in the eye. Everything was being done remotely. Sven had a textbook's worth of calculations to do. He needed to work out the flight times of the ordnance, times on task for the CAS, a list of targets, the order in which to hit them and he would have to be sure the enemy had been positively identified at each.

And so the performance began.

'Doug, throw smoke. CAS inbound.'

'Roger, green smoke.'

A minute or two later a 500lb bomb lanced the enemy position to the north of us. As it impacted, the walls of our compound shuddered and shrugged off a cloud of dust. The second strike was just as awesome, delivering a bomb into a stream hidden amongst a tree-line just eighty metres away, sending men diving for cover. As for me, I half-fell down some steps I had just climbed up to get a better view of the unfolding drama. There were yet more explosions, this time to the west, caused by shells from the Leopard tanks detonating. Back up the steps I could clearly see mutilated bodies lying out in the churned-up cornfield, the red blood combining with the green crops and the brown mud to create a vivid, visceral canvas.

Never before had I been in a position to call in so much varied firepower. I hadn't really envisaged a situation in which I would need it, let alone have it available. The amount of destructive – not to mention extraordinarily expensive – ordnance at my beck and call would have been frightening had it not been so bloody welcome.

On my say-so I had everything a commander could need. Air support. Tanks. Artillery pieces. Rockets. This was the closest to total war I had come. It was the might of the ISAF arsenal being deployed to ensure the survival of a handful of men. Counting the Brits, and the Danes, and the American marines, plus the ANA, Task Force Helmand might have been over 12,000 men strong. But at that very moment it seemed as if every technological resource in theatre was being focused on keeping us – a mere baker's dozen men from 1 R IRISH – alive. And thank God it was.

Next there was thunderous fire from the 105mm guns to give the enemy to the north-west something to think about until the GMLRS was ready. When it was, it fired a salvo of four rockets: two landing in compounds to the north-west, underlining the good work just done; the other pair hitting much closer to our compound, forcing the enemy to slip back into the undergrowth. For the first time in two hours we had a breathing space. From the four corners (it seemed as if there were many more, so thinly were we spread) of our redoubt the shouts went out. Ammo! Water! The cries were just as much about establishing contact with colleagues as they were about securing supplies, each soldier finding reassurance in the sound of English voices.

I did a circuit of my territory, talking to every man, trying to offer some encouragement, asking what activity each had seen, hearing about his own experience of repelling the enemy. And they all had a story to tell – about how the Talibs had tried to rush the position, only to be held back and gunned down at a range of no more than a few metres. How the enemy had emerged out of nowhere to launch an RPG at point-blank range, only then to melt back into the surround-ings. And in every case the men had stood their ground, fought their positions, defended their patch, driven on by self-preservation, but also a burning desire not to be the weakest link, the one who let the others down. It was a real show of grit and determination. I wouldn't have expected any less.

I called Bugsy and Gordy over to me to tell them the plan. 'Right, we are going to head out due west, covered by the tanks.'

The aim was to get the fuck out of Oz and back to Kansas

as quickly as possible. Having briefed them, I spoke to Stevo at Attal and gave him the same information. Finally I double-checked with Sven what range of instruments was left playing. The CAS had left the pit to rearm, but the 105s were still ours.

There was no point in hanging about. Deep breaths and then it was out of the compound and out of the village. A few rounds flew way over our heads but the cavalry had taken the wind out of the enemy's sails. Not that they were probably too bothered. From their point of view, there would always be tomorrow. This was their home. They were going nowhere. It didn't really matter whether they killed us one day or the next. As long as the job got done . . . sooner or later.

And at that moment I was quite happy to wait until the next day to die. I had had enough. I was worn out.

But there must have been some Talibs who had not read the script because all of a sudden the air was once again full of contact reports and the sound of enemy fire.

'Contact, right!'

'Contact, high ground!'

'RPG!'

Everyone seemed to have seen and heard the enemy action at the same time. With the enemy firing through a cornfield, from an elevated position to our right – the north – we all made a beeline for the only cover available to us – a ditch with a stream running along the bottom. As the small-arms fire scythed through the crops and over our heads there was little we could do. Even Gordy, who was at the front and closest to exiting the Green Zone, was left impotent by the weight of the insurgent fire. We required back-up.

Sven came through on the radio and asked us to mark our position with green smoke so the tanks wouldn't end up bombarding our locations. I yanked a smoke grenade from my belt and threw it just in front of me. It was possibly the most stupid thing I had ever done. Whilst it might have given the tank commanders some indication of where I was, I'd also offered a great big come-on to every fanatic who wanted to see me dead. I couldn't have made myself more conspicuous if I had stood up with a target over my heart and shouted 'Shoot me' to the enemy. Which is what they did next.

An instant later an RPG was launched towards us. Sitting towards the top of the stream bank I watched mesmerised as it landed perhaps five metres in front of me. Still entranced I saw it explode and a large chunk of shrapnel sliced through the greenery before flying, by a margin of mere centimetres, over my head – and Kev's, who was sitting right next to me. More metal splinters showered from the sky.

I looked at Kev. And he looked at me. And then we both slid back down the muddy bank and into the water, happy to get our arses wet for the sake of keeping ourselves alive.

I felt as if some contrition was appropriate. 'What a dick-head. I won't be doing that again.'

'Yeah, please, mate.'

My moment of embarrassment was broken by the voice of Sven: 'Doug, you can move now.'

The Leopard 2 battle tanks, plus the artillery guns, were hitting the enemy locations. The contact was all but over.

Watched by our Afghan allies, we staggered through Attal's main gate, each of us covered in dirt and dust and debris from the engagement. The physical and mental tiredness was evident. Heads were held low, weapons were held low. Many of the men had lost magazines when they had had to furiously reload. My wrist satnav was gone. So was my Silva compass, which had – once – been secured to my body armour. I was tired, the men were tired, dog-tired.

But I still had work to do. Ammunition sorted, there were sitreps to be sent to Gereshk, battle damage assessment (BDA) to be sent. Then a report to HQ in Lash, who passed it to the top of the tree – Regional Command South, those in charge of the whole ISAF effort in southern Afghanistan, including not just Helmand but also Kandahar province. Their response was one of incredulity. 'How could so few men do so much damage?' Jon Huxley, the OMLT liaison officer working in Lash, passed on the query to us and also the associated message: 'Tell Task Force Beattie, there are questions being asked as to how all that ordnance could be used during the contact.' Of course Jon already had the answer to that one. He was the guy who had built Attal. He understood its situation as well as anyone. And now I was sure he was explaining to our superiors the realities of life, not on the front line, but way beyond it.

I was making no friends, perhaps there were even those asking for my head on a plate, but what was I to do? Abandon the mission? Sit in the base and take casualties? Fuck them all. Perhaps those with a problem should get out of their air-conditioned tents and come and enjoy hospitality Attal-style. All the naysayers combined weren't worth one of my men and I would do what I had to do to keep them alive. Damn me if I didn't.

FIFTEEN

NINE LIVES GONE

CAPTAIN DOUG BEATTIE, 1 R IRISH

13 SEPTEMBER 2008

I had lied just a little bit.

Told HQ what they wanted to hear.

Explained we would be going out in company strength.

But that wasn't quite correct. I had managed to persuade some of the ANA to leave the confines of the camp to join us on patrol in the Green Zone, but not all of them – actually only about a third of the sixty who were at Attal. Throw in the OMLT members and we were still little more than platoon strength. No matter. Our little mission had been cleared.

My aim was once again to get to the main supply route – and then beyond it to the river where, according to intelligence reports, the enemy was using the bank as another conduit for transporting themselves and their equipment up and down the valley. They had also found an easily fordable section of the Helmand River that enabled them to move east to west with little effort and keep the pressure up on both Attal and Gibraltar.

Leaving the camp at around 10:00 hrs, we first pushed

south-east until we hit the MSR, then turned slightly left to head due east towards the watercourse. We made progress, using a formation we'd deployed a million times. Two teams: one the primary, extending forward; the other the secondary, offering backup and assistance. It took an hour of creeping through the Green Zone to reach the river. Concealed in our positions I looked across the flow, some forty metres wide. On the far side I could see a sprinkling of small villages, all defiantly and brazenly under Taliban control. Our enemy realised we were in no position to take the fight over the river. All we could do was sit and watch. After a while we started working our way north, parallel to the Helmand, keeping in amongst the fields full of crops that ran almost to the banks. Through the maze of maize I could see locals going forth and back through the river. It emphasised the point. If children and goats could get over the obstacle, then it wasn't going to be hard for the enemy to hurdle it, carrying weapons and ammo. My only real chance of disrupting the supply chain was to intercept it at a point somewhat away from the expanse of water. The idea was to head a bit further north and then wheel west to occupy an isolated compound between the river and the village GF8, where we had had much of the earlier trouble. There we'd wait for the enemy to reveal themselves.

Keeping in amongst the vegetation, we ploughed on through the corn, negotiating the numerous tree-lines straddling our path. Then there were the frequent streams draining in and out of the Helmand that created yet more bars to our progress. I didn't know what it was – perhaps better irrigation – but the area we were in, right next to the river, seemed to be much 'tighter' even than what we'd been used to, the greenery more dense and more vigorous. Every few minutes we seemed to be tackling an obstacle. Channels and trenches. Trees and shrubs. Low-hanging tangles of limbs, closely set trunks, jumbles of roots. The ruins of long-since abandoned compounds and pens. Walls that marked boundaries of land. Through, over and under each of these barriers the men had to pass. It was slow, painstaking stuff. One group of soldiers would cover, whilst the other moved through the impediment, having taken off everything likely to snag and halt progress further – rucksacks, radios, weapons, these were all handed from man to man as if part of a grown-up game of pass the parcel.

From our waists to the soles of our boots we were soaked through. Not just from sweat, but by the water and mud we had endlessly to wade through to gain a few more metres of ground. But we were getting somewhere. We'd nearly reached the point where I wanted to turn back towards the desert.

'Go slightly further north and hit the tree-line that heads west.'

We continued on. Up a bit, then left a bit, before we arrived unannounced at compound GF8-12. I could describe it, but there's no real need. It was no different to the vast majority of other compounds we had come across in Helmand. Plain, simple. What made it special was not its design, but its commanding location, which allowed views towards the village in one direction and the river in the other. My worry was that if I understood its tactical importance, then so would the Taliban and they might already be manning the position. This wasn't the time for softly-softly – we would hit the building with a 'hard knock', a forceful, aggressive entrance, a boot to the door and then crash in, screaming and shouting as we went. A 'soft knock' would have been the absolute opposite. A gentle tap with the knuckles as if calling on a friend, weapons held non-threateningly, barrels pointed to the floor. In the politest of manners we'd ask people for their help, seek permission to search their premises. Of course we'd never take no for an answer, but it would appear as if we might. It was all about keeping friendly with the locals who weren't the enemy.

More often than not we'd use the subtle approach, but not today. Not in an area we were all but guaranteed to come under attack in.

It was Gordy's team that rushed the door, the ANA leading the way, supported by OMLT soldiers giving cover. We might have been going in hard, but pushing the Afghan soldiers in first was still a sop to relationship-building with the natives. If all they found was an innocent family rather than hardened Talibs, then the women could be discreetly shepherded out of sight of the infidels. Us confronting females was a big no-no – a real cultural *faux pas*. No matter we had just kicked the owner's door down; at least we wouldn't then be embarrassing him by getting an eyeful of his wife and daughters.

The women safely escorted to one corner and men to another, the mentoring team got down to clearing the compound whilst a couple of the Afghans heaved their PKMs and RPGs up on to the flat roof of the main building to keep a wider lookout.

'Boss, Gordy. The compound is clear.'

'Roger, mate. I am going to push Bugsy's team to the garden beyond the western wall and bring Sven and his boys in so we can set up.'

Stepping into the compound I could see the Afghan soldiers had given it a good going-over. But there didn't seem to be any hard feelings between them and the head of the household, who was chatting animatedly to the ANA commander. Everyone seemed to have a smile on their face. It was almost as if the ANA were glad to get out of Attal after so much time confined to camp.

With the man of the house distracted I risked a glance towards the women. Covered head to toe in burqas – or *chadri*s as they are known in Afghanistan – with only a thin-netted grille to see through, they squatted behind a low wall in the area set aside for cooking.

Now on the roof with the ANA, Sven called down. 'Doug,

if it kicks off, my starting point for the 105s is going to be 250 metres to the north.'

This would take the initial rounds into a patch of open ground.

Leaving Sven on the roof, I headed off to see Bugsy's team and gave them the order to push on further west to another compound 100 metres away. As they moved I wondered what response we might get from the Taliban. Even if we didn't come across a supply patrol, we were having an effect by passively dominating the area. They couldn't do what they wanted to due to our presence. Surely they wouldn't be happy to have us sitting in their backyard? Our presence must be winding them up. The answer was yes.

First there were a few isolated shots from a point where the Talibs had a sentry post, then quickly the whole of the eastern edge of the village seemed to come angrily to life.

Leaves from the trees began to flutter towards the floor as if it were autumn, plucked from the branches by the enemy bullets. There was the sound of more rounds slamming into wood, splintering trunks and branches.

'Amber 92, this is Alpha. Contact GF8. Wait. Out.'

Sven came on the radio. 'I have movement to the north in the fields, people heading east.'

Desperate not to incur any civilian casualties, I asked him if they were firing at his position or at least carrying weapons. When he told me he couldn't be sure, we decided to let them go and keep one eye on where they headed. Besides, we had plenty to worry about from the intense fire being laid down from the village. The difficulty with my current position – in the corn – was that, although the enemy had a hard job seeing me, I was finding it equally tough accurately pinpointing them. The Afghans with us didn't seem to have my difficulty, not least because they seemed to have taken up rather more exposed positions, trusting their fate not to training and skill, but God. And knowing how inaccurate they themselves often were when shooting, perhaps they calculated the Taliban were equally woeful. It wasn't a strategy I'd be adopting. Still, I needed to know where they thought the enemy were.

I crawled over to the nearest ANA soldier.

'Dushman! Dushman!' he shouted, gesturing towards a compound due west, very close by. Straining my neck a bit further to look in the direction in which he was pointing, I saw a muzzle flash and a small puff of smoke. The next instant a bullet from an AK cracked over my head. Fuck, the bastard was shooting at me. Raising my SA80 I fired back, a short burst. One, two, three, four, five rounds.

'Stevo, push west into the edge of the village. Sven, can you hold the compound and secure the rear?'

I didn't want to turn this into yet another major engagement, and keeping Sven behind us meant we should be able to just slip back once we had given the enemy something to think about.

'Contact. Contact!' It was Stevo, his voice accompanied by a whole mass of noise just fifty metres ahead, out of sight round the back of a compound.

There was the unmistakable sound of an SA80 being fired on automatic. Then a Minimi joined in, plus a GPMG. In there, too, the audio signatures of the enemy's AK47s.

It was sustained, heavy, murderous stuff. This was each side trying to put down a massive amount of fire to break the other and push them back. There was nothing measured about the shooting. It was about the sheer volume of rounds. It was about who had the fastest finger on the trigger. Who had the most raw aggression, who was the most professional. Who was prepared to do whatever it took to stay alive, even if that meant killing in large numbers. This was opposing soldiers coming face to face at a range of ten to fifteen metres – point-blank range – in a situation where success was measured in terms of blood spilled and blood saved. All the 105s, GMLRS, mortars and fast jets in the world weren't of any relevance in this type of personal battle. It was about men and not machinery. Individual bravery, not indirect fire.

As I stumbled forward to try and reach my young commander, I didn't know who was going to emerge victorious.

So it was with immense relief then that I turned the corner of the compound perimeter and saw Stevo and his men, sitting in open ground still under heavy fire but at least alive.

It turned out Stevo had stepped in front of members of a Taliban patrol – all eight of them – who had just left the mosque. Without hesitation he had taken the initiative and charged towards the Talibs, firing from the hip. His immediate resolve had left the enemy on the back foot. Despite their strength of numbers, two had been killed and at least one seriously wounded as the others dragged themselves away. But whilst Stevo had won that exchange we looked in danger of losing the battle.

Bugsy and some ANA were confronting a further eight or so Talibs at the southern end of the village. He also had eyes on another enemy team trying to outflank us and get behind us.

Stevo was in contact with the rump of the patrol he had just shot up and also more Talibs to the north.

Then I heard from Sven and Gordy. The compound I'd left them at was being attacked from the direction of the river at a distance of less than 100 metres.

In the blink of an eye things had got out of control. We were becoming encircled, with a real danger our group would be cut in half.

I needed to tighten everybody up. 'Sven, Gordy, move to my location now!'

And with that, together with the rest of the Afghans, they were on their way, crashing, whilst shooting, through the undergrowth towards the compound I was in. Whatever hope I had of withdrawing east back towards the river was gone. It would be madness. Instead we'd go 180 degrees in the opposite direction – straight through the village and back to Attal that way. But I was going to have to get the toys out of the box again.

'Amber 92, this is Alpha, requesting CAS or AH over.'

'Roger, 92, Alpha, you have two Fennec helicopters re-tasked to you from FOB Gibraltar in ten minutes.'

Built by Eurocopter, the Fennecs weren't exactly what I had had in mind. Being unarmed flying observation platforms they couldn't actually shoot at anything. The best I would get from them was a report of the enemy positions. And that I didn't really need, because it was already clear where the Taliban were – bloody everywhere. Certainly there were enemy in at least six separate positions and they seemed to be closing in on us by the second.

Cautiously I raised my head over a low wall and found myself staring at another enemy group, about fifty metres away – a distance Linford Christie would have covered in about five seconds. Even allowing for a lack of athletic ability, the Talibs could be on us in next to no time. I raised my rifle, pointed it at them, squeezed the trigger and held it down.

Four seconds later and I was back on my arse, the magazine empty. 'Karl! Get over to this fuckin' wall and hold them back.'

I crawled to Sven. 'I need those 105mm rounds in, fuckin' danger close, mate, a hundred metres to the north, nearer still if you can manage it.'

I could tell he didn't like what I was asking, but there was no alternative. 'Sven, we have no choice. They are closing in and we can't hold them off for ever.'

'OK, OK, but pull Stevo's team back, will you.'

'Right, leave that to me, but you call them in now to grid 66043461.'

'I'll call them into the open, and then adjust them down to that grid.'

'OK, mate, but you have to be bloody quick.'

Again I placed my trust in the FST boys – Sven, Morgs, Kev and Karl. They were skilled operators and in this situation they had to be.

As Stevo and his boys made it back to the compound, Sven shouted out, 'Shot!'

Two shells came scudding over our position and slammed into ground to the north. The next two came a lot closer and then Sven got the guns firing for effect. As we hunkered down for cover, rounds repeatedly pounded the area where a minute or two earlier I had emptied a mag at the Taliban. At sixty metres away, the points of impact were much closer than I had dared hope – or in my heart really wanted. The air seemed to vibrate with the sound of the detonations and the shock of the blast waves. The compound walls convulsed, shaking dust free. And still the shells kept coming, round after round slamming into the enemy location.

'Fuck me, Sven, I don't like this!'

'This is as close as you will get without calling the guns on to your own position,' he yelled over the sound of the barrage.

For a second I questioned whether the glint in his eye hinted at the relish he'd get from doing just that.

Finally the artillery pieces went quiet.

Time for the next act. It was the turn of the GMLRS battery at FOB Edinburgh in Musa Qala. They would target the western side of the mosque.

And it was then that everything nearly went horribly, horribly wrong.

As the 105s had hit I ordered Gordy to use them as cover to assault another compound – compound 6 – in preparation for our breakout. But just as Sven called, forty seconds before the rocket impact, I checked my map against the position I could see Gordy and his men in. And it wasn't right. They were in the wrong place. Not at compound 6, but at compound 7. I had given them the wrong information and now they were within a stone's throw of the spot where a 200lb warhead was about to land. Oh shit.

'Gordy! Pull back now! GMLRS strike forty seconds. Your location!'

I was screaming into the PRR mic and at the same time getting to my feet. Not that I would have been able to get to Gordy's position any time before the missile landed, and anyway, what would I have done even if I had got there? Other than share in their demise? I felt helpless.

Over the radio I could hear Gordy yelling to his men, rounding them up, urging them to make a run for it. Even as the rocket landed and exploded, Gordy was still giving orders to his squad. Just as the weapon impacted and exploded with an earth-shattering crash, I recognised my own vulnerability and hit the deck too. Then everything went hideously silent. It hadn't, of course, there was still a battle going on, but I was listening out for only one thing – Gordy's voice – and every other sound had been filtered from my brain.

'Gordy, Doug.' My heart was in my mouth. I was sweating more than ever, my pulse racing at a million miles an hour.

'Gordy, Doug.' What had I done?

'Doug, Gordy, send.'

Thank the Lord. The wave of relief was immediate. It came out as humour. Bad humour.

'Mate! Stop dicking about out there, will you?'

Now the sounds of the rest of the battle started to seep back into my consciousness.

Amongst them Sven's voice: 'Doug, we will have CAS in two minutes and I have a second GMLRS. What targets?'

I looked down at his small team. Sitting in the dirt, in the middle of the fighting, they had created their own little world of maps and radios – the TacSat, VHF, HF, PRRs. Using them they appeared to be in touch with just about everyone who was anyone in Helmand – Armadillo, Opal 82, Sierra 60 in Gereshk, Norseman, Amber 92 and 92 Alpha. They were sending and receiving an encyclopaedia full of information. One wrong grid, one slip of concentration, and we were fucked. Completely and utterly fucked. Dead. All I could do was trust these guys and make sure what I was telling them – and indeed Gordy and the others – was accurate in the first place. I needed to up my game. I was in overall command and I had to act like it. Yet again I pushed myself up to see over the wall. Despite the indirect fire, rounds were still spinning past my head, leaving a sick-inducing ringing in my ears. It was relentless.

Stevo, with Robbo and Q, had now reoccupied his original position. Once again Q was in the thick of it, blasting away with his GPMG, screaming for more ammunition. Next to him, standing up, with his Minimi to his shoulder, Robbo was also giving the enemy something to think about, the ammo belt hanging from the left side of the weapon visibly shortening as he pulled the trigger.

The others were holding the ground; it was up to me to get us all out of there. I set the mosque as the first rally point.

'OK, GMLRS now. Tree-line junction at 65923469,' I shouted to Sven as he continued to pore over his maps. Next I gave him the co-ordinates for the CAS.

The rockets arrived, rearranging the scenery 175 metres away.

Then came the cavalry. A pair of Dutch F-16 jet fighters.

I had been here many times before. In Garmsir in 2006 it was only the air-strikes called in by my JTAC, Bombardier Sam New, that kept us alive. And on one occasion they very nearly cost me my life, a rogue bomb tearing up the ground just in front of our positions, large chunks of molten bomb casing sweeping out over the top of us. With that to the fore of my mind I lay flat on the floor and retreated into my shell, pulling my head turtle-like as far back into my shoulders as I could, helmet facing the direction of the blast, a drill you are taught for nuclear explosions. We often joked about it, saying you are only given this position to adopt so that when they came round later, collecting what's left of you after the force of the blast has pile-driven your tin hat down over the rest of your body, they can simply retrieve your helmet and there inside, neatly scooped up, you'll be.

I tried to make myself smaller still.

Even if you don't see the bomb detach from the belly of the aircraft, you can tell it has been released from the sound of the plane's engines, the pilot kicking the afterburner into life as he pulls up, trying to put some vertical distance between himself and several hundred pounds of high explosive going off.

There were three separate strikes, all made by a single aircraft. Each time the plane streaked low along the horizon from left to right, on each occasion dropping a 500-pounder that drilled into the Afghan landscape before going off, causing monstrous damage and reducing the enemy fire to a trickle.

It was our cue to move.

'Stevo, hold your ground, we are going to pass through.'

'Roger, Boss.'

Through the greenery, Gordy and his team at the front, we made for the village, out of the fields, past the contorted bodies of the Talibs Stevo had cut down during his earlier chance encounter.

For a second I stopped and looked at the dead, suddenly feeling the weight of the radio on my back, as the straps cut even further into my shoulders and sapped what was left of my strength. Could have been worse, though; I could have been dead – like this lot. The Talib closest to me was lying on his back, his death mask shaped into a look of total surprise – it was evident he hadn't seen Stevo coming.

'Make sure they're well searched,' I shouted as I discovered some last reserves of energy with which to pick up my feet again and start walking.

And then we were into the confines of the narrow alleys, heading for the mosque. It wasn't somewhere I wanted to hang around. The enemy was silent for the moment but from bitter experience I knew they always had another trick up their sleeve that they'd produce just as you thought you were safe and sound. No point giving them too much time to pull it out. From the mosque we dodged down yet more narrow streets, hemmed in by compounds, until suddenly we emerged from the western edge of the village, out of the shadows and into the blazing sunshine. From here it'd be a quick yomp through the GZ, first to the MSR and then on to Stars Wars Wadi and, finally, home sweet home. As I pushed forward to assess the way ahead, the lads took a breather and a few moments to slag off Karl. As we'd got to the mosque, men had moved in different directions to take up covering positions. As they did so, Karl suddenly found himself standing there alone, not sure where everyone had disappeared off to.

His big mistake was to say so over the radio, so everyone could hear: 'I'm all alone. Where are you all?'

In answer to which, Stevo had appeared out of nowhere, grabbed him by the scruff of the neck and dragged him away. No big deal, except the scene was now being re-enacted for laughs by men eager to find a way of offloading the stress of the day. In rapid succession came the mimicking of Karl's already notorious question.

'I'm alone. Where are you all?' A bleat.

'Help me. Help me.' A whimper.

'Don't leave me.' A camp whine.

'I'm scared.' The voice of a woman.

'Is anybody there?' The sound of a frightened child.

I was just about to break up the revelry and get everyone moving again, away from the village, when the insurgents produced their surprise. A fusillade of RPGs from behind us and from the left. And here we were floundering in linear formation – a straight line, no depth, no way of properly supporting one another. Again I had failed in my role. We should have been spread out but we weren't.

'Sven, what chance of any more air support?'

His response was positive. We had a B-1 bomber *en route* as follow-on CAS. Only thing was he didn't know how long it would be until it reached us. So there we were again, a small contingent, backs not to the wall, but to each other, battling to hold our tiny patch of ground – shit position or not, it was the one we were in.

Stevo, Bugsy and Gordy rose to the challenge magnificently, commanding their own men, mentoring the Afghans, fighting ferociously. The MSR was a mere 100 metres west but, if we had moved at that moment, we would have been cut down in the corn before we'd travelled twenty metres. Then came a message from the Messiah.

'Doug, B-1 in two minutes,' said Sven. 'What grids, Norseman is asking?'

I reeled off a stream of numbers, all referencing points to the south, where the enemy seemed to be closest. Flying way above us, the B-1 crew would simply take my co-ordinates, key them into their computer and then release the GPS-guided munitions. Bombs away. Three of them released together. Easy. So long as I hadn't got the numbers wrong. We'd soon find out.

The weapons landed and detonated within a split second of each other. Perversely the noise and visual effects were not as awe-inspiring as I had expected but the overpressure was immense. And if it was bad for us, it must have been hideous for our enemy, whose fire quickly all but dried up, either because they were now dead or wounded; or because they didn't want to be dead or wounded and feared the B-1 would strike them next if they continued to give us trouble.*

---

* Sometime later I saw the cockpit video of the attack, on which I could clearly make out our position as well as the enemy locations that were hit. One of the three bombs landed a mere fifty metres from where we were.

'Move. Move,' I yelled and we were up and away, crashing into and then through the maize, reaching the MSR in a couple of minutes and Star Wars Wadi soon after that. In just ten minutes we had made it back to Attal. Totally shattered, I walked to the ops room and closed the TiC. The fighting was over but not the aftermath.

We had used up an incredible amount of ammunition and indirect fire support to dominate our area and get ourselves out of trouble. On the most basic level – the level I was working at – what we had done was extremely successful. Judging from the Taliban radio traffic subsequently intercepted we had killed or wounded over thirty of the enemy.

But there were those who now decided Task Force Beattie was getting into just too much trouble. The day's events, combined with what had happened a few days earlier, had unnerved some of the top brass. And so we were put on the shortest of leashes, limited to travelling no more than 500 metres beyond the camp walls, and even these excursions had to be sanctioned by HQ in Lash. In effect we had been grounded.

I explained to the men that their magnificent efforts had not gone unnoticed. That in a way we had become victims of our own success. We were making people nervous and essentially we would be sitting on our hands until the relief, men from 1 RIFLES, arrived in about ten days.

Somewhat more welcome corroboration of what we had achieved arrived about forty-eight hours later in the form of a delegation of elders from the local villages. First of all they scotched rumours put about by the Taliban information officer in the area (for all that they dress like peasants, the Taliban were sophisticated fighters used to shaping public opinion through propaganda as well as guns) that we'd killed eighteen children during our last engagement. The elders said, so badly had the Taliban been bloodied that they'd retreated north up the valley and east across the river. Through the villagers the Taliban even offered us an unofficial truce, one the civilians were keen to see accepted. The deal was straightforward. The Taliban would launch no more attacks on the base if we didn't cross the MSR. It was an easy one for us to agree to, given our new orders meant we weren't allowed to patrol as far as the supply route anyway.

Royal Irish 1. Taliban 0.

I had another reason to celebrate. For the first time in twenty-seven days I managed to have a crap which didn't resemble chocolate custard. Small victories.

Then on 23 September 2009 my replacement arrived, a young, eager captain. But he wouldn't be getting rid of me straight away. There were a couple of days put aside for a hand-over which seemed as if it would be made easier by the accord we had secured with the enemy.

During the six months of my tour I had racked up forty-nine major contacts. I was certain of the number not because I was cutting notches in the bedpost, but because I had to write a bloody report on each one of them. Even in the middle of the Afghan desert there was no escaping bureaucracy. Damned form filling, it followed us everywhere, even into battle.

The list of skirmishes would have been greater still had we responded to every provocation that came our way. But there were times where we refused to take the bait and rise to the challenge, occasions when the Taliban would open fire on us, but for some reason or other – more often than not because we were so tired – we would not engage them, as there was nothing to gain from a confrontation and everything to lose. Anyway, forty-nine it was. And I had no desire to reach my half-century. I had well and truly reached the stage of my tour where all I wanted to do was keep my head down and get home safely. I had done my bit – the men of 1 R IRISH and all those attached to us had done their bit – and now my sights were set not on the enemy but the chopper that would take me away from Attal for ever.

Funny how things never go quite as you plan them.

On the very last day before we were due to be extracted I took the new commander on one last familiarisation patrol. We headed north from the FOB. I still hadn't been cleared to enter the Green Zone but I was determined to give my replacement some sense of just how stark the contrast was between the dry, dusty, unproductive desert where you could see for miles, and the lush, verdant landscape that flanked the river in which you would be lucky to see more than a few metres.

As we descended into the other world, the team I had left up on the high ground was shot at by some Talibs using small-arms and RPGs. So much for the cease-fire, however they were well over half a kilometre to the north and at that range they were wasting their time. And, as it turned out, their lives. Once again it was Q who led the response with his GPMG. He didn't give the enemy a chance to shoot again, his ferocious and accurate return fire cutting a number of them down. For good measure Sven then brought in the artillery. 105s pummelled the area the enemy had attacked from.*

Manoeuvring through the undergrowth we didn't escape completely unnoticed, a number of 7.62mm rounds from enemy AK47s making us duck. This little contact did have one benefit though, it brought home to the young captain just how precarious and difficult life was in the Green Zone. It also graphically answered one of the questions he had asked me almost as soon as he arrived in Attal: 'In the tight country of the Green Zone, when you're being fired at, how do you know where it's coming from?' Simple question with a simple answer. Often you don't.

Two days later, in the middle of the afternoon, I stood at the edge of the HLS with my men, bergan at my feet, as the

---

* For his repeated courage and life-saving actions during our time at Attal, Sven was awarded a Mention in Despatches.

Chinook came swinging in low from the south-west, the rhythmic clatter of rotor-blades quickly growing louder. As the aircraft descended to land I turned my back on it and closed my eyes, ready for the dust storm it was about to whip up. As the cloud first enveloped us and then started to disperse, I turned round in time to see soldiers of 1 RIFLES spilling down the ramp at speed, their entire lives stuffed into their rucksacks or the pockets and pouches of their uniforms and webbing. Amongst their faces I saw one I recognised, that of Corporal 'Evo' Evans, a man I knew well from the Infantry Training Centre where we'd both worked together. But there was no time to talk – only just enough to give him the thumbs-up – before we hurried forward to take the seats he and the others had just vacated. As we lifted I twisted to look over my shoulder out of a small window in the fuselage. As the aircraft banked I caught a glimpse of the camp we were leaving behind. Even when we were in it, it had seemed small and vulnerable, now, from the air, it looked pathetic. Isolated and forlorn in the heart of enemy territory, far off the beaten track, it was not the sort of place likely to receive much attention other than from the enemy. To me it symbolised the war in Afghanistan. Here we were in the twenty-first century, yet the scene laid out below me, and the actions that took place there, could have been straight out of the Beau Geste era. An ISAF outpost made of mud, situated in a harsh environment, in a country that itself seemed stuck in a bygone age, manned by a tiny contingent of coalition soldiers, working with the ANA, surrounded by adversaries who hated us and locals who didn't understand us. I wasn't sorry to be leaving.

As Attal slid out of view I shifted in my seat and studied the faces of the soldiers around me. Gordy and his men had already left, pulled out with the Danes and their tanks. But there, just a few metres away, were the others who had given so much during the seven weeks we'd spent at Attal – Q, Bugsy, Stevo, Robbo and Jon Kerr amongst them. Most had smiles on their faces. Several were taking photos or posing for them. Yet the strain of what they had been through was still apparent. The worry lines on their faces, something in their eyes alluding to the fear they'd felt, and thoughts of the lives they'd saved and the lives they'd taken. I had asked a lot of every one of them and to a man they had given me what I'd wanted and more. They never questioned, just toiled away. Most probably didn't even appreciate the finer points of what we were trying to achieve in Attal. To them it didn't matter. They were there to do a job with their mates. Each day was about surviving until the next day. Somebody else, sitting on their arse, could work out the strategy. Somebody else could give the orders. These boys just followed them. Uncomplaining, unstinting, unswerving, unfailingly brave.

I stood at the back of the hollow square of men listening to the words of the padre, and the CO, Ed Freely. It was a memorial service to our dead. The dead of 1 R IRISH battlegroup. Jon Mathews. Barry Dempsey. Justin Cupples*. All around me troops stood stiffly. Many of them were surprisingly clean, freshly shaved, wearing washed and pressed combats, and appropriate head-dress. Newly arrived from Attal, just in time for the ceremony, I noticed how much of a mess I was. I stank. My clothes were filthy, covered in Afghan dirt with bloodstains on the trousers. I hadn't shaved and the only thing I had to put on my head was the helmet now lying in front of me. I saw people I hadn't come across in a while. We'd served in the same country, in the same province, but for all the contact we'd had we might as well have been on different planets. There was Brian McNabb and Hughie Benson,

---

* Justin Cupples – the ranger I briefly spoke to whilst out on exercise in Kenya – died in Sangin on 4 September 2008 after an IED detonated. Corporal Barry Dempsey of 2 SCOTS was also killed by an IED.

two more late-entry officers like me. They looked immaculate. Where had I gone wrong?

Over the next twenty-four hours I got the chance to make myself look more like they did. I washed, shaved, changed, handed in ammunition and other bits of kit, did everything necessary to get out of there, first to Kandahar and then to the UK.

Arriving at Kandahar, disembarking from the Hercules and taking shelter in the tent that doubled as a departure lounge, we were met by those newly arrived in theatre. They appeared just as me and the others had when we first flew into Afghanistan half a year previously. Fresh-faced, pale, slightly chubby, eager, keen. They stared at me in the same way I had stared at the outgoing soldiers all those months earlier, with a mixture of surprise and disgust. In me they would have seen a man who was a shadow of his former self. The hair I had shaved off in Kajaki had yet fully to grow back. There was a deep colour to my skin. My uniform, although newly clean, now hung limply from my shoulders, the belt of the trousers pulled as tight as possible around my waist. I had lost three stone in weight in Helmand and it showed all too evidently. I stood amongst a large group of soldiers all waiting to leave. Most were different to me. They looked healthy, they didn't have hollow cheeks, there was laughter in their voices. Whilst we were fighting for our lives in Attal, goodness knows what they had all been doing.

And then the inevitable happened. There in Kandahar, just as we were about to board the plane, the Taliban decided to give us one last thing to remember them by. The alarm went off. The base was under attack from rockets. Men scrambled for their body armour and helmets, some even crawled under the tables, a drill you are taught to follow when in a building under fire to protect yourself from falling masonry. Here under canvas, I didn't think seeking cover beneath the furniture would make a lot of difference to my wellbeing. In fact I felt pretty disinterested in the whole episode. Lethargy and exhaustion had caught up with me. And anyway, during all that had gone before, I'd used up my nine lives. If this was it, if – after all I'd been through – a 107mm rocket was about to claim me, then so be it. Inshallah. I sat down on a chair to wait for the all-clear.

As I drove along the A1 on my way from Clive Barracks in Shropshire, back home to Catterick, I tried to remember everything I had been told about the difficulties of returning from war and being reunited with loved ones. We had been given a video to watch at Kandahar. And then during twenty-four hours of 'decompression' in Cyprus, before reaching the UK, there was the chance to have a beer and talk stuff through with some of the guys.

What we'd heard was sensible enough. Before telling your wife about everything you've been through, ask what things have been like for her. Remember she too has been through a difficult time, worrying about your safety, running the household, making important decisions alone rather than as a couple. And for six months your house has been her house. Your wife, your children, will have become used to having the run of the place – it has become their space. You return as an outsider invading their privacy. You are told your mood will change without warning. You will get angry, sad, depressed, resentful and you won't know why. You might start drinking too much, driving too aggressively, arguing unnecessarily, picking fights for no good reason. The first step is to walk away from these situations. Find a place to calm down. But in the longer run you are told to confront what you did. Talk it through with someone. Tell someone. Seek help.

The thing was, I was well aware of this. I had experienced it all twenty-one months previously. And because of that I was absolutely certain where my help would come from. Not shrinks or experts or through the system. It would come from

Margaret. All I had to do was ask for it. For twenty-two years she had been with me, keeping my feet on the ground and reminding me what was really important. And after Afghanistan 2006, when I had had serious problems upon my return, I eventually told her, showed her through my scribblings, things I feared would repulse her and make her hate me as a person. But in the end it had been OK. Back then I should have had more faith in my wife. This time I would.

Reaching home, I pulled up outside the house and turned the engine off, got out and went to the boot to get my gear. I walked up the path to the front door where Margaret was already waiting. As I stepped inside she slid the rucksack from my shoulder and put it on the hall floor. I shut the door behind me.

Three days after my forty-third birthday, on 17 October 2008, all those soldiers of 1 R IRISH, and those attached to us, who had served in Afghanistan received their campaign medals.

'Almighty God, whose love knows no bounds, grant that we the Royal Irish Regiment, may do our duty courageously whether at home or abroad, so that undaunted by the difficulties which beset us, Your will may be done. And united as members one with another may we, mindful of the valour and sacrifice of those who have gone before us, clear the way for those that follow. Through Jesus Christ our Lord. Amen.'

As the collect finished, the soldiers on parade marched off the square to the strains of 'Killaloe', played by the regimental band, together with the Bugles, Pipes and Drums, Bugsy out in front. As the men disappeared from sight, I was mindful of those who weren't taking part. Not because they didn't want to, but because they couldn't. One was Ranger Andy Allen. Just nineteen years old, he was missing both his legs and – at that time – some of his eyesight. But if I was inclined to feel any pity for him, he immediately put me straight.

'Things aren't so bad,' he said, peering up at me, holding my gaze. 'At least I've still got my arms with which to hold my child.'

If I had been an ordinary soldier, then truly he was an extraordinary one.

Alone, I walked off to my car, got in it and went home. As a civilian.

EPILOGUE

Barely a day seems to go by without some mention, often critical, of the way British troops have been equipped – today in Afghanistan, before in Iraq. Much of what is said is incorrect, coming as it does from armchair generals with little or no experience (or indeed concept) of the places where the men and women of this country's armed forces are sent to fight. Yet there is also legitimate comment.

At the outset I should make clear that in twenty-seven years of serving Queen and country, I never had better personal equipment whilst on operations than during my time in Helmand. It was just that some had even better kit than me and my colleagues. And when it came to the big-ticket items – helicopters, vehicles, radios – there were real holes in our inventory.

Whatever anyone at the Ministry of Defence might say, as I write this, there are not enough helicopters. And in my mind this costs lives. Soldiers are making journeys by road that really should be completed by air.

However, there are times when soldiers need to be out and about in vehicles. This might be for tactical reasons or as a way of interacting with ordinary Afghans – the people we are in Helmand to help.

We found the best way to do this was by using the lightly armoured Snatch Land Rovers and relatively new Jackals, or the unarmoured WMIKs. The alternative was to drive about like the Danes did in Piranhas or Leopard 2 tanks, pretty much cocooned from the outside world. Which did little to win over the hearts of the local population.

The Snatch Land Rover has received a bad press over recent months. Its unpopularity is not because it has only limited armour – indeed, given a choice, most soldiers would choose the totally unarmoured WMIK every time over the Snatch – but down to a lack of visibility and firepower. In the Snatch the commander and the driver ride in a tightly enclosed cab that severely limits their view of the surrounding area. Acting as their eyes and ears is the man on top cover, sticking out of a hatch. His only armament is his personal rifle or a Minimi. Both of which are next to useless when in a contact on the move because of an absence of stabilised gun-mounts. The Snatch is also cumbersome and difficult to manoeuvre.

Conversely the WMIK is open, offers near-360-degree visibility, does have mounts and can be armed with an assortment of weapons, ranging from a GPMG for the commander through to another GPMG, a .50-cal or even a GMG for the gunner. And there is another reason the WMIK is popular, which not everyone might admit to – it looks the part. It is 'Ali' as soldiers say. Real *Boy's Own* stuff. At times it can be about image – look good, feel good, act good.

The Snatch has its place. In tight urban areas where there is a high risk of attacks from suicide bombers it is first-class. Just don't take it out into rural areas or the desert, where it is next to useless.

That said, regular soldiers (the so-called 'green army' as opposed to special forces) are used to making do with what they are given. They might gripe and moan, but still they get on with the job. Yet the SF are used to getting a rather different class of kit to the majority of British soldiers. In Afghanistan in 2008 it was clear I was fighting in a two-tier army. Never was this starker than when I met with the SFSG in Marjah in July. Not for them the indignity of stopping every couple of miles to try and get a signal on the radio by waving the antenna about in the air. No, they had omni-directional aerials that allowed them to get comms on the move. Then there were the differences in body armour, hel-mets and personal weapons. Why don't all soldiers get access to the same pool of resources when they are all in the same war zone, doing ostensibly the same job – fighting the enemy? Are SF members seen as less expendable than the rest of the British Army?

The SAS and SBS are second to none in the world at what they do. I have never doubted the courage and skills of the SF fraternity – indeed I tried more than once to join the SAS (and failed miserably) – but I do wonder why any man is asked to put his life on the line without access to equipment that is clearly regarded as essential for some of his colleagues carry-ing out a very similar role.*

A dangerous role.

As I write this on 14 June 2009, almost nine months after returning from Helmand and six months after leaving the army, the MoD is confirming the death near Sangin of Lieutenant Paul Mervis of 2 Rifles, killed in an explosion, the 168th British soldier to die in Afghanistan since the start of operations in 2001. I met Paul just before his deployment in March. He was energetic, enthusiastic and engaging – together with his colleague Captain Ed Poynter we talked long into the night over more than a couple of drinks.

The news proved that, just because I have entered civilian life, I cannot turn off my past. And as much as I look forward to a future with Margaret, my children and grandchild, the reminders of what has gone before are everywhere. They are in my head. They are on the TV. Perhaps most of all they are

---

* It is true to say that some of what I describe is being rectified. For example, the Mk7 helmet and new Osprey body armour are due for introduction in the autumn of 2009.

in the conversations I have with the colleagues I served with in Afghanistan and elsewhere.

I have never regarded myself as anything special. Whilst my family – like, I suppose, all servicemen and women's – has put me on a pedestal and treated me like a hero, I am nothing more than an ordinary soldier. There is an old saying that I unashamedly repeat as often as I have to: 'I am no hero, but I served alongside heroes.' Many of these brave soldiers have drifted off into obscurity, their exploits never to be recognised by anyone other than friends and family, though there are some who achieve celebrity status. Amongst those I must include Colonel Tim Collins, my former commanding offi-cer, with whom I served as regimental sergeant-major during the invasion of Iraq in 2003. He fought his battles over twenty-two years of service with the Royal Irish and the SAS, but it will be for his eve-of-conflict speech on the Kuwait/ Iraq border that he is best remembered. As much as anything, that oration helped get the British public behind its armed forces. Iraq was not a popular conflict, yet Colonel Tim helped persuade people that it was OK to 'hate the war, but love the soldiers'. And he knew what that love was all about, because he too loved his men. I remember a trip the battalion made to Canada in 2002. We lost a man in a parachuting accident. Straight away the CO drove several hundred miles so that he could, in his words, 'take care of the lad'. I stood and watched as the Colonel spoke to the dead soldier as if he could understand every word. It was like a father speaking to a child; caring, tender. It was moments like this that endeared Tim Collins to his troops. And there were many more such moments, though, to be sure, when the fighting started he became the devil himself. Yet I don't think the boys would have had it any other way.

Of the others that stick in my mind from more recent times, none does so more firmly than Sam New. In September 2006 he came to Garmsir in southern Helmand with me, working as a JTAC, calling in air-strikes. For two weeks it was his skill and coolness under fire that kept me and several others alive; his repeated interventions in precarious situations meant I survived, often when I had little right to expect to.

On our return from Garmsir he was written up for a medal. In my opinion he deserved the highest honour, yet he received nothing. At a time when some parts of the media are suggesting medals are too easy for this generation of soldiers to come by, Sam New is the foil to such arguments. Today he lives in Kent, where he works as a paramedic; still serving his country – and still saving lives.

As with Sam, I only spent a matter of days with Tim Illingworth, flung together as we were by events, only to be pulled apart again by operational requirements. For his exemplary courage in Garmsir Tim was awarded the Conspicuous Gallantry Cross, incredible recognition for someone so young and relatively inexperienced. I can vividly remember the day his actions saved me and my men. He was not physically injured by his exploits but I know he still bears the mental scars. I also know he faces them as stoically as he faced the enemy.

As for Paddy Williams, the commander of our Garmsir excursion, he returned to the UK, only for him then to head to America and pick up a posting at staff college. He has also managed to find time to get married. He is another who combined flair and aggression with compassion and understanding.

As for those who feature in this book, 'Colonel' Kennedy's tour was distinguished throughout, though it was only in Kajaki that we served together. What I remember most of him is the day at compound 808 when he not only dealt with a seriously wounded Afghan casualty but also managed to control the man's colleagues and direct them in the fight to hold their ground. For this display of cool professionalism he received the Joint Force Commander's Commendation – though I thought he should have got more. On returning to the UK he announced he would quit the army, but – given that the notice period is one year – many were hoping that over time he would change his mind and stay in. I agreed with them that he should. And indeed that is what happened. Colonel is now instructing at the Infantry Training Centre.

I am often asked what inspires me. And I say that men like Al Owens inspire me. A young ranger in Afghanistan, he was doing things way beyond what his age and level of experience would normally demand of him. If generals (and colonels) give the speeches, then it is the actions of the small man that win their wars.

As for the men in Marjah, my path has not crossed that of Rab McEwen since the day he disappeared into the belly of the Hercules, following the coffin of his closest friend Jon Mathews.

'Stewarty' Stewart – someone I often see in my dreams, covered head to toe in the blood of the man he was trying to save – had his eardrums burst later on in the tour, and now he is set to leave the battalion and the army. Matt House has gone back to being a paramedic in the Lake District. As for Brummie Hagans, he is lucky to be alive. On 11 September 2008, in Garmsir, any future he might have had as a frontline soldier was torn from him by an IED that detonated under his WMIK. His legs were badly damaged, and – even after a long period of rehabilitation and course of treatment at both Selly Oak and Headley Court – his battle for fitness continues. Yet he remains in the military and pledges to do what he can to prepare the next generation of 1 R IRISH for places like Afghanistan.

Slightly injured alongside Brummie was 'Monty' Carson, who later returned to his day job as a clerk with 4 SCOTS in Germany.

Amongst those I spent the latter part of my six months in

Afghanistan with, there are many brave men to remember. Not least, Stevo. At the end of Op Herrick 8, he was promoted to sergeant and slipped back into his role as part of the battalion's recce platoon. Later he received the Conspicuous Gallantry Cross in recognition of the work he did in the most difficult and dangerous of environments. As a civilian, I shook his hand at the St Patrick's Day celebrations in Tern Hill in March 2009, a year after we first deployed. It was clear he was proud of his award and relieved he had the chance to share the honour with his family. Sven Hay did his time in Afghanistan and then went back to Germany only to find himself tossed out of the frying pan and into the freezer, swapping the sweltering temperatures of Helmand for the frigid ones of Norway, where he was to lead his unit's Nordic skiing team.

Then there was Q; a truly outstanding soldier, one who was always to be found in the thick of the action. And yet at the same time he was a man of the utmost benevolence. A medic, he treated casualties in Afghanistan without care for their status, nationality or age. His was the toughest of jobs. And it left its mark on him. Back in the UK he was plagued by nightmares and flashbacks. He started to sleepwalk. In the end he took himself off to Fiji and it was there he started to come to terms with what he had seen and done. Today he is back with 1 R IRISH and, after being promoted, is now Lance-Corporal Qalitakivuna. Which might be some consolation for not being honoured for his time in Helmand. Of all the people I believed deserved decoration, and who received nothing, Q was at the top of the list.

Of course, despite the mental and physical trauma Q and others suffered, they did make it back. There were those who did not.

Justin Cupples.

Jon Mathews.

Barry Dempsey.

I should be counting my blessings, that I was one of the fortunate.

Earlier this year, to the strain of pipes, I buried my father, killed by cancer. During his lifetime he served for thirty years in the Ulster Rifles, the Royal Irish Rangers and the Ulster Defence Regiment. As much as anything, my own army career was a way of proving to him my worth – something to make him proud of me. And with his passing, and my own miraculous escape from the hell of Helmand, there should be no reason on earth why the uniform that hangs in my wardrobe need ever see the light of day again. And yet. And yet. There is a part of me – a bigger part than I dare admit to Margaret – that hankers after a return to the regiment that gave me so much. I dare not think what way things will go in the future. Dare not think of what I would say if the phone rings again and the voice at the end of the line offers me the chance to return to a world of loyalty, history and violence.

GLOSSARY

AH	Attack Helicopters – US-designed AH-64 Apaches
AK47	Soviet-designed 7.62mm-calibre assault rifle. Over 100 million have been manufactured. Cheap, robust and simple to use.
ANA	Afghan National Army
ANP	Afghan National Police
CAS	Close Air Support
CH-47	Chinook helicopter
CO	Commanding Officer
C130	Hercules transport aircraft
CSM	Company Sergeant-Major
DC	District Centre
EODD	Explosive Ordnance Disposal Detachment. The bomb disposal team.
ETT	Embedded Training Team. US equivalent of OMLT.
FOO	Forward Observation Officer
FOB	Forward Operating Base
FSG	Fire Support Group
FST	Fire Support Team
GMG	Grenade Machine Gun. Made by Heckler and Koch of Germany, the weapon can fire 40mm grenades distances of up to two kilometres.
GMLRS	Guided Multiple Launch Rocket System, nick-named the '70km sniper'. The weapon fires

GPS-guided rockets over long distances. It is manned by a team of three gunners and is mounted on a tracked armoured launcher.

GPMG   General Purpose Machine Gun. 7.62mm-calibre machine gun that can be used on a bipod, tripod or else mounted on a vehicle or in an aircraft. Rate of fire: 750 rounds per minute.

GZ   Green Zone

HE   High Explosive

HF   High Frequency

HLS   Helicopter Landing Site

HMG   Heavy Machine Gun

Humvee   High-Mobility Multipurpose Wheeled Vehicle

IED   Improvised Explosive Device. For example, a so-called roadside bomb or other type of booby trap.

IRT   Incident Response Team, the group of medics and soldiers on constant standby at Camp Bastion to carry out medical evacuations across Helmand province. Also known as the Medical Emergency Response Team (MERT).

ISAF   International Security Assistance Force. The umbrella organisation for international intervention in Afghanistan, it was created in December 2001 after the Taliban were ousted from power by Operation Enduring Freedom. It is not a United Nations force but is deployed under the authority of a UN Security Council mandate. Since August 2003 ISAF has been led by NATO.

Jackal   Patrol vehicle mounted with weapons.

JTAC   Joint Tactical Air Controller. JTACs manage the movement of aircraft within their areas of responsibility. This responsibility ranges from the safe movement of helicopters delivering supplies, through surveillance operations, to calling for, or

	clearing the use of, air-delivered munitions in support of ground forces.
Kandak	Afghan National Army battalion
MFC	Mortar Fire Controller
MoD	Ministry of Defence
MSR	Main Supply Route
MT	Motor Transport
NATO	North Atlantic Treaty Organisation
NDS	National Directorate of Security. Afghanistan's internal security service.
OC	Officer Commanding
OMLT	Operational Mentoring and Liaison Team. Made up of British soldiers, the OMLT helps train the Afghan Army and supports them on missions.
105mm guns	British artillery pieces that have a maximum range of 17 kilometres. First introduced in 1975 they are manned by a crew of six.
PB	Patrol Base
PKM	Russian machine gun
PRR	Personal Role Radio. Range: 500 metres.
PRT	Provincial Reconstruction Team. PRTs are part of the ISAF mission in Afghanistan and are a combination of international military and civilian personnel based in provincial areas of the country, extending the authority of the Afghan government, supporting reform of the security sector, and facilitating development and reconstruction.
PTSD	Post-Traumatic Stress Disorder
RPG	Rocket-Propelled Grenade
RMP	Royal Military Police
RSM	Regimental Sergeant-Major
SA80	The British Army's standard individual rifle. 5.56mm-calibre.
SAF	Small-Arms Fire
SFSG	Special Forces Support Group. Formed in April

2006, the SFSG draws on men from the Parachute Regiment, the Royal Marines and the RAF Regiment to provide infantry and specialist support to the SAS and SBS.

SPG9	Russian tripod-mounted man-portable gun
TacSat	Tactical Satellite communications equipment
TiC	Troops in Contact
2IC	Second In Command
UGL	Underslung Grenade Launcher
U/S	Unserviceable
VCP	Vehicle Checkpoint
VHF	Very High Frequency
VP	Vulnerable Point
WMIK	A Land Rover fitted with a Weapons Mount Installation Kit that allows it to become a platform for a variety of armaments.

PICTURE CREDITS

INDEX

(The initials DB in subentries stand for Doug Beattie. Digits
beginning names are indexed as if spelled out.)

acronyms and initialisms, 62
Afghan National Army (ANA), 12,
    21–2, 30, 42, 59, 73–4, 76–7,
    94, 104
  Afghan elders glad to see, 162
  at Attal, 207, 211–12, 224–30,
    237–308 *passim*
  bigger picture not obvious to,
    58
  child-shooting incident and,
    209
  'Hero' Brigade of, 15
  infighting amongst, 68
  map reading and, 69
  Marjah 'home' to members of, 113
  Marjah missions of, with OMLT,
    114–27, 132–94, 259
  OMLT 4 mimic, 22
  prisoner executed by, 238–9, 249–53
  RPG attack causes injuries among,
    80–2
  suicide bomber's body parts
    displayed by, 178–9
  Taliban's collusion with, 211
  water supplies and, 55–6
Afghan National Directorate of
    Security, 248
Afghan National Police (ANP), 44,
    73, 104
  attack on vehicles of, 106–8
  fears of leaks from, 65

  mentoring of, 32, 40
  Taliban attack checkpoints of,
    187–8
  Taliban attack vehicles attacked of,
    106–8
Afghanistan:
  All Man Thursday recreation of,
    70–1
  Alozai tribe of, 44, 211
  Arghandab River in, 104
  Babaji, 129
  Bagai Kheyl, 47, 74, 94
  Balochi ethnic group in, 183
  Bamiyan Valley, 184
  Big Top, 53, 56, 58, 59
  Camp Bastion, *see main entry*
  coalition troop numbers in, 26*n*
  dental problems in, 89, 95
  Garmsir, 8, 115, 154, 163, 204,
    284, 302, 318–19, 320
  Gereshk in, 32, 33, 34, 182, 204,
    256, 264, 265
  Green Zone in, 42, 53, 210,
    219–20, 222, 239, 241, 250,
    255, 257, 259–61, 270, 276,
    292–3, 308
  Helmand Province of, *see main
    entry*
  Helmand River in, 33, 42–3, 44,
    49, 52, 72, 205, 218, 292,
    293

Afghanistan: – *continued*
International Security and
    Assistance Force (ISAF) in,
    xxiii, 26, 47, 53, 60n, 65, 91,
    162, 182, 259–60, 287
Kajaki, 35, 42, 51, 63–4, 87, 88,
    95, 98
Kajaki Olya, xxi, xxii, 47, 52, 53,
    56, 60, 65
Kajaki Sofla, 47, 52, 53 60
Kandahar, 104, 183, 291, 311–12
Kandak 1 in, 35, 41
Kandak 2 in, 72
Kandak 4 in, 105n
Kanzi, 47, 48, 66, 67, 74–5
Khalawak, 74
Lashkar Gah in, xxv, 27, 54, 104,
    114, 166, 182, 216
Machi Kheyl, 47, 74
Marjah, 113–27, 132–94, 197–8,
    202, 259, 316
Musa Qala, 44, 72, 182, 228
Nad-e-Ali, 182
National Army (ANA), *see* Afghan
    National Army
National Police (ANP), *see* Afghan
    National Police
Northern Alliance in, 49
Now Zad, 182
Operational Mentoring and Liaison
    Team in, *see* Operating,
    Mentoring and Liaison Team
    (OMLT)
Qal-e-Gaz, 277
Regional Command South in,
    290
Russian occupation of, 87
Sangin, 15, 35, 53, 71, 182, 202
Shabaz Kheyl, 47, 66, 89, 98
Shomali Ghulbah, 75, 93–4
Shrine vantage point, 49, 62
soldiers expected to learn about,
    14
summary justice in, 70
Taliban in, *see main entry*
Tangye, 44, 47, 48, 73

Upper Gereshk Valley in, 33, 204,
    210, 211–12, 228, 265
see also Helmand Province
AK47s, *see* Kalashnikovs
Akhundzada, Sher Mohammed, 44, 65
Alexander the Great, 27
Ali, Mohamid, 68–9, 72, 77, 78, 80,
    83, 87–8
    Rasol replaces, 88
Allen, Ranger Andy, 313–14
Alozai tribe of, 44, 211
Al-Qaeda, 26
American M16A2 rifles, 51, 73–4
American National Guard, 205
Amputees in Action, 20
Andrews, Dan, 241, 245, 249, 250,
    253n
Armstrong, Bombardier Morgan
    ('Morgs'), 208, 222–3, 224, 241,
    243, 244–5, 247, 248, 266,
    277–8, 279, 281, 300
Armstrong, Major Rob, 21
Athens peak in, 47, 52
Atonement, 20

Bagai Kheyl, 47, 74, 94
Balochi, 183
Beattie, Captain Doug:
    becomes grandfather, 90
    flying disliked by, 28
    forty-third birthday of, 313
    in Garmsir, 8, 115, 154, 204, 284,
        302, 318–19
    home again, 312–14
    IED encounter of, 266
    in Iraq, 318
    in Kajaki, 38–99
    in Kosovo, 12–13, 164
    major contacts racked up by,
        307
    Marjah missions of, 113–27,
        132–94, 259
    in Nairobi, 13–14, 16–18
    at Patrol Base Attal, 206–30,
        237–308 *passim*
    previous operational tours of, 5

R & R leave of, 194–8
religious belief and, 186–7
see also Operational Mentoring and
    Liaison Team (OMLT)
Beattie, Leigh (daughter), 4, 195,
    196, 317
    Tristan born to, 90
    wedding of, 180, 196–7
Beattie, Luke (son), 4, 194, 195, 317
Beattie, Margaret (wife), 3–9 *passim*,
    23, 72, 194–5, 197, 313, 317,
    322
Beattie, Tristan (grandson), 90,
    195–6, 317
Beattie, William (father), 322
Benson, Major Hughie, 11, 310–11
Big Top, xxii
Bloomers (driver), 108
Bollywood (interpreter), 173, 174,
    175, 180, 184–5, 187, 188, 189
Boyne, Battle of, 165
Broughton, Major Chips, 171
Brown, Lance-Corporal William
    ('Brownie'), 19, 133, 147, 148–9
Bryant, Corporal Sarah, 111

Camp Bastion, 248
    expansion of, 27
    fences and watchtowers of, 27
    main British base, 22
    memorial service at, 203
    soulless nature of, 28
Camp Shorabak, 30, 35, 37, 42, 67
Camp Tombstone, 30, 37, 42, 123,
    194, 204
Card A, 143–4
Carney, Sergeant Jim, 45–6, 50, 95,
    104, 106, 133, 138, 139–41,
    144–6 *passim*, 148–9, 151, 157,
    158
Carson, Lance-Corporal 'Monty',
    114, 119, 120, 121, 123, 125,
    320
    mentioned in Despatches, 125*n*
Cartwright, Captain James, 18, 34,
    105, 111, 132, 136, 163

Chinook helicopter:
    'brown-outs' caused by, 110
    interior of, 38
    vulnerability of, 39
Christiansen, Sergeant First Class
    Henrik Christian, 256
Clive Barracks, 312
Collins, Colonel Tim, 10, 318
combat estimate, 134
combat stress, 93
Connaught Rangers, 9
Conspicuous Gallantry Cross, 9
Crocky, 208–9, 227
Croft, Ranger 'Crofty', 46, 55, 57,
    59, 94
Cross, Corporal, 45
Cupples, Ranger Justin, 15–16, 310,
    321
Cupples, Vilma, 15

D-Day, 162
Dempsey, Barry, 310, 321
dickers, 242
Dublin Fusiliers, 9

Embedded Training Team (ETT),
    205, 206, 212, 229–30, 239,
    250–1, 254
    departure of, 257
    'front-of-house' role of, 224
    lack understanding of Attal role,
    229
Engineer Robbo, 268–70, 272
Evans, Corporal 'Evo', 309
Explosive Ordnance Disposal
    Detachment (EODD) teams, 54,
    57, 112

facial hair, importance of, 30
Faizullah, Haji, 44
Fennec helicopters, 299
Fire Support Group (FSG), 47, 62,
    79, 96
Fire Support Team (FST), 47, 62, 79
Flodden, Battle of, 202
FOB Edinburgh, 47, 300

FOB Price, 32, 204, 228, 251
FOB Zeebrugge, xxi, 38, 50, 54
forward observation officer (FOO),
    62, 67, 96
Foster, Captain Ben, 116, 157, 163,
    164, 194
Freely, Colonel Ed, 11, 12–13, 35,
    36, 163, 229, 310
    in Nairobi, 17

Garmsir, 8, 115, 154, 163, 204, 284,
    302, 318–19, 320
Gereshk, 32, 33, 34, 182, 204, 256,
    264, 265
Getty, Corporal (formerly Ranger),
    32–3
Gladiator, 20
Glorious Twelfth, 165–6
glossary of terms, 323–6
GMLRS battery, 32, 47, 50, 59, 82, 96
Great War, 9, 67
Green Zone, 42, 53, 210, 219–20,
    222, 239, 241, 250, 255, 257,
    259–61, 270, 276, 292–3, 308
Gullam, Sergeant, 72

Hagans, Sergeant-Major Brummie,
    18, 105, 133, 134, 137, 139–40,
    142, 144–52 *passim*, 154–9
    passim, 320
Haighton, Dennis, 40
Haighton, Lance-Corporal Will, xxii,
    40, 56, 57, 74, 94
Hamilton, Colonel, 206, 228
Harrison, Major Dave, 228, 251–2,
    255
Harry, Prince, 26
Hay, Captain Robert John ('Sven'),
    208, 214–16, 223–7 *passim*, 239,
    241, 242, 243, 249, 256–7,
    261–2, 266–7, 270–1, 272, 278,
    279, 280, 282, 283, 286–7, 289,
    290, 295–6, 297, 298, 299–300,
    302, 305, 308
    mentioned in Despatches, 308*n*
    to Norway, 321

Hayward, Major Grant, 61, 62, 63–5,
    66, 72–3, 74–9 *passim*, 91, 93, 98
Helmand Province:
    Athens peak in, 47, 52
    Camp Shorabak in, 30, 35, 37, 42,
        67
    Camp Tombstone in, 30, 37, 42,
        123, 194, 204
    compound 261 (Sentry Post) in,
        91–2
    compound 627 in, 62, 95
    compound 650 in, 76–7, 82, 84–5
    compound 676 in, 94
    compound 808 in, 61, 77–82,
        95–7
    Fire Support Group (FSG) in, 47,
        62, 79, 96
    Fire Support Team (FST) in, 47,
        62, 79
    FOB Armadillo in, 211, 216, 217,
        239, 243, 244, 256, 262, 265,
        271, 283
    FOB Edinburgh in, 47, 300
    FOB Gibraltar in, 88, 209, 211,
        292, 299
    FOB Price in, 32, 204, 228, 251
    FOB Sandford in, 255, 256
    FOB Zeebrugge in, xxi, 38, 50,
        54
    Harry, Prince, in, 26
    Helicopter Landing Site (HLS)
        Broadsword in, 43
    Joint District Co-ordination
        Centre (JDCC) in, 45
    Medcap conducted in, 89–90
    Operational Mentoring and Liaison
        Team in, *see* Operating,
        Mentoring and Liaison Team
        (OMLT)
    Pashtu the local tongue in, 41
    Patrol Base Attal in, 204–9,
        237–308 *passim*
    Provincial Reconstruction Team
        (PRT) in, 112
    Sparrowhawk peaks in, 47, 52,
        58

Special Forces Support Group (SFSG) in, 183–4, 190, 191–4, 316
Star Wars Wadi in, 210, 221, 257, 304, 306
weapon-malfunction incident in, 128–132
Witch's Hat PB in, 209
see also Afghanistan
Helmand River, 33, 42–3, 44, 49, 52, 205, 218, 292–3
rickety bridge over, 72
HESCOs, 46, 207
House, Matt, 108, 114, 115, 117, 118–19, 121–5 *passim*, 126, 133, 134, 140, 142, 147, 149–50, 154, 164, 167, 168–70, 173–4, 188, 189–90, 191, 194, 320
Huxley, John, 205, 291

Illingworth, Tim, 319
improvised explosive devices (IEDs), xix, 12, 20, 52–4, 67, 71, 75, 256, 266, 320
effect of, explained, 231–6
metal detectors used to locate, 52, 74
pressure-pad (PPIEDs), 108
suicide (SIEDs), 166
Incident Response Team (IRT), 81, 171
Infantry Training Centre, 10, 116, 309, 320
Intelligence Corps, 111
International Security Assistance Force (ISAF), xxiii, 26, 47, 53, 60*n*, 65, 91, 259–60
Afghan elders glad to see, 162
might of arsenal of, 287
resentment of, 182
worries of leaks from, 65, 212
Iraq War, 5, 10, 15–16, 113

Jackal vehicles, 14, 315
James II (of England), 165

Javelin anti-tank missiles, 18, 38, 96
Joint District Co-ordination Centre (JDCC), 45
Joint Tactical Air Controllers (JTACs), 33, 147,` 216, 319

Kajaki, xxi, 35, 36, 38–99
dam, 60*n*, 87
numerous villages of, 39
OMLT's last act in, 98
OMLT's last patrol in, 95–8
Kajaki Olya, xxi, xxii, 47, 52, 53, 56, 60, 65
Kajaki Sofla, 47, 52, 53, 60
Kalashnikovs, xxii, 51, 73
Kandahar, 104, 183, 291, 311–12
Kandak 1, 35, 41
Kandak 2, 72
Kandak 4, 105*n*
Kanzi, 47, 48, 66, 74–5
enemy activity in, 67
Karzai Hamid, 26
Kay, Peter, 71
Kennedy, Corporal Chris ('Colonel'), 39, 55, 56–7, 59, 61–3, 74, 75–85 *passim*, 94, 131, 319–20
Ali mentored by, 68
Joint Force Commander's Commendation for, 320
Kerr, Ranger Jon, 213, 216, 257, 309
Khalawak, 74
'killed in action' explained, 231–6

Labalaba, Trooper Talaiasi, 46
Lashkar Gah, xxv, 27, 54, 104, 114, 166, 182, 216

McEwen, Sergeant Rab, 94, 106–7, 108, 109, 118, 120–1, 125–6, 194, 197, 202–3, 320
McGovern, Colonel Mike, 3, 6, 9, 11
Machi Kheyl, 47, 74
McNabb, Brian, 310–11

Mair, Sergeant Gordon ('Gordy'),
     267, 269, 270–2, 277, 278–80,
     282, 285, 286, 288, 289, 295,
     298, 300–2, 303, 305, 309
Malone, Acting Sergeant ('Bugsy'),
     206, 213, 221, 224–6 *passim*,
     241, 243 247, 250, 257, 261,
     262, 263, 273, 275–6, 277–8,
     279–80, 281–2, 285, 288, 295,
     296, 298, 305, 309, 313
Marjah, 113–27, 132–94, 197–8,
     259, 316
  deteriorating situation in, 163
  OMLT pulled from, 202
  SIED explodes in, 166–81
Mark (son-in-law), 196–7
Massoud, General, 49
Masterson, Sergeant, 6
Mathews, Sergeant Jon, 116, 117,
     162, 164, 167, 168, 170, 175,
     178, 179, 187, 188, 189, 190,
     194, 310, 320, 321
  death of, 198, 201–4
Medcap conducted, 89–90
Meddlines, Captain, 265, 268, 270,
     272
media:
  Time, xxvi
Mervis, Lieutenant Paul, 317
Mike (adjutant), 18–19
military terms, explained, 323–6
Ministry of Defence (MoD), 21, 32,
     136, 315, 317
Mirbat, Oman, 46
Mohaiyoden, General, 34, 35
Mohammed, Captain Basim, 43–4,
     209
Mohammed, Raz, 50
Mount Kenya, 13
Muldrew, Dennis, 40
Muldrew, Ranger Andy, 40, 55, 56,
     57, 59, 62, 72, 73, 74, 79, 94
Musa Qala, 44, 72, 182, 228, 300
Muthaiga Club, Nairobi, 16

NAAFI, 112

Nad-e-Ali, 182
Nanyuki Show Ground, Kenya, 13
Naughton, Brigadier Adrian, 17
New, Bombardier Sam, 302, 318–19
night-vision goggles, 20
9/11, 26
nine-liner, xxv, 81, 109, 169
  explained, 162
Northern Ireland, 3, 9, 113, 135,
     165, 242*n*, 259
Now Zad, 182

Oliver (American National Guard),
     211, 212, 218, 223–4, 227–8,
     229, 239
Operation Herrick 8 (H8), 32, 321
Operational Mentoring and Liaison
     Team (OMLT):
  ANA mimicked by, 22
  'boulevards' code word transmitted
     to, 149–51
  child-shooting incident involving,
     209
  first assembly of, 21
  to Gereshk, 32
  GF8-12 compound rushed by, 295
  Helmand role of, 15
  important to solving long-term
     problems, 40
  in Kajaki, 38–99
  leading by example, 68
  Marjah 'home' to members of, 113
  Marjah missions of, with ANA,
     114–27, 132–94, 197–8, 259
  at Patrol Base Attal, 206–30,
     237–308 *passim*
  to Shorababak, 35
  village GF1 engagement by,
     267–74
  village GF8 engagements by,
     277–90, 296–305
  water supplies and, 56
opium, 105, 164, 211
Orange Order, 165
Ordinary Soldier, An (Beattie), xix
O'Sullivan, Colonel Joe, 63

Owens, Ranger Al, 46, 55, 57, 95, 96–7, 104, 108, 133, 139, 141, 144, 146, 156–7, 158, 320

Pakistan, 41, 183
Parachute Regiment:
  2nd Battalion (2 PARA), 15, 40, 43, 63–4, 71, 73, 74, 88, 136, 211
  3rd Battalion (3 PARA), 40
  rescue mission by, 32n
Patrol Base Attal, 204–30, 237–308 passim
  no-go area for Danes, 256
Penny, Bombardier Kevin, 208, 241, 247, 257, 277–8, 279–80, 281–2, 290, 300
Phantom of the Opera, 20
Poor, Sergeant Shah ('the Russian'), 50, 67–8, 71, 72
Poynter, Captain Ed, 317

Qal-e-Gaz, 277
Qalitakivuna, Ranger ('Q'), 217, 219, 222–3, 240, 241, 244, 245, 246, 252, 257, 262–3, 277, 280–2, 285, 302, 309
  promoted, 321
RAF Brize Norton, 24, 194
Ramadan, 255
Rasol, Sergeant, 88
Razik, Abdul, 44, 47
Rifles Regiment:
  1st Battalion (1 RIFLES), 306, 309
  2nd Battalion (2 RIFLES), 317
Robbo, Engineer, 268–70, 272
Robinson, Ranger Mark ('Robbo'), 257–8, 264, 302, 309
Rory (doctor), xxiv, xxv, 47, 85, 89–90
Roy, Sergeant-Major Billy, 205, 207–8, 210, 219, 224
Royal Anglian Regiment, 18, 265
Royal Engineers, 18
Royal Horse Artillery, 228
Royal Inniskilling Fusiliers, 7

Royal Irish Fusiliers, 6, 9
Royal Irish Regiment, 1st Battalion of (1 R IRISH):
  Bugles, Pipes and Drums platoon of, 206, 313
  campaign medals for men of, 313
  five companies required of, 15
  Helmand role of, described, 15
  long history of, 6
  Operating, Mentoring and Liaison Team of, see Operating, Mentoring and Liaison Team (OMLT)
  'other family', 5, 10
  Shropshire move by, 11
  Sierra Leone capture of men from, 32n
  in World War One, 9
Royal Irish Regiment, 2nd Battalion of (2 R IRISH), 177
Royal Military Police (RMP), 129, 177
Royal Regiment of Scotland:
  2nd Battalion (2 SCOTS), 18–19, 112, 132
  4th Battalion (4 SCOTS), 45, 94, 116, 197, 267
  5th Battalion (5 SCOTS), 40, 72, 112
'runaway gun' phenomenon, 130–2

SALTA report, 216
Samuel (American National Guard), 212, 213, 218, 223–4, 227, 229, 239
Sangin, 15, 35, 53, 71, 182, 202
Sarajevo, 10
Saving Private Ryan, 20
Shabaz Kheyl, 47, 66, 89, 98
Shabia, xxi–xxvii, 90, 91, 195, 196
Shahrukh Major, 154
Shomali Ghulbah, 75, 93–4
Shaun of the Dead, 20
Sherafadin, Captain, 48–9, 57–8, 59, 67–8, 88, 95
  beating administered by, 70

Shervington, Major Mike, 43–4, 47, 49–51, 52–60 *passim*, 64
   imaginary reference lines drawn up by, 54
   to Sangin, 63
Shields, Gunner Karl, 208, 239, 257, 282–3, 299–300, 304
Shirley, Major Simon, 71
Shrine vantage point, 49, 62
Sirisavana, Corporal Billy, 46, 70–1, 94
Snatch Land Rovers, 14, 315–16
Somme, Battle of, 8
Sopranos, The, 44
Sparrowhawk peaks, 47, 52, 58
Special Air Service (SAS), 317, 318
   rescue mission by, 32n
Special Boat Service (SBS), 317
Special Forces Support Group (SFSG), 183–4, 190, 191–4, 316
SPG-9 recoilless rifle, 214
Stanley, Captain Dave, 104–5, 106–7, 108, 136, 190
Stevens, Corporal Alwyn ('Stevo'), 213, 220, 221, 224–6 *passim*, 241–51 *passim*, 257, 262, 269–72, 275, 289, 297, 298, 299–300, 302, 303, 304–5, 309
   Conspicuous Gallantry Cross for, 321
   promoted, 321
Stewart, Junior, 94, 133, 147, 148, 163, 164, 166, 167, 169, 170, 176, 193, 194
Stewart, Lance-Corporal Malcolm ('Stewarty'), 158, 164–5, 167, 168, 170, 171, 173–4, 188, 194, 320
suicide bombers, 88, 115, 166
   small boys and women used as, 176–7
   see also Marjah: SIED explodes in

TacSat, 21, 121, 123, 133, 162, 192
Taff, 32–3
Tali Alley xxii

Taliban:
   Al-Qaeda harboured by leadership of, 26
   ANA's collusion with, 211
   ANA–OMLT Marjah missions attacked by, 119–22, 142–51
   ANP checkpoints attacked by, 187–8
   ANP vehicles attacked by, 106–8
   Attal attacks by, 212–17, 222–3, 225–6
   avoidance of local victims by, 53
   Big Top a recognised stronghold of, xxii
   booby-trap speciality of, 82
   Buddha statues blown up by, 184
   changing tactics of, xix
   compound 808 attacked by, 79, 96
   driven north, 33
   foliage strongholds of, 42
   Garmsir wrested from, 204
   in village GF1, 267–74
   in village GF8, 277–90, 296–305
   Northern Alliance overthrow, 49
   opportunist attack mounted by, 67
   patrol attacked by, 243–5
   possible ISAF leaks to, 65
   press-to-talk radios of, 221
   resurgence of activity by, 125
   Shamali Gulbah used by, 93
Tangye, 44, 47, 48, 73
Tommy (in ops room), 227
Topping, Major Ken, 5
Tourjan, Lieutenant, 184–5
Townson, Lee, 162–3, 164, 166, 167, 169, 177, 179, 188, 194
Trauma Risk Management (TRIM), 180
Turkmenistan, 41
Twin Towers, 26

Ulster Defence Regiment (UDR), 34
Ulster Rifles, 9
Unarmed Aerial Vehicles (UAVs), 47
US Marine Expeditionary Unit, 27

Waterloo, Battle of, 7
Weapons Mount Installation Kits
   (WMIKs), 14, 49, 53, 106, 118,
   315, 316
Wellington, Duke of, 7
West Side Boys, 32*n*
William of Orange,
   165

Williams, Paddy, 319
Williams, Sergeant-Major Michael,
   88
World War One, 9, 67
Wright Corporal Mark, 45

Yorkshire Regiment, 2nd Battalion
   (2 YORKS), 31